Industrial Location and Economic Integration

Industrial Location and Economic Integration

Centrifugal and Centripetal Forces in the New Europe

Barbara Dluhosch
University of Koeln, Germany

Edward Elgar
Cheltenham, UK • Northampton, USA

Published by
Edward Elgar Publishing Limited
Glensanda House
Montpellier Parade
Cheltenham
Glos GL50 1UA
UK

Edward Elgar Publishing, Inc.
136 West Street
Suite 202
Northampton
Massachusetts 01060
USA

A catalogue record for this book
is available from the British Library

Library of Congress Cataloguing in Publication Data
Dluhosch, Barbara.
    Industrial location and economic integration : centrifugal and centripetal forces in the new Europe / Barbara Dluhosch
    Includes bibliographical references (p.) and index.
    1. Industrial location—European Union countries. 2. European Union countries—Economic conditions—Regional disparities. 3. Europe—Economic integration. 4. European Union countries—Foreign economic relations. 5. International economic relations. I. Title.

HC240.9.D5 D58 2000
338.094—dc21   99–053988

ISBN 1 84064 210 6

Printed and bound in Great Britain by MPG Books Ltd, Bodmin, Cornwall

Contents

Figures

Tables

Preface

Over the last decades Europe has been characterised by deepening and broadening integration. European Monetary Union is expected to promote even further the process of integration. Yet since its very beginning European economic integration has also caused worries as regards how much regions and countries might benefit from integration. In particular laggards have been frequently considered to be at a disadvantage. In response, European structural policy was implemented which aims at furthering the development of lagging parts of Europe by fostering market access and competitiveness of local firms. Recently, contributions to the new economic geography have again lent support to this notion as they claim that differences in local market size might lead to a process of self sustaining geographical agglomeration of industries. In doing so they sparked the theoretical and political debate anew.

This study seeks to shed additional light on the process of integration and the evolution of the division of labour with particular focus on European economic integration. In contrast to the new economic geography which focuses on transportation costs, it stresses the role of communication costs and their recent decline in the intra-European division of labour. In addition, it puts emphasis on the role of integration in fostering cost competition and influencing technology choice which is largely neglected in contributions to the new economic geography. It concludes that while transportation costs and the kind of competition envisaged by the new economic geography play some role, the cost competition triggered by integration tends to promote a more fragmented and geographically dispersed production process.

Research on the subject began in 1994 at the Bank of Spain's Research Department which offered insight into the experience of Spain as a newcomer to the European Union and whose invitation to do research on the subject at the Bank of Spain is acknowledged. Another part of the research was undertaken while visiting the Economics Department at Stanford University in 1995/96 whose hospitality is also very much appreciated.

The study very much benefited from comments and suggestions provided by Michael C. Burda, Michael Dalton, Juergen B. Donges, Henri L.F. de Groot, Thorsten Hens, Anne O. Krueger, Malte Krüger, Kurt R. Leube, José Viñals, Pia Weiß, Carl Christian von Weizsäcker, Patrick Welter, Hans Willgerodt and seminar participants at Universities in Freiburg, Jena, Köln,

Konstanz and London, Ontario as well as at annual meetings of the AEA, the EEA and the Verein für Socialpolitik where preliminary versions of some of the chapters were presented.

Chapter 5 first appeared in the *Journal of Constitutional Political Economy*, Vol. 8 (1997), pp. 337-52, under the title 'Convergence of Income Distributions: Another Measurement Problem'. Permission from Kluwer Academic Publishers to include the paper in this book is very much appreciated. Financial support by the German Science Foundation is gratefully acknowledged. The usual disclaimer applies.

Koeln   Barbara Dluhosch

1. Integration and Economic Development: is History Destiny?

I. The concern about regional evolutions

The question whether an outward-oriented economic policy fosters income growth or not has long concerned the economics profession. Instead of stimulating convergence in economic development (i.e. centrifugal forces), it was argued, the forces of integration might imply that economic activity gravitates towards the already more prospering centres (centripetal forces). In particular due to a larger market the centre would be able to attract additional economic activity while the periphery would lose business. The result would be that some countries are left at the periphery of economic activity. This reasoning frequently nourished the view that laggards could not expect gains from integration – broadly defined as the removal of barriers to trade and mobility – unless their economy has (or particular local industries have) reached a critical size compared to the economies of their trading partners.

Worries about development potential probably being regionally skewed because of differences in local market size had already been raised in the 1940s and 1950s (Rosenstein-Rodan (1943); Nurkse (1953); Myrdal (1957); Hirschman (1958)). Many contributions to early development theory stated that due to forward and backward linkages between different industries, the process of take off would be difficult because of local demand being too small to sustain a business. In order to protect local industries from foreign competitors until they matured, development economics was long in favour of import substitution (e.g. Chenery (1955: 463); Chenery and Clark (1959); see also Bruton (1989; 1998) for a more recent discussion). Much of early development policy, as well, was motivated by the idea that protection would push industrialisation. Industrialisation in turn was considered *the* key to economic development (see Krueger (1995a; 1997) for surveys).

Experience with development policies of the 1950s, 1960s and 1970s raised doubts about whether this line of reasoning holds true. By and large, they failed to deliver the expected development push. Instead, they resulted in overvaluation, exchange shortages, capital flight, and a deterioration of the terms of trade. At first, problems were traced back to policies being wrongly implemented (for a historical assessment see Krueger (1997)). Today, however, in development economics, most of the profession shares

1

the view that an outward-oriented trade regime as opposed to an import-substitution regime fosters economic development (Donges and Hiemenz (1985); Edwards (1993); Havrylyshyn (1990); Krueger (1980/1990; 1984/1990; 1997)). Exceptions are few in numbers (for a dissenting view see, for instance, Murphy, Shleifer and Vishny (1989a; 1989b)). Apart from the overwhelming empirical evidence that developing countries following an outward-oriented trade regime were comparatively more successful in terms of income growth than their inward-oriented counterparts (e.g. Ben-David (1993; 1996); Sachs and Warner (1995); and the historical assessment by Williamson, J.G. (1996)), problems of managing the process of integration have been identified as mainly being of a different kind. Today, they are considered much less a matter of backwardness and lack in local demand per se, but a matter of (domestic) distortions. Therefore, in development economics the tide has turned from running a demand-side policy towards a supply-side policy.

Unlike in development economics recent contributions to economic geography have again lent support to the notion that sustained differences in regional development might emerge in the course of opening up (e.g. Henderson (1988); Fujita (1989); Krugman and Venables (1990); Krugman (1991a); Dehesa and Krugman (1993); Arthur (1994); Krugman (1996a; 1997), see also the surveys by Feix (1996); Venables (1998a) and Krugman (1998a))[1]. One of the economic arguments put forward in support of the centralisation hypothesis is that if markets become more integrated, economies of scale will be exploited far better by concentrating production locally. Given the cost structure in production, differences in local demand rather than supply-side factors are considered to be crucial for competitive positions. Because of increasing returns prevailing in many industries, those facing a larger domestic market would enjoy a higher ability to sell. A larger market would thus offer a locational advantage. The result would be that the locally larger market attracts additional business at the expense of the smaller periphery. Following this argument, market size has a cumulative effect with respect to the localisation of industries.

Naturally, trade liberalisation and integration in general are precisely supposed to eliminate differences in local market size. However, the new theory claims that because of the costs of shipping the goods to the market, differences in local demand would remain even if trade were completely

---

[1]   A compilation of some contributions is also found in Buchanan and Yoon (1994). For evolutionary models akin to the models developed by Krugman et al. see Störmann (1993). On the links between the new economic geography and early development economics see Dluhosch (1996) and Krugman (1996c). Fisch (1993; 1994) investigates how differences in economic development might shape European economic integration in particular.

liberalised: as long as transportation costs are high, it is argued, a pattern with production both at the centre as well as at the periphery would be sustainable. A decline in the costs of distance, and transportation in particular, is thought to make it increasingly difficult for producers at the periphery to successfully compete for consumers.[2]

Along with the regional pattern of industries, the regional distribution of real GDP per capita would become skewed. Consumers in the larger market would save on transportation costs,[3] whereas residents in the smaller market would have to bear additional costs in case of the industries lost. Together with local market size, technology not only determines the distribution of the gains from trade, that is from any *additional* division of labour created by integration. Rather, technology and market size decide about who receives the income emanating from production *in general*: by losing industry, those starting behind in terms of local market size may even fail to keep their ex ante real income. Ex post, they can be *worse off* (Krugman (1991a: 78)). If this argument holds true indeed, prospects of catching up for countries that are backward in relative terms will be rather disappointing. Instead of being ironed out, already existing differences in economic development might even be reinforced when barriers to trade and mobility are removed.

Following the new theory, the dividing line between regions and countries managing to take off and those failing to get started could be simply a matter of the starting position. Even slight differences in initial conditions might trigger a process by which a centre-periphery pattern of industries and per capita GDPs proves to be sustainable (e.g. Krugman and Venables (1990); Krugman (1991a); Venables (1996)[4]). In this case, history would be destiny: the geographical distribution of incomes before integration would be crucial for the one experienced after integration. Like many contributions to evolutionary economics,[5] the new economic geography thus stresses the existence of multiple equilibria.

These results stand in contrast to standard trade theory. In particular theories of integration based on factor proportions nourished exactly the

---

[2]   As costs of transportation approach a negligible size, the regional allocation of production might bounce back, so that the pattern can be reversed (Krugman and Venables (1995)).

[3]   For some early work on the influence of transportation costs for the localisation of industries see Weber (1909).

[4]   Refinements of the basic idea have mushroomed in the early 1990s. The most recent development is the link to self-organisation and rugged landscapes. On this see Prigogine and Stengers (1984); Kauffman (1993); Arthur (1994); and Krugman (1995a; 1996a). The basic reasoning, however, extends back to Giersch (1949). See also Schelling (1978) for related thoughts.

[5]   See in particular the literature on evolutionary game theory with frequency-dependent pay-offs of which Smith (1982, Chapter 5) is one of the pioneers.

opposite expectation, namely that centrifugal rather than centripetal forces dominate in economic integration. Standard Heckscher-Ohlin-Samuelson (HOS) reasoning (Heckscher and Ohlin (1919/24), transl. by Flam and Flanders (1991)) and the factor price equalisation theorem (Samuelson (1948; 1949)) has it that the process of market-led integration promotes a *more even* rather than a more uneven income distribution. This at least applies with respect to the earnings of the same factors of production, for instance labour of the same quality. Differing capital-labour ratios might surely contribute to sustained gaps in national per capita incomes (e.g. Slaughter (1997)). However, generally speaking, centrifugal as opposed to centripetal forces are said to be strengthened. Unlike the new approach to integration, which is essentially a demand-side story, the HOS story is basically a supply-side story: differences in endowment among trading partners give rise to a specialisation pattern that is associated with a decline in earnings differences. Earnings of locally abundant (scarce) factors are expected to rise by more (less) than otherwise. Provided that economies are sufficiently small and unspecialised, the law of one price implies that the regional distribution[6] of incomes narrows rather than widens.

II.   EU policy vis-à-vis regional evolutions

EU policy seems to share in the sceptic view that an excessively skewed regional distribution of per capita incomes within the European Community is regarded a policy issue. According to the Treaty on European Union (Preamble, Art. 2, Art.130a), cohesion of the community is defined as progress in real convergence. The extent to which real convergence is achieved is measured by the cross-regional and cross-national dispersion in per capita incomes.

As a matter of fact, the reduction of income gaps was considered an essential part of EU integration and its institutional design from its very beginning (see Art. 2 of the 1957 Treaty of Rome; CEC (1993: 335 et seq.); Begg and Mayes (1993); Leonardi (1995)). In 1986, the task of actively promoting a more even regional development became part of the EU constitution. If not achieved by integration proper, economic policy is supposed to fill the gap. Following the Single European Act, regions with average per capita incomes of less than 75 per cent of the overall EU average (so-called objective-1 regions) are eligible for EU transfers (see the overview in European Commission (1996) and the surveys by Reichenbach

---

[6]   In this argument regions and countries are both considered to be characterised by a lack of factor mobility. Naturally, institutions make an important difference.

and Beck (1997) and Waniek (1994)).[7] At the Berlin summit in March 1999 the European Council agreed on policy reforms concerning the common agricultural policy (CAP) and structural policies for preparing the EU for enlargement, however, without changing the basic concept.[8] As funds for the most part are raised in proportion to national GDPs, EU policy is in effect channelling transfers from richer to poorer EU member states. Though not considered an outright incomes policy and though quantitatively still modest, these EU transfers are expected to exert a leverage effect on incomes of laggards. The leverage effect is supposed to take place either indirectly by increasing public spending or directly by promoting private investment. In any case, EU structural policy is deemed to help equilibrate regional per capita incomes. Government assistance for less developed regions and countries within the EU has been further extended in 1993 by implementing a special 'cohesion' fund which is thought to provide a development push for the so-called 'cohesion four' (defined as countries with a per capita income of less than 90 per cent of the EU average), that is Ireland, Greece, Portugal and Spain.[9] Even though put into effect in preparation for European Monetary Union, the cohesion fund is tied to relative income. Thus, it seems to rest on the notion that laggards face more problems in achieving the convergence criteria (in particular the fiscal criteria) laid down in the Treaty of Maastricht than the more advanced European economies. Though EMU has been in place since January 1999, the European Council at its Berlin meeting in March 1999 'considers the basic objectives of the Cohesion Fund, which was set up to further economic and social cohesion in the Union and solidarity among Member States by providing a financial contribution ... still relevant today' (European Council (1999: note 50)). Accordingly, the Council decided to continue funding for the current four beneficiaries with a review now scheduled for the year 2003.

Following frequently voiced fears, differences in regional development become even more of a policy issue as the economies of Eastern Europe apply for membership in the EU (see Jackman (1995) for a summary). Measured in current prices and exchange rates the Czech Republic reached only one fifth of the EU 15 average per capita income in 1995; Hungary attained slightly less; and the ratio of the Polish per capita income to the EU 15 was approximately one seventh (see Chapter 2). Hence, the gap between richer and poorer countries within the EU will certainly widen, should these

---

[7] Most recently, EU structural policy is scheduled for reform, however without changing EU regional policy conceptually. For a discussion see, for instance, Cuny (1997).

[8] For details see European Council (1999).

[9] See the protocol on economic and social cohesion to the 1992 Treaty.

countries join the EU. The same applies with regard to the Baltic States. With this huge a difference, it is argued, EU membership might not only fail to lend macroeconomic stability to Eastern Europe in the period of transition from socialist planning to a market driven economy. Without additional financial support by the EU, the expectation that EU membership provides a development pull effect might prove to be ill-founded as well. To provide assistance on the same scale as currently to the four EU laggards is considered to demand too much of the EU member states. Therefore, it is frequently argued in an infant-industry manner that EU membership of Eastern Europe should be postponed (see Barber (1995) for a report on this issue[10]).[11]

In the light of recent theories on the gains from integration, EU policy might be interpreted as being driven by the concern that without transfers to disadvantaged regions and member states the latter are not able to participate in the benefits. The notion that EU transfers are necessary for safeguarding the cohesion of the EU would then stand on some economic ground. They could be interpreted as a sort of side payment ensuring the cooperation of the periphery in the division of labour. Otherwise, one might argue, the periphery will withdraw its support in attempts to further liberalise markets. If the theory held true, it would thus provide a political-economy explanation for EU structural policy.

However, EU structural policy is open to two other political-economy explanations. In both of these cases the question is not whether or not laggards benefit at all from integration but how the gains from integration are distributed. First, EU transfer schemes may be considered as the outcome of social norms about the 'appropriate' income distribution. Second, they can be the result of successful rent seeking by those lagging with the latter trying to improve their terms of trade by extorting transfers from richer EU member countries. This strategy might prove particularly successful if EU member states have to decide on a whole bundle of policy measures. Differing interests might then give rise to a log-rolling process. As is well known since Buchanan and Tullock (1962: Chapter 10), log-rolling processes may yield inefficient outcomes. The fact that the no-gains-from-integration argument is frequently put forward by some of the current

---

[10]   In the run-up to the Amsterdam summit of the EU in June 1997 Spain's Prime Minister José María Aznar made it perfectly clear that EU enlargement must not come at the expense of the EU's southernmost members. Otherwise, Spain would bloc EU decision making and EU enlargement in particular (Barber and Robinson (1997); *Handelsblatt* June 2, 1997; *Handelsblatt* June 10, 1997; Weimer (1997)).

[11]   However, see Willgerodt (1992) and Baldwin, Francois and Portes (1997) for an opposing view.

EU members rather than from Eastern European countries gives rise to the suspicion that the true reason for EU structural policy is to preserve rents.[12]

Is the concern about centripetal forces dominating at the disadvantage of laggards justified? Or, more generally, how does the division of labour evolve as markets become increasingly integrated? Can one indeed expect the pattern of the division of labour to be driven by recent changes in transportation costs or, more generally, changes in the costs of distance? If changes in the costs of distance have been important recently, how do they exactly influence the division of labour? Does the nature of the division of labour promoted by integration provide a legitimate case for EU transfers because of the gains being biased towards those ahead in economic development? More precisely, is there an economic reason for compensating the losers by means of intra-EU transfers? Or do they primarily accommodate rent-seeking behaviour and poor economic performance?

If the notion that below-average per capita incomes are in themselves a stumbling bloc for economic development were true, one would expect all laggards to have suffered the same fate in economic integration. Their relative per capita incomes should have declined vis-à-vis countries ahead in economic development. However, experience tells us something different. Generally speaking, periods of trade liberalisation have been characterised by the periphery attracting industries and enjoying above-average income growth. After World War II, for instance, European countries managed high income growth, despite the strength of the US economy; and the so-called second enlargement of the EU in the mid-1980s was characterised by considerable convergence in per capita incomes, indicating that centrifugal rather than centripetal forces dominated.[13]

In addition, individual experiences differed. Some laggards succeeded in catching up in the aftermath of integration whereas others did not. The Newly Industrialised Countries are the most widely cited example for successfully managing their integration into the world economy (for example Young (1992)) even when taking into account that not all sustained their income growth (though for reasons different from local market size).[14] However, one need not go that far for finding examples of catching up. Even within Europe there is a diversity in experiences, both from an

---

12 See also the remarks on the political economy of enlargement in Baldwin (1994: 176); and Baldwin, Francois and Portes (1997: 158 et seq.).
13 See, for instance, the 1993 UN statistics (United Nations (1993)) and in particular the empirical assessment by Ben-David (1993; 1996), Sachs and Warner (1995) and Strack, Helmschrott and Schönherr (1997).
14 On the recent Asian crisis see Corsetti, Pesenti and Roubini (1998); Krugman (1998b); Sachs and Radelet (1998); Shultz and Simon (1998); Stiglitz (1998).

intratemporal and an intertemporal perspective (see, for instance, Dluhosch (1996)). Why, one might ask for instance with the new theory in mind, have Portugal and Spain experienced a development push upon joining the EU whereas Greece has not managed to achieve comparable income growth? Why has the Saarland never made it – even though receiving public funds on a large scale and even though being located in the centre of Europe? Or to put it differently, why, if transportation costs and technology drive the pattern in the way described by the early development economics and its new geographical counterpart, can one still observe so diversified a regional pattern in economic performance nowadays – despite the process of trade liberalisation the world economy and Europe in particular has witnessed since World War II? Wouldn't one expect everything to more or less take place at (one) centre? At any rate, the observation of differences in economic performance despite similar starting positions in terms of per capita GDP is hard to reconcile with a theory stating that backwardness per se prevents countries from realising gains from integration. In a word, casual evidence already suggests different reasons for post-integration performance rather than merely lagging behind or being ahead in per capita GDP at the outset (or more generally market size). But what is missing in the new theory? What sort of driving forces of the division of labour are neglected? The answer to these questions is not the least important for the question whether there are economic reasons for an EU-wide transfer scheme or whether EU funds have to be considered as being primarily the outcome of the political process.

III. The study

The study is an investigation of the evolution of the division of labour triggered by integration with particular focus on the European Union. In analysing the impact of integration on production patterns the study will employ a trade theoretical setting. Integration will be broadly defined as the removal or decline of costs of trade. These might involve politically determined costs like tariff and non-tariff barriers to trade, but also costs of ordering goods according to some specification as well as the shipping and handling of goods. Consequently, changes in these costs may be due to political decisions or technological progress, such as recent advances in the telecom industry.[15] The economic costs of distance (as opposed to the politically determined costs) range from costs of transportation to costs of

---

[15]   The fact that communication costs plummeted recently is also partly due to the deregulation of telecommunication markets.

communication. However, as pointed out by Harris (1995), there are fundamental differences with regard to the economic nature of various costs of distance which will be examined in more detail below.

There has been a number of studies approaching the topic of centrifugal and centripetal forces in economic integration from a growth-theoretic perspective.[16] In particular, with the recent surge in the new growth theory there have been numerous contributions challenging the canonical Solowian view (1956) of economic growth having an equalising impact, predicting instead a centre-periphery pattern as many contributions from the trade and geography fields do.[17]

However, growth theory focuses mainly on steady states years from now. Therefore, it provides a rather limited view of the economics and politics of EU integration. This does not mean that there are no insights to be gained from adopting a long-term perspective. Rather, the limitations are twofold: first, circumstances change over time. That means that most of the time the economies are out of the steady state which makes this time much more interesting to analyse. Second, the incentives politicians face and in response to which they design economic policy are much more of a short-term nature. Developments which may occur many years from now (if nothing else changes) are somewhat out of their time horizon (e.g. the election period). If, because of the time horizon of politics, short- and medium-term developments are even accentuated by economic policy, the short-run impact of integration will carry even more weight for the actual path of economies.[18] Therefore, our analysis will be restricted to a trade framework.

Two results of the study are particularly noteworthy. The first point concerns the role of transportation costs in shaping the intra-EU division of labour. The second refers to the question of how openness affects competition and the production mode chosen by firms. Transportation costs turn out to be crucial in the new economic geography in so far as without

---

[16] Hence, whereas in the 1960s and 1970s the consequences of local growth for the pattern of international trade were fiercely debated in the economics of integration (e.g. Johnson (1967)), the perspective has now changed: the question has been turned around, with growth as the dependent variable rather than the independent one.

[17] Starting with Romer (1986), there have been many studies on the possibilities of endogenous growth. For a survey see Sala-í-Martin (1990), Stolpe (1995), and the contributions to the 1994 symposium on new growth theory in the *Journal of Economic Perspectives* 8: 3-72. See also Rivera-Batiz and Romer (1991) and Grossman and Helpman (1991/1995) who share a particular reference to the economics of integration. On this see also the spatial approach by Stadler (1995). For a particular focus on German Unification see, for instance, Blien (1994). For some early formulations of the idea see Young (1928) and Kaldor (1972).

[18] In addition, recent empirical studies have shed substantial doubts on major results of the new growth theory (Young (1992)).

them the so-called integrated economy, that is the reference model with perfect intrasectoral and international factor mobility, might be reproduced even in case of increasing returns to scale and economies differing in size. Yet, the importance attached to transportation costs and their evolution stands in contrast to actual developments. Even though transportation costs are of some relevance today, recently, the more dramatic change has been in other costs of distance. Most recently, the decline in the costs of distance is much more due to a decrease in the costs of coordinating economic activities across space, in particular in the costs of communication (see the evidence documented in Herring and Litan (1995); the World Bank (1995); Van Bergeijk and Mensink (1997) and Baldwin and Martín (1999) among others). Major changes in the costs of transportation instead took place as ships and railroads were built, as cars and aeroplanes were invented, and as their use spread around the world. In addition, there is scattered empirical evidence that the costs associated with institutions and jurisdictions matter more than the pure costs of shipping the goods to the market (e.g. McCallum (1995); Engel and Rogers (1996)). The implications are threefold: (a) if transportation costs have not changed by much recently, they can hardly be blamed for centripetal forces; (b) in fact, a decline in the costs of communication tends to strengthen centrifugal forces; (c) the answer to the question whether integration actually has a centrifugal impact or not is also a matter of getting the institutions right.

The second point worth noting is that the Dixit and Stiglitz (1977) approach to monopolistic competition on which most of the new economic geography and trade theory rests captures a special kind of competition when integration proceeds. In particular, there is no role for cost competition in this framework. Technology, broadly defined as the way goods are produced, and therefore costs (as well as the cost structure) are exogenous in standard models. The division of labour primarily unfolds *horizontally*. Integration triggers a proliferation effect as the larger market sustains a greater variety of goods while production methods remain the same. Despite operating in a more liberalised environment, firms offer the same quantity in the same manner before and after integration (though they might move regionally). However, while on the one hand market size is irrelevant for technology choice and the mode of production in particular, on the other hand it turns out to be crucial for results; and since production methods and cost structures are exogenous, the division of labour is basically demand-driven rather than supply-driven.

Yet, generally, evidence tells us exactly the opposite. Usually, the more open the economy (that is the lower the costs of trade), the tougher competition will be. Competition, however, also results in downward pressure on the price-marginal cost margin. If the elasticity of demand is endogenous, that is if it climbs with the range of available goods becoming larger, the perceived demand curves faced by individual firms will become flatter. If producers are forced to look for cost-reducing measures due to competition intensifying, the mode of production after integration will differ from the one before. Indeed, one observes that firms revise their policies when barriers to trade are removed as they either have to save on costs or they have to offer superior goods for staying in business.

The study shows how a larger market tends to trigger a process towards a technology in which production is characterised by larger economies of scale on the supply side and a greater fragmentation of production processes into different production blocs in particular. The value added chain tends to be sliced more extensively with the various tasks in the production of a commodity being more narrowly defined. The outcome appears as if due to exogenous technical change though in fact it is due to integration as production methods are endogenous in this setting. This is a key departure from traditional trade and geography models based on DS preferences.[19] In fact, it is more of a classical approach to the division of labour (see also Section I of Chapter 4) in which competition has a horizontal dimension (new entry) as well as a vertical dimension (fragmentation).

As tasks within production processes become more narrowly defined, Ricardian differences in production functions across regions or countries can be exploited to a greater extent. Therefore, integration may actually make it easier rather than harder for the periphery to participate in the division of labour. Or in different words: centrifugal as opposed to centripetal forces may be strengthened by integration. Actually, it is the exploitation of economies of scale on the supply side that brings about a better exploitation of Ricardian differences as well. This is also where the costs of communication come in. For a number of reasons a decline in the costs of communication tends to promote a more fragmented and a more regionally dispersed production which is not captured in models of transportation costs which usually employ the iceberg assumption, namely that part of each good shipped gets lost in transition.

This supply-side impact of integration is lacking in most of the new models of economic integration with their emphasis on the demand side. Note the difference: from a purely *horizontal* perspective the pattern of the division of labour before liberalisation is basically replicated in the aftermath of integration. Oddly enough, and contrary to all experience, integration in this framework takes place without structural change in the

---

[19] Though in principle they could be incorporated. See Burda and Dluhosch (1999a,b).

sense that something really new happens on the supply side. However, taking account of the fact that integration also fosters cost competition and recognising that communication costs differ with respect to their economic nature from costs of transportation adds a *vertical* dimension to the division of labour. In this case, integration is indeed associated with structural change. This source of centrifugal forces is missing under a purely horizontal perspective in which all producers have to compete on the same terms. Hence, even if the new theory is right in pointing out that the centre enjoys some advantage due to its larger market, the vertical perspective will reveal that there are also strong incentives at work which promote a more regionally dispersed production.

In stressing the extent of the division of labour in the production of final goods the study is related to work by Feenstra and Markusen (1994); Feenstra, Markusen and Zeile (1992) and Grossman and Helpman (1991). However, in their work output is driven by the availability of new inputs due to integration (that is a love of variety in intermediates), while in our case output and cost competition drive technology choice and the extent of fragmentation in production. In focusing on the fragmentation of production the theory sketched out in detail in Chapter 4 shares aspects with contributions of Francois (1990a,b) and Jones and Kierzkowski (1990; 1997) as well as Kierzkowski (1998) to the economics of integration and the structure of production.[20] Chapter 4 develops this idea further by explicitly tracing the fragmentation and the globalisation of production back to considerations about cost competition and optimal technology choice as markets widen.

The study is organised in six chapters. After the introduction Chapter 2 will present some stylised facts on the evolution of cross-national differences in EU per capita incomes. Income gaps are the most commonly used indicator for pinning down whether centripetal or centrifugal forces dominate in economic integration. It is also the main indicator employed in the formulation of EU structural policy. Therefore, the EU-wide income distribution is quite naturally a starting point for the analysis. If centripetal forces dominated indeed, macroperformance of countries ahead and behind the EU average would diverge. In particular, one would expect to observe a polarisation of economic activity with the more prospering countries realising disproportional gains from integration. As will be shown, however, generally speaking, the stylised facts of EU income evolution do not lend support to the notion of a more pronounced centre-periphery pattern as

---

[20]   Arndt (1996) and Deardorff (1998) explore more genuine trade issues with respect to fragmentation.

integration proceeds. In addition, the data confirms that there has been a variety of experiences across EU members. The empirical findings raise doubts as to whether currently observed income gaps among EU member countries can indeed be traced back to the forces of integration per se. In any case, the data provides some motivation to take a closer look at the factors in economic integration which according to the new view give rise to centripetal forces.

Therefore, Chapter 3 is devoted to an investigation of the driving forces of the division of labour in the new theory. In examining the centralisation hypothesis put forward by recent theory the study will address three issues in particular. The first section will investigate whether economies of scale per se promote an uneven geographical allocation of industries and whether the geographical bias implies cross-national differences in real incomes. The second section will sketch out the general argument that a decline in the costs of distance will lead to industries being tied locally, that is, a more pronounced centre-periphery pattern; and the third section is devoted to an analysis of cost differences and the role of comparative advantage in these models. Being the traditional argument for centrifugal forces in economic integration, it is of interest why these supply-side factors should be of secondary importance for the regional evolution of production patterns.

Chapter 4 is in five sections. It starts in Section I with an outline of the basic differences in the nature of the division of labour in the horizontal and the vertical perspective. Section II will document historical evidence from the European and the US systems of production in support of market size inducing a technological change which is associated with a finer vertical division of labour. Section III will develop a unifying approach to the division of labour from which both the purely horizontal division of labour underlying standard trade and geography models and the purely vertical division of labour emerge as special cases. Section IV then will investigate the change in the vertical division of labour triggered by integration in more detail. In particular, it will be shown with the help of a model of induced technological change how the increase in market size due to integration sustains a finer vertical division of labour and thereby strengthens centrifugal forces. The final section of Chapter 4 is devoted to policy conclusions arising from the theoretical findings of Chapters 3 and 4. In particular, policy conclusions emerging from the theoretical chapters of the study will be confronted with current EU policy towards regional evolutions. Notably, according to theoretical results of the study the nature of the division of labour triggered by integration does not provide a case for EU transfers out of economic reasons. Rather, as it turns out, costs of coordinating economic activities across different countries and regions crucially influence production. However, these costs are to a considerable extent being shaped by institutions and national economic policy. In fact, similarly to a decline in the costs of communication, institutions and economic policy can exert a leverage effect on the spatial division of labour.

Since there is no reason to assume that laggards are systematically at a disadvantage in the process of integration, Chapter 5 will investigate whether EU cohesion is a matter of income distribution. In this chapter, it will be shown that tracing EU policy back to notions about the 'appropriate' income distribution is problematic because of the normative measurement involved in the criterion income convergence.

Finally, Chapter 6 will summarise basic results of the study and pick up the question of the first chapter again, namely whether history is destiny – with the answer being in the negative.

2. Stylised Facts on EU-wide Geographical Disparities

I. Within-set and between-set macroperformance

If the notion that integration fosters income divergence between participating countries were true, macroperformance in the EU would show an increase in regional disparities as integration proceeded – or as Schelling (1978) has put it with reference to sorting and mixing equilibria, micromotives would find their expression in the macrobehavior of the system.[1]

Admittedly, even if actual EU macroperformance were characterised by regional incomes diverging, the conclusion that EU policy is driven by concerns about development prospects of those lagging average EU income would not yet be warranted. Contrary to many official statements put forward, actual EU policy might nevertheless be the outcome of a deal or a log-rolling process for getting all EU members to agree on a set of common institutional arrangements within the EU. However, investigating EU macroperformance, in particular income performance, is an important first step in analysing the consistency of EU (regional) policy. If the divergence argument were lacking empirical support, the argument in favour of intra-European transfers for equilibrating otherwise divergent development processes would be difficult to maintain.

Results of any convergence analysis clearly depend upon the perspective: on whether productivity data or GDP data is being chosen, on whether it takes account of national characteristics such as demographics, participation rates, employment, education, the size of the underground economy, differences in capital gains and so on (for details see Johnson (1996)).[2] Results, too, depend on the precision and methodology of national statistics, the indicator employed and the level of regional disaggregation.

As far as the data is concerned, the focus will be for two reasons on GDP per capita data at purchasing power parity (PPP). First, EU policy is – at least according to the Treaty on European Union – geared towards equilibrating geographical differences in GDP per capita on a PPP basis. Second, this chapter wants to trace the evolution of the local capacity for earning income due to the forces of integration proper rather than the impact of a particular set of national institutions (such as local labour

---

[1] Under the implicit assumption that integration is proceeding apace.
[2] On equivalence scales for various compositions of the population, see Blundell, Preston and Walker (1994).

market institutions) on macroperformance. Productivity or earnings data would capture more of the latter than of the former.[3] However, even when focusing on GDP data one has to keep in mind that institutional characteristics of the EU members do affect the regional dispersion of per capita incomes. In addition, they might influence their evolution as some of them are also crucial for the way shocks are regionally transmitted and absorbed.

There is a growing body of literature on income convergence within EU member countries and among European regions employing the disaggregated regional data set EUROSTAT provides. In contrast to EU structural policies and eligibility criteria for EU funds, most of the studies focus on β convergence, that is whether lagging regions experience above-average growth rates.[4] β convergence has to be distinguished from σ convergence which focuses on the evolution of income dispersion proper.[5] Following Solowian growth theory two forms of β convergence can be distinguished, unconditional and conditional convergence. The former assumes that all regions converge to the same steady state (that is the same capital-labour ratio from a long-run equilibrium perspective), while the latter concept allows for different steady states by controlling for a number of variables which can contribute to differences in long-run equilibria. Conditional convergence therefore states that lagging regions enjoy faster economic growth the further apart they are from their steady state. Studies by Barro and Sala-í-Martin (1995) and Sala-í-Martin (1996a,b) which analyse the regional evolutions in the period 1950-90 within a subset of 90 regions of the European Union show unconditional and conditional β convergence as well as σ convergence. Similarly, Armstrong (1995) arrives at unconditional and conditional β convergence employing data of 85 regions from the EU-12. Busch, Lichtblau and Schnabel (1998) draw on a

---

[3]   Portugal and Spain are a case in point. According to GDP data, they were pretty much alike in their economic development after entering the EU. Productivity data, however, differs, indicating different labour market institutions and employment records in the process of catching up. During 1979-96, the annual rate of change in labour productivity was only 2.4 per cent in Portugal, but 2.8 per cent in Spain. The standardised unemployment rate in Portugal hovered around 8 per cent in the mid-1980s (1986) and declined to 4.1 per cent in the period of catching up (1986-91). Spain, in contrast, had a much higher level of unemployment with 20 and 16 per cent respectively, though labour force participation rates are approximately 10 per cent lower in Spain than in Portugal (OECD (1997b), A22, A25, A66). The difference in macroperformance indicates that labour market institutions implied different combinations of employment and wage growth (see also Peñalosa (1994) for details). Similarly, though with slightly different growth rates, recently Ireland and the UK (see Burda (1997)).

[4]   This is usually done by checking whether levels of per capita incomes in a chosen base year are negatively correlated with subsequent growth rates of per capita incomes.

[5]   On the major differences see, for instance, Sala-í-Martin (1996b: 1020-22).

sample of 143 regions (from the EU-12) with per capita incomes converted at purchasing power standards. Their data refers to the NUTS II level, except for regions where there is no complete disaggregated data on the NUTS II level in case of which they refer to the NUTS I level instead. Like many of the empirical studies, the work by Busch, Lichtblau and Schnabel is (for reasons of data availability) limited to the period 1980-93. Employing least-squares estimates they find evidence of unconditional β convergence which implies that poorer regions catch up as they experience higher growth rates than richer regions (in terms of per capita incomes). Concerning conditional convergence they come up with a rate of 1.6 per cent per year among the 143 regions of the EU-12 between 1980-93 when they take into account the share of employment in agriculture. According to their studies the rate of convergence almost doubles if R&D employment is included in the regressions (due to data availability the latter refers to a subset of 97 EU regions), a result which comes close to the one of Barro and Sala-í-Martin (1995). Following Busch, Lichtblau and Schnabel convergence occurs especially with reference to regions which fall under the objective 1 of EU structural policy (that is regions with a per capita income of less than 75 per cent than the EU average).[6] The convergence among objective-1 regions reveals that this subset of regions is also mainly responsible for the observed EU-wide convergence. However, Busch, Lichtblau and Schnabel also analyse the role of EU structural policy (defined as the ratio of EU expenditures for spurring regional growth and development to the respective regions' GDP) and find no significant impact of EU structural policy no matter whether the regressions include all 143 regions or whether they are confined to objective-1 or objective-2 regions.

According to the majority of studies undertaken so far, convergence among European regions seemed to have slowed down recently. Thomas (1997), in focusing on β convergence in the period from 1980-92 finds evidence of European regions slowly converging in terms of per capita incomes (with Greece and Luxembourg as outliers). However, as Thomas (1997) points out, the shorter the period the more cautious results have to be interpreted as differences in macroperformance may be due to temporarily asymmetric shocks. As most of the studies, he also finds stronger convergence among the EU-12 countries than on the regional level (NUTS II). Fagerberg and Verspagen (1996) find evidence of conditional convergence when controlling for various variables such as differences in

---

[6] At the 1999 Berlin summit the six objectives of EU structural policy were regrouped into three, however, without changing major objectives and with two-thirds of EU structural funds under the financial framework 2000-2006 still allocated towards objective-1 regions (see European Council (1999)).

the share of agriculture in total employment, the rate of unemployment, R&D, and investment in physical capital. Neven and Gouyette (1995) estimate some unconditional convergence among 141 EU regions between 1980 and 1989, though at a very low rate. Within a smaller subset of 107 regions they estimate unconditional convergence for the period 1975-89 at a rate of 1.95 per cent. To a lesser or larger extent most of the studies find some indication of the existence of convergence clubs, that is within subsets of regions there is stronger convergence than within the whole set. Table 2.1 gives an overview of major results of selected studies.

Table 2.1:   Estimates of β convergence among European regions: major results of selected studies

Author(s)	Reference Period	Number of regions in the sample	Form of β convergence	Rate of β convergence in per cent
Busch, Lichtblau and Schnabel (1998)	1980-93	143 (EU-12)	Unconditional	0.8
	1980-93	143 (EU-12)	conditional	1.6
	1980-93	39 (EU-12 object.-1 regions)	Unconditional	2.2
	1980-93	39 (EU-12, object.-1 regions)	conditional	3.8
Neven and Gouyette (1995)	1980-89	141	Unconditional	0.53
	1975-89	105	Unconditional	1.95
Sala-í-Martin (1996a,b)	1950-90	90	Unconditional	1.5
Thomas (1997)	1981-92	164	Unconditional	0.3
	1981-92	164	conditional	1.3

For details see the cited studies.

The second concept, σ convergence, refers to the dispersion of per capita incomes through time. Therefore, it is more closely connected to the notion of convergence employed by the EU. Rather than tracking movements of regions within a given distribution of per capita incomes of all EU regions EU policy is geared towards the EU income distribution. Both of the concepts, β convergence and σ convergence, need not arrive at the same result. Instead, there may be β convergence, but no σ convergence. Hence, the reasons for focusing on σ convergence are twofold: First, results for σ convergence may differ from those delivered by studies drawing on β convergence. Second, EU policy is much more associated with the notion of σ convergence. Busch, Lichtblau and Schnabel (1998) in calculating the standard deviation of the logs of GDP per capita from 1980 to 1993 for a set of 143 regions find that it hovers within a very narrow band showing only a slight reduction from 0.128 to 0.121. While also displaying a slight reduction (from 0.083 to 0.077), dispersion of per capita incomes among objective-1 regions seems to be more strongly affected by business cycles than the whole set of 143 regions. Together with results for the objective-2 regions which show basically no convergence, they conclude that σ convergence among regions is slow at best. Neven and Gouyette (1995), while also using the standard deviation of the logs of output per capita, find some evidence of convergence in the 1980s in a sample of 141 EU regions. Convergence concentrated in particular in the second half of the decade. A subset of 107 regions also is indicative of σ convergence from 1975 to 1989 in case of which most of the narrowing of the income distribution took place between 1985 and 1989 as well. Thomas (1997), in referring to the weighted standard deviation of per capita incomes between EU member states finds that the dispersion narrowed considerably between 1984 and 1992 with the process of convergence slowing down somewhat at the beginning of the 1990s. Despite the fact that in the first half of the 1980s there is no clear trend, there is considerable evidence of σ convergence in the period from 1980 to 1992. However, in any case, income per capita in 164 regions[7] displays σ convergence to a much lesser extent than between EU member states. In this sample the standard deviation fluctuates considerably from 1981 to 1987, while from 1987 to 1992 it declines slightly. Nevertheless, with respect to the whole period from 1981-92, he finds evidence of some σ convergence also at the regional level. The latter results are also consistent with estimates of the EU Commission in the Commission's *First Report on Economic and Social Cohesion* (European Commission (1996)).

---

[7] Due to lack of data results refer only to a sample of 129 regions for some of the years.

Hence, according to the majority of studies undertaken so far, there is indication of β and σ convergence among EU regions, though at a low rate and with most of the σ convergence taken place in the 1980s. For the remainder the study will focus more closely on cross-national rather than cross-regional data in measuring dispersion. This is due to two reasons. From a policy perspective, cross-national performance is particularly relevant since EU institutions (such as the structural funds) for balancing differences in per capita incomes are the outcome of agreements between representatives of EU member states rather than between local (that is regional) authorities. Thus, we can expect that EU regional policy is subject to a national cost-benefit analysis - in terms of votes or economic welfare – as regards the volume and the distribution of funds (see also discussion about Germany's net contributions – *Handelsblatt* July 28, 1997; Hort (1997); Welter (1997a,b); Diekmann (1998) and at the 1999 EU summit in Berlin).[8] The cross-national focus is supported by the EU Commission stating that purely regional problems (as opposed to income gaps between member states) first and foremost remain a national matter (European Commission (1996: 6)), despite regional eligibility criteria for EU funds (with the exception of the cohesion fund). Another way of putting this is that as long as regional problems arise within rather than between EU countries, member states themselves can take care of regional matters. Also there is the problem that EU transfers to EU regions might provide an incentive for member states to reduce their own subsidies to regions in response to an increase in EU aid. On the contrary, income gaps between EU member states might be a genuine European issue.[9]

The most interesting period for measuring EU income dispersion is from 1980 to 1996. In the 1980s, three countries joined the EU, all of them earning substantially less in per capita incomes than the European Economic Community of nine. Before the so-called second EU

---

[8]   On the net contributions of various EU member states see also the 1998 report of the European Commission on the operation of the own resources system. European Commission (1998).

[9]   There is some dissent within the EU Commission, though. The DG IV, the section of the European Commission dealing with competition policy, is arguing against this political 'division of labour' for the reason that it would distort competition between producers of different locations. To avoid these kind of distortions, the EU imposes caps on regional aid. In addition, there is some inconsistency within the regional division. On the one hand, regional problems are considered primarily to fall into the national realm, with the subsidiarity principle applying. On the other hand, there is a concern that the assignment in favour of national rather than European authorities might even aggravate intra-European income disparities since rich countries are considered to afford higher transfers to their regions than the relatively poor can (EU Commission (1996: Ch. 3)). From the perspective of the theory of bureaucracy, the true explanation might differ from the distortion argument: an incentive on the side of the Commission to expand its competencies.

enlargement, the Community formed a rather homogeneous group with almost all per capita incomes concentrating around the Community's average. The only major exception was Ireland entering in 1974 with Irish per capita incomes slightly short of 59 per cent of the Community-8 average (that is including the UK which joined at the same time and excluding Ireland itself). Thus, even though the nine member states knew regional income gaps well before the 1980s (see the Mezzogiorno problem), it was not until the early 1980s that they appeared to be a European issue (that is on a cross-national scale). This makes the early 1980s a natural starting point for the empirical analysis.[10]

However, the integration of markets went into effect well in advance of Greece, Spain and Portugal joining the EU. A couple of preferential trading arrangements already applied to them being candidates for EU membership. Because of their association with the European Economic Community and in the expectation of entry, they succeeded in attracting FDI flows on a substantial scale even before they became a full-fledged member of the Community. In case of Greece the association with the European Economic Community became effective in 1962 putting exports to the Community on an equal footing to those within the Community while import barriers were gradually removed within the next 12 to 22 years (for so-called sensitive products). Spain was on a free trade agreement with the Community; Portugal has participated in EFTA since 1960 (see Donges et al. (1982) for details). Further links between the economies of Europe's southern periphery and the Europe of nine were established in the 1960s as in particular the overheated German economy attracted hundreds of thousands of guest workers. Due to easing the pressure on local labour markets and due to their remittances per capita incomes in the southern periphery increased by more than otherwise. Though, generally speaking, under free trade arrangements the specialisation pattern is inter alia being shaped by differing trade policies and the distorting impact of rules of origin (ROOs),[11] there was a gradual process of integration which finally fed into

---

[10] The so-called third EU enlargement in 1995 with Austria, Sweden and Finland joining the EU is less interesting from the distributional perspective as all of the entrants had approximately average per capita incomes with reference to the EU-15. However, proponents of the divergence hypothesis might argue that every enlargement shakes up the intra-European division of labour. The trade and mobility induced structural change might be associated with a change in the (regional) distribution of incomes. Worse, with the number of member countries earning average or above average incomes becoming larger, catching up of those behind might even become more difficult. This argument might be challenged, however, as the specialisation pattern of the entrants is biased towards the pattern of those on top of the EU income hierarchy, thus increasing competition amongst them and thereby improving the terms of trade for the periphery.

[11] On this peculiar feature of ROOs see Krueger (1995b) and Krishna and Krueger (1995).

institutional integration under the roof of the Community. Of course, a number of exceptions from free trade still prevailed until full membership (or even beyond). In addition, in some markets competition was distorted because of the southern periphery not participating in common EC policies, in particular in the CAP. The explicit and implicit effective protection kept them from fully exploiting their comparative advantage.

In the course of the 1960s and later on, the three countries became increasingly outward looking. Gradually, they started to remove remaining barriers to trade and mobility vis-à-vis the EU and vice versa. Tariff and non-tariff barriers to trade vis-à-vis third countries were adjusted to the, mostly lower, European levels, thereby fostering indirectly the integration of the Europe of nine and the periphery's economies as they could do without ROOs. In short, Greece, Portugal and Spain were on a schedule towards full-fledged integration well before they entered the European Economic Community. On the other hand, a couple of 'privileges' which preserved specialisation patterns were kept for a while even after they became members.

The gradual character of integration makes it necessary to focus on both periods, the early period before institutional integration, that is 1950-79, as well as the period of the EU-12 (later EU-15), that is 1980-96. Because of their different characters, we present the results for the two periods in separate tables and figures. For the first part, we draw on the Heston and Summers (1997) data set (PWT 5.6) of real incomes in 1985 international prices. PWT data allows for a long-term perspective. EUROSTAT, though offering data on real incomes in PPP as well, only covers a rather short period of time (starting in 1978). Calculations for the second period are based on own calculations based on OECD and IMF data with GDP at 1985 prices and converted at PPPs.[12] As far as the methods of measurement are concerned, two indicators which are commonly used for summarising distributions and measuring their concentration in particular, namely the Theil index and the Gini coefficient, are employed.[13]

Contrary to what policy and the new theory of economic geography might suggest, the long-run trend shows no increase in the dispersion of average per capita incomes between EU members (data refers to the 12 European countries later to become the EU-12). Results for the first period from 1950 to 1979 are summarised in Table 2.2 and Figure 2.1. Though the Theil index and the Gini coefficient differ somewhat with regard to details,

---

[12] Data provided by the Heston-Summers set is limited to 1950-90; IMF and OECD data, on the other hand, is not complete for the 1950s and 1960s. As far as the two sets overlap, there are slight differences.

[13] On the mathematical properties of the various indicators, see Cowell (1995).

in the long-run perspective, they have one thing in common: None of the indicators shows a trend towards a widening of geographical disparities. This is also consistent with evidence on OECD convergence based on growth data (Barro and Sala-í-Martin (1991)).

Figure 2.1:   Cross-national dispersion of per capita incomes between 12 European countries 1950-79

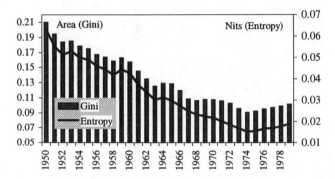

Source: See Table 2.2.

The Theil index measures the entropy of per capita incomes between EU member states weighted by income shares.[14] As displayed in Figure 2.1, the entropy declined almost continuously from 0.063 nits (that is information units based on natural logarithms) in 1950 to 0.015 nits in 1975. Among the twenty-five years, there are only three showing a slight deviation from the trend: 1953, 1959 and 1964. Compared to the substantial decline in income dispersion between 1950 and 1975, the increase in the entropy during the worldwide recession of the late 1970s (from 0.015 to 0.019 nits) appears rather minor.

The Gini coefficient, based on the Lorenz curve, basically shows the same intertemporal pattern. The coefficient declines sharply from 1950 to 1975 and it increases slightly during the cyclical downswing following OPEC I (1975-79) and the internal political transition of Portugal, Greece and Spain from dictatorships to representative democracies (starting in April 1974 in Portugal, in July 1974 in Greece, and in December 1975 in Spain). Note that the dispersion has risen in a time of particular political events rather than in the unfettered process of integration.

---

[14] In all of the tables (2.2, 2.3, 2.4 and 2.5), income shares were used to calculate the entropy measure. However, differences in the pattern between income and population shares are minor.

Table 2.2: *Cross-national dispersion of per capita incomes between 12 European countries 1950-79*

Year	Entropy[a]	Gini coefficient[b]	Year	Entropy	Gini coefficient	Year	Entropy	Gini coefficient
1950	0.063	0.210	1960	0.043	0.157	1970	0.022	0.107
1951	0.055	0.194	1961	0.037	0.145	1971	0.020	0.105
1952	0.051	0.184	1962	0.034	0.134	1972	0.019	0.102
1953	0.053	0.185	1963	0.030	0.125	1973	0.017	0.095
1954	0.050	0.178	1964	0.031	0.129	1974	0.015	0.090
1955	0.049	0.175	1965	0.030	0.128	1975	0.015	0.092
1956	0.046	0.167	1966	0.027	0.119	1976	0.017	0.095
1957	0.044	0.163	1967	0.025	0.108	1977	0.017	0.096
1958	0.042	0.158	1968	0.023	0.106	1978	0.018	0.099
1959	0.044	0.162	1969	0.022	0.107	1979	0.019	0.101

[a] The between-member states entropy was calculated according to $I_0(y:x) = \sum_{i=1}^{12} y_i ln(y_i/x_i)$ with y_i being the income share of country i in total income of the EU of 12, and x_i its population share, again with reference to the total population of the EU. Basically the same pattern emerges if population shares are used as prior and income shares as posterior probabilities. Absolute numbers differ though (for differences in the pattern see Chapter 5 of this study). On the characteristics of both concepts see Theil (1967), in particular p. 126.

[b] The Gini coefficient was calculated according to the following formula $G = 1/2\left(\sum_{i=1}^{12}\sum_{j=1}^{12} x_i x_j |y_i/x_i - y_j/x_j|\right)$ with x_i and y_i being again the population share and the income share of countries i and j respectively.

Source: Summers and Heston (1997) data set, own calculations. Calculations are based on real GDP per capita (RGDPL) in 1985 international prices. The reference is the EU average of 12. A rise of the respective indicator signals an increase in dispersion.

Figure 2.2:   *Cross-national dispersion of per capita incomes in the*
                  EU-12 1980-96

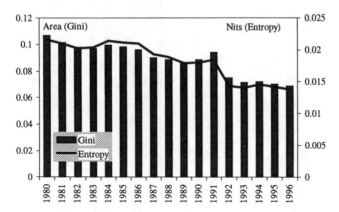

Source: See Table 2.3.

The second period, that is the period of institutional integration under the roof of the EU, shows no income divergence either (see Table 2.3 and Figure 2.2). Instead, the dispersion declined slightly in the early 1980s and flattened out in the mid-1980s. In the second half of the 1980s, following the entry of Spain and Portugal, the stagnation gave way to another decline. Though, in absolute terms, the decline was not as pronounced as before, it reversed the slight increase which occurred during the years of political change, OPEC I and the recession of the late 1970s within only three years (1987-90). After 1992, the downward trend stopped and the pattern became quite stable again with the dispersion now continuing to flirt with the 0.014 line. Note that in the 1990s, both the Theil index and the Gini coefficient reach an all-time low (since 1950). This holds true even though most of the decline in dispersion between 1991 and 1992-96 is to be traced back to German unification dragging down average per capita income in one of the richest of the EU countries.

Taking a birds-eye perspective, the evolution can thus be split into three sub-periods. The first period stretches from 1950 to 1975, showing a strong decline in dispersion. There is a second period of decline covering the years 1986 to 1996. In between these two periods there is a third (1976-85) which is characterised by a slight up and down of income disparities.

Table 2.3: Cross-national dispersion of per capita incomes in the EU-12 1980-96

Year	Entropy	Gini coefficient	Year	Entropy	Gini coefficient	Year	Entropy	Gini coefficient
1980	0.022	0.107	1986	0.021	0.096	1992	0.014	0.075
1981	0.021	0.101	1987	0.019	0.090	1993	0.014	0.071
1982	0.020	0.098	1988	0.019	0.088	1994	0.015	0.072
1983	0.020	0.097	1989	0.018	0.086	1995	0.014	0.070
1984	0.021	0.099	1990	0.018	0.088	1996	0.014	0.069
1985	0.021	0.098	1991	0.018	0.094			

Source: IMF (1996; 1997b); OECD (1997b; 1997c); own calculations. Calculations are based on GDP per capita in prices and purchasing power parities of 1985. The reference is the EU average of 12. As in Table 2.2, a rise of the respective indicator signals an increase in dispersion. From 1992 on data includes the unified Germany. The dispersion of 1996 is calculated by using population data of 1995 (mid-year estimates). Due to a slight deviation between the Summers-Heston data set and the OECD-IMF data numbers show an increase in dispersion in 1979/80 while within the same data set they do not. As far as data sets overlap (that is for the decade 1980-90), there are no major differences in the intertemporal pattern of dispersion though.

26

Admittedly, according to these calculations differences in macro economic performance among EU member states have at least proven to be persistent between 1976 and 1985. However, two things have to be kept in mind when interpreting the data. First, the periphery's economies were ridden by a couple of shocks. Two of them were already mentioned: OPEC I and the rollover of the political system in Greece, Portugal and Spain. The second enlargement of the Community constituted a third shock though. Note that the slight increase in 1984 which is responsible for the income distribution being almost stable in the first half of the 1980s occurred right before Portugal and Spain entered the EU.

That being so, the rise in dispersion might be due to the removal of barriers to trade (or the expectation of them being removed shortly) rather than indicating the forces of integration proper. That the dispersion increases right after the removal of barriers to trade seems to be quite natural. For the liberalisation constitutes a disturbance of an old pattern which takes some time to settle down into a new allocation. However, the removal of barriers to trade and mobility amounts to a transitory shock.

Therefore, its impact cannot be at the heart of the centre-periphery concerns by which EU policy is being driven. Rather, the increase in dispersion should bring about a new allocation which is (probably) characterised by a lower dispersion than was the case pre-integration.[15] EU policy, instead, is assumed to counterbalance the forces of integration proper, if the latter are associated with an increase in the geographical dispersion of per capita incomes. Hence, shocks are the first reason why the persistence of cross-national income gaps between 1976 and 1985 cannot with confidence be traced back to the dynamics of integration.

The second reason why income disparities in the third period might be shaped by transitory evolutions rather than the forces of integration proper is because of cyclical swings. In particular the late 1970s were a time of worldwide recession. Thus, the increase in 1975-79 might be due to the periphery of the EU being more affected by recessions than the centre. Less of a diversification might be one such reason that the periphery is more prone to cyclical swings. Yet, again, these ups and downs are something different from centripetal forces of integration proper.

In summing up the data on cross-national income dispersion one thing is for sure: integration has not fostered an overall increase in income dispersion between EU member states. Note in particular that since 1986,

---

[15] This GDP pattern with GDP growth first slowing down and later picking up again is most evident in the case of the former socialist countries' transition to market-led economies.

that is in the EU-12, macroperformance measured in GDP per capita is characterised by convergence rather than divergence.

Yet, both from a policy perspective and from a theoretical perspective, it might be interesting to know whether the dynamics of the overall evolutions since the mid-1980s mainly stem from

- evolutions which took place *within* EU member states, or
- evolutions which took place *between* EU member states.

A decomposition into these two components (for technical details see Theil (1967: 101 et seq.)) reveals that the decline in the overall entropy since the 1980s was considerably shaped by the evolution of per capita incomes *between* EU member states.

The evolution of the entropy[16] of per capita incomes *within* EU member states is summarised in Table 2.4. The calculations are based on EUROSTAT REGIO data. EUROSTAT provides disaggregated GDP data on three different regional levels, NUTS I, NUTS II and NUTS III with the NUTS III data being the most disaggregated. NUTS II data is employed for eligibility criteria with respect to EU funds (with the exception of resources distributed under the cohesion fund). Because EU policy is referring to NUTS II data the analysis will also draw on NUTS II data for comparing the evolution of incomes within and between EU member states – though regional policies themselves might be the outcome of a political tug-of-war between EU member states (rather than between regions). The regional components entering the dispersion in our calculations thus refer to the dispersion as measured on the EU NUTS II level. Aside from the EU taking NUTS II, the NUTS III perspective might also be too disaggregated a view: NUTS III regions are in some cases rather small with a mid-sized town sometimes already being split into two regions. That being so, a more disaggregated perspective (that is NUTS III data) may be biased by residential mobility. Residential mobility can have an impact on the income dispersion measured, though the earnings capacity of a region need not have changed. Zoning is a related problem probably arising stronger on a NUTS III than on a NUTS II level. However, we are less interested in capturing mobility for purely residential reasons. Rather, what we are interested in is the regional evolution of prospects to earn income, which is quite different from the former. In addition, NUTS III data is strongly influenced by the concentration of the public sector and its growth in larger cities. In any case, the data has to be interpreted with caution as no matter whether NUTS

---

[16]   Due to being additively separable, the entropy is quite suitable for this procedure.

II or NUTS III data is being used, the regional disaggregation differs substantially across EU member states.[17] Nevertheless, even on the NUTS II level boundaries of the regions are redrawn from time to time and data is very incomplete: Considering the EU-12, data for comparing the entropy *between* sets (that is countries) and *within* sets is only available for a couple of years. To capture also the impact of the anticipation of EU membership of Spain and Portugal on European-wide income disparities we include numbers for 1981 and 1984. The most recent complete NUTS II data set is for 1993.

As can be seen from Table 2.4, regional evolutions *within* EU countries are by no means confined to countries at the lower end of the income scale. Rather, the regional dispersion climbed in Spain and in Portugal which both are at the lower end of the income scale as well as in France and Germany which are at the top. Neither is the entropy generally higher in low-income countries as compared to high-income countries.

In addition, evolutions *within* EU member states were outpaced by those taking place *between* EU member states. Table 2.5 shows the decomposition of the overall entropy in the within-set entropy (column three) and the between-set entropy (column two) for the years 1984-93.

Table 2.4: Within-set entropy for selected EU countries 1981-93

Year	Belgium	Italy	Netherlands	UK	Greece
1981	0.0358	0.0326	0.0277	0.0184	0.0283
1984	0.0294	0.0277	0.0303	0.0166	0.0204
1987	0.0258	0.0315	0.0100	0.0195	0.0273
1990	0.0249	0.0336	0.0069	0.0196	0.0274
1993	0.0248	0.0302	0.0089	0.0171	0.0268

Year	France	Germany	Spain	Portugal
1981	n.a.	0.0145	0.0169	0.0288
1984	0.0240	0.0158	0.0161	0.0283
1987	0.0277	0.0172	0.0194	0.0457
1990	0.0293	0.0175	0.0205	0.0398
1993	0.0292	0.0180	0.0194	0.0389

Calculations are based on average per capita incomes in current prices and purchasing power parities on the EU NUTS II level. Concentration is measured in nits. n.a.: data not available.
Source: EUROSTAT REGIO data tape, April 1997 edition, own calculations.

---

[17]   On this issue see Estebán (1994: 24 et seq.).

Table 2.5: Entropy decomposition of per capita income distributions in the EU 1984-93

Year	Total entropy	Entropy (measured in nits) Between member states entropy	Within member states entropy (NUTS II)
1984	0.0394	0.0187	0.0207
1987	0.0393	0.0168	0.0226
1990	0.0386	0.0154	0.0232
1993	0.0349	0.0128	0.0221

Calculations are based on average per capita incomes in current prices and purchasing power parities on the EU NUTS II level and the national level respectively.
Source: EUROSTAT REGIO data tape, April 1997 edition, own calculations.

According to these calculations the between-set entropy declined throughout the decade whereas in case of the within-set entropy no trend can be discovered. That being so, the share of the between-country entropy in total dispersion declined from 47 per cent in 1984 to 40 per cent in 1993. The disaggregated view thus indicates that the evolution of the overall entropy of the geographical income distribution was basically shaped by the decline in dispersion between EU member states.

Hence, there are actually four reasons for adopting a cross-national rather than a narrowly defined regional perspective. First, the major course of EU policy is set by the heads of the governments of the EU member states which means that there are public choice theoretic reasons for focusing on the between-set evolution in particular. Second, in contrast to evolutions within member states those between them might be a European issue indeed (they need not, though). Third, at any rate, with approximately 40 per cent of the overall entropy of the European income distribution the between-set evolution carries substantial weight. And finally, and probably most importantly, the overall evolution has been mostly shaped by the change in the distribution *between* EU member states.[18]

More precisely, the new theory of economic geography considers the polarisation of the income distribution a likely outcome of integration. In

---

[18]   For a regional focus see again, for instance, CEC (1991); Barro and Sala-í-Martin (1991); Carlino (1992); Estebán (1994); Sala-í-Martin (1994; 1996a); Thomas (1995); Neven and Gouyette (1995); Busch, Lichtblau und Schnabel (1998) and with particular reference to Spain Dolado, González-Páramo and Roldán (1994) and to Germany RWI (1996). Some of these studies measure both the rate at which per capita incomes converge towards the mean (β convergence) on the regional level, as well as the evolution of the dispersion of the distribution through time (σ convergence).

particular those on the bottom of the European income hierarchy are expected to fall behind. From this perspective it matters for instance whether the overall evolution of the geographical income dispersion is due to changes within the periphery or within the centre or whether it is due to the evolution of the periphery vis-à-vis the centre. To which extent the latter was the case can be inferred from the so-called Atkinson index (Atkinson (1970: 257 et seq.)).[19]

Basically, the Atkinson index attaches different weights to countries in the measurement of dispersion. The weight with which a particular country enters the index depends on its location on the scale of average per capita incomes in the EU. The more one wants to focus on how well those on the bottom of the income hierarchy do, the larger have their weights to be. The Atkinson index captures these weights by means of a variable $\in$. The index is the more focused on the lower tale of the distribution the higher $\in$.

Figure 2.3:   *Atkinson index with $\in=100$ for 12 European countries 1950-79*

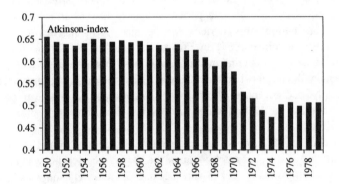

Source: Own calculations based on real GDP per capita in 1985 international prices as published by Summers and Heston. The Atkinson index has been calculated by use of $A=1-\left[\sum_{i=1}^{12} x_i (y_i/x_i)^{1-\in}\right]^{1/(1-\in)}$. x_i and y_i again refer to the population share and the income share of country i respectively (see Atkinson 1970: 257 et seq. on the concept)

---

[19] For an alternative method of measuring center-periphery income patterns see Estebán and Raj (1994). Here, the Atkinson index is used as a technical device rather than for considerations of social welfare (for a discussion of the latter see Chapter 5).

Figure 2.4:   Atkinson index with ∈ =100 for the EU-12 1980-96

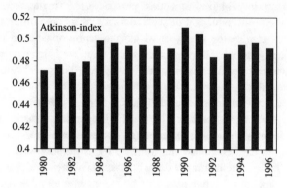

Source: Own calculations based on GDP per capita in 1985 prices and purchasing power
parities. Source of data: IMF (1996; 1997b), OECD (1997b; 1997c).

In Figures 2.3 and 2.4 the focus towards the periphery is quite skewed as ∈
is set equal to 100 for both periods, 1950-79 and 1980-96. According to
these calculations, four periods can be distinguished. The first stretches
from 1950 to circa 1964. In Figure 2.1 and Table 2.2 this period was
characterised by a decline in the overall dispersion. However, as Figure 2.3
reveals with an almost stable Atkinson index, the decline in dispersion was
basically due to those ahead of the income distribution (in particular
Luxembourg, the United Kingdom, Belgium and Denmark) falling back in
relative terms.

In contrast, the second period, covering the decade from 1964 to 1974,
constituted a period of catching up of the EU periphery. This was the period
as Greece, Portugal and Spain became increasingly outward-oriented.
Thereafter, the Atkinson index stabilises again and moves only slightly up
and down.[20]

One might split the following two decades from 1975 to 1996 into two
sub-periods though, distinguishing the years from 1975 to 1983 from the
last thirteen years (1984-96). Both are characterised by an almost constant

---

[20]   The lack of homogeneity in the evolution between 1974 and 1985 is underlined by the fact
that for a couple of years the Atkinson index disagrees with either the Gini coefficient or the
entropy-based Theil index. The differences in evaluation indicate that the Lorenz curves of
two subsequent years intersect rather than shifting either totally inward or outward. This
means that different income segments pulled forward in the distribution, in one year those in
the middle of the income scale got a bigger slice from the normalised cake while in the other
year lower percentiles managed to pull forward.

relative performance of the periphery vis-à-vis the EU average. However, since 1984, the level of performance was slightly less favourable.

To put it into a nutshell: there is no indication of a trend towards a polarisation between the periphery and the centre in the EU. Indeed, since the mid-1960s the periphery managed to catch up vis-à-vis the centre, with the centre-periphery pattern basically stabilising since the mid-1970s. However, a more disaggregated perspective reveals some interesting facts about the reasons for the stabilisation.

If the divergence hypothesis were true, all countries at the bottom of the EU distribution should have experienced a similar evolution as integration proceeded. At least in relative terms all should have suffered from a set back. However, there was no such common experience. Rather, some countries succeeded in pulling forward, whereas in case of others integration proved to be less rewarding with the balance on the side of the former. Countries earning below average per capita incomes in the EU are Greece, Ireland, Spain and Portugal (they are also those most remote from the centre).[21] Yet, though all of these countries are considered as periphery in EU terminology, the country-specific pictures are rather diverse.

In particular, the economic performance of the southernmost newcomers to the EU display no marked similarity. Instead, case studies reveal a variety of experiences. Over the whole period from 1950 to the mid-1970s (see Figure 2.5), all of the peripheral countries experienced a substantial increase in relative terms, with the exception of Ireland. Spanish incomes climbed from 53 per cent to 81 per cent of the average of 12 European countries, Portuguese incomes from 33 per cent to 48 per cent and Greek incomes from 39 per cent to 58 per cent. Ireland, in contrast, suffered a setback in relative terms with per capita incomes declining from 75 per cent of the European average (1950) to 62 per cent until it entered the Community (1974).

From the mid-1970s to the mid-1980s the periphery by and large managed to hold its position on the European income scale. While Irish incomes climbed vis-à-vis the average of 12 European countries, Spanish and Portuguese incomes declined. Relative macroperformance of Greece was basically unchanged. However, keep in mind, that Portugal and Spain underwent a major political change in the mid-1970s. Hence macro-performance has to be seen in the light of political uncertainty making it difficult for investors to form expectations about the future course of the economy and the real return on investment.

---

[21] Despite of catching up during the thirty years from 1950 to 1980, most recently Italy once again belongs to this below-average group. However, except for the Mezzogiorno, Italy as a whole has not been considered as peripheral in EU language.

Figure 2.5:   Per capita GDP of Greece, Ireland, Portugal, and Spain in
*   1985 international prices vis-à-vis 12 European countries*
*   1950-79*

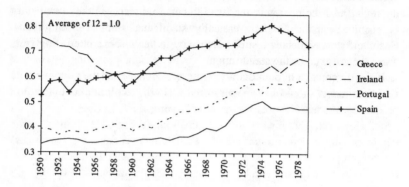

Source: Summers and Heston (1997) data set, own calculations. GDP is in 1985 prices
          and purchasing power parities.

Figure 2.6:   Per capita GDP of Greece, Ireland, Portugal, and Spain in
*   1985 international prices vis-à-vis the EU-12 1980-96*

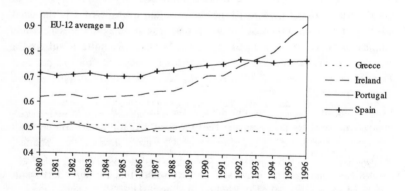

Source: IMF (1996; 1997b); OECD (1997b; 1997c); own calculations. GDP is in 1985
          prices and purchasing power parities.

Since the mid-1980s there is more of a dynamic in the European income
distribution. In fact, since entering the EU, all countries of the periphery
were able to improve their relative position on the income scale, except for

Greece. In particular relative performance of Ireland amounts to a success story in catching up with an outstanding increase of relative GDP per capita of almost 30 percentage points (63 per cent in 1985, 92 per cent in 1996). At the same time, growth also picked up again relatively strong in Spain[22] and Portugal if compared to the EU-12 average. Spain gained 7 percentage points vis-à-vis the EU-12 average. Portugal came almost close to that. Spain and Portugal show a strong similarity in the whole pattern. Proximity and similarity in endowments might be the reason, providing for natural trading partners.[23] On the contrary, Greece suffered a relative decline with GDP per capita incomes dropping from 51 (1985) to 49 per cent (1996) of the EU-12 average.[24]

Table 2.6: Relative per capita GDP: EU periphery vis-à-vis EU-12 average 1980-96

Country	Year								
	1980	1982	1984	1986	1988	1990	1992	1994	1996
Ireland	0.62	0.63	0.62	0.63	0.65	0.71	0.75	0.81	0.92
Spain	0.71	0.71	0.70	0.70	0.73	0.75	0.78	0.77	0.77
Portugal	0.51	0.51	0.48	0.49	0.50	0.53	0.55	0.55	0.55
Greece	0.53	0.52	0.51	0.51	0.49	0.47	0.50	0.49	0.49

GDP data is in 1985 prices and purchasing power parities.
Source: IMF (1996; 1997b); OECD (1997b; 1997c); own calculations.

The disaggregated perspective thus shows that it was basically the weak performance of the Greek economy which was responsible for the slight increase in the Atkinson index in the mid-1980s as well as its recent

---

[22] Compared to previous periods, the relative performance of Spain was almost rock-bottom in the mid-1980s (see Peñalosa (1994), Dluhosch (1996) for details – on Spain's development during integration see also Viñals et al. (1990), Viñals (1992) and Galy (1993)). The notion that relative growth in per capita income is not showing primarily benefits from integration, but merely regaining of lost ground, would be too short a perspective though. An argument like this would only be valid if relative performance was the outcome of a cyclical swing lagging or leading the EU average. Nonetheless, relative GDP per capita slowed down steadily as from the mid-1970s, quite independently from any cyclical fluctuations, before it took off in the mid-1980s. That the slide of the economy in the period 1974-84 was mainly due to structural factors (e.g. labour market rigidities; economic policy reluctant to change course; the change of the political landscape – and therefore a high degree of uncertainty on the side of investors about the actual rate of return –) has been pointed out by Dolado and Viñals (1990: 306).

[23] On natural trading partners see Frankel, Stein and Wei (1996) and Krugman (1991b). Both of these studies suggest that the issue of natural versus unnatural trading partners is a matter of the magnitude of transportation costs.

[24] On the role of economic policy in the performance of laggards see Larre and Torres (1991).

stabilisation. Note also that the ranking of the four countries in terms of relative per capita GDP was subject to change in recent history.

The variety of experiences suggests that the reasons for relative macroperformance are country-specific rather than being geographically located at the periphery per se. Neither does the data provide a backing for the argument that backwardness per se prevents countries from catching up. Rather, the evidence is supportive to the notion that integration fosters income growth of laggards. In both periods of increasing outward-orientation (that is 1962-74, 1986-96), the majority of the four enjoyed above-average income growth.

The heterogeneity case studies display is also counterfactual to the argument that there was no widening observed because of EU regional policy. In fact, poorly performing Greece received between 1989 and 1993 three times as many funds per capita than Spain did. In absolute terms, Greece received EU structural funds on a similar scale as Portugal, while getting twice as much as Ireland (Nunnenkamp (1997: 197-8))[25]; Ireland experienced outstanding growth rates with transfers substantially reduced. There is simply no indication that transfers have a positive impact on macroperformance (see also Busch, Lichtblau and Schnabel (1997) for details; and with similar results for Spanish regions Cuadrado, Dehesa and Precedo (1993)) – recall also the famous Mezzogiorno problem.

In any case, the further enlargement of the EU (by granting membership to the Czech Republic, Poland and Hungary, for instance) is frequently considered to put much more of a stress on the European income distribution than integration did in the past.[26] However, aside from the fact that – as just seen – backwardness in itself has not proven to be a stumbling bloc for development, income gaps between the EU-15 and the newcomers are not without a precedent. Admittedly, in terms of current prices and exchange rates the ratio of national per capita incomes to the EU-15 is 1:5 at best (in the case of the Czech Republic) in 1995 (1:5.3 in the case of Hungary and 1:7.1 in the case of Poland). However, at current prices and purchasing power parities Czech per capita income was about 9479 US dollars in 1995 which amounts to 47 per cent of the EU-15 average (see OECD (1997c) for data). For comparison: in 1985, right before joining the EU, Portugal had a per capita income of 46 per cent of the EU-10 (in terms of 1985 prices and purchasing power parities).

An additional aspect is to be noted: all of these countries are still in a transition from a centrally-planned to a market-led economy. Therefore, two

---

[25] Numbers refer to funds under the so-called objective 1 which amount to more than 70 per cent of all funds distributed under the EU structural policy.

[26] For an optimistic evaluation, however, see DIW (1997a).

sorts of adjustment can be expected. The first is the impact of the abandoning of socialist policies on average per capita incomes. The second is the impact of integration itself. As far as the former is concerned all of the countries can be expected to catch-up thus clearly improving their income position, if they continue to provide market friendly institutions. This process of catching up will enlarge local market size if the latter is measured in terms of relative economic performance drawing on GDP per capita data. From this perspective, EU enlargement puts much less of a strain on EU institutions such as the regional transfer scheme currently in place than might be expected in comparing actual data.

II.   The US as a point of reference

In many respects, the United States constitute a natural point of reference for the impact of integration. With free trade of goods and services (and free mobility of capital and labour as well) between US states, the hypothesis that the US might also be informative as far as the regional dispersion of incomes is concerned immediately suggests itself.[27]

Exactly because of lower costs of mobility and trade within the US as compared to Europe for much of the history one would expect according to the centralisation hypothesis that the dispersion in the US is higher than in the EU. However, at least in actual exchange rates the level of the 1990-dispersion across US states was *lower* than the one across EU member states. Figure 2.7 highlights the case in point. It shows the distribution of the country-specific (state-specific) average per capita income in terms of the overall EU average (US average).

In each case, the overall weighted average is indicated by the grey shaded vertical line in the middle. The one to the left marks the weighted average in countries (states) that are relatively backward, whereas the one to the right shows the respective average for those ahead. Data for the EU member states was derived from national data by using PPP as well as actual exchange rates as neither provides for an exact aggregation.

---

[27]   For an investigation in the evolution of the regional distribution of industries instead of per capita incomes see Krugman (1991a: Ch. 3) and Crandall (1993) for the US (and for evidence within North America Hanson (1998)) and Amiti (1997; 1998) for the EU.

Figure 2.7:   Geographical dispersion of per capita incomes in 1990:
EU-12 versus United States

(a) EU-12: national data aggregated at PPP

number of countries

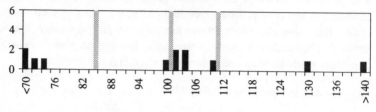

EU average = 100

(b) EU-12: national data aggregated at actual exchange rates

number of countries

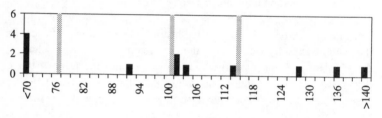

EU average = 100

(b) US states

number of states

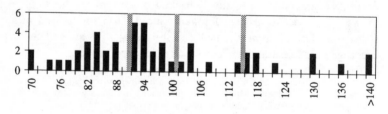

US average = 100

Source: US Bureau of the Census (1994); EUROSTAT REGIO data tape April 1997;
own calculations.

According to the 1990 calculations displayed in Figure 2.7, the distribution in both economies, the US and the EU-12, differs in three respects: first, the spread between the mean of states earning below-average per capita income and those earning above-average per capita income is smaller in the US than in the EU (the distance between the grey-shaded vertical line on the far right hand and the far left hand).

Actually, the spread differs not so much with regard to states ranked among the highest in terms of average per capita income, but with the lowest. On average, per capita income in states with an income below the overall mean amounted to only 76 per cent (at actual exchange rates) or 84 per cent (at PPP) in the EU, whereas in the US it came up to approximately 90 per cent.

Second, looking upon the state or country marking the lower boundary, relative differences between the US and the EU turn out to be even greater. For in the case of lowest ranking Mississippi average per capita income was at least 70 per cent of the overall US average. In the EU, Portugal brought up the rear in 1990, showing an average per capita income of only 39 per cent of the EU average at current prices and exchange rates. Penultimate ranked Greece is not much better off, with 43 per cent. At current prices and PPPs, the order is reversed, with Greece approaching 58 per cent and Portugal 62 per cent. Yet, although somewhat higher, the average per capita income is still substantially lower when compared to the EU average than in case of the US.

Third, measured by the coefficient of variation the dispersion of incomes between the states is higher within the EU than within the US, namely 24.93 compared to 16.45. However, if in the case of the EU national data is converted at PPP, there is no notable difference between the US and the EU (EU: 17.84).

If US data provides a benchmark[28] for the consequences of integration for the regional distribution of incomes, then the message is that there is no

---

[28] Those who call for a stronger regional focus of European economic policy often refer precisely to the United States. In the US, it is argued, built-in stabilisers are operating on a much larger scale than those established within the EU. An often neglected fact would be that, although explicit intergovernmental grants play only a minor role in the US, there is an implicit vertical compensation mechanism at work which tends to cushion regional disparities in economic development. This would iron out at least some of the differences in regional economic strength, whereas in the EU there would be no comparable mechanism in place (among those who are of the opinion that real adjustment problems in the US are cushioned much more than in Europe because of fiscal federalism is, for instance, Eichengreen (1990); see also calculations by Sachs and Sala-í-Martin (1991), who come to the conclusion that in the US almost 40 per cent of the impact of regional shocks is absorbed via vertical flows between the different levels of government). However, these calculations are not undisputed. See, for instance, von Hagen (1991).

indication that a single market necessarily fosters a centre-periphery pattern in the geographical income distribution. On an overall account there is not that much of a difference in the regional dispersion in the EU and the US. In several respects cross-state dispersion is even smaller in the US than in the EU. This applies in particular to the relative performance of the bottom of the distribution vis-à-vis the average. Naturally, the data has to be interpreted with caution as US-EU comparisons have limits for systemic reasons. Labour market institutions differ substantially, and mobility is known to be considerably higher in the US.

According to the new economic geography, factor mobility is alleged to widen rather than to reduce regional income disparities. However, US-EU data suggests that mobility exactly works in the opposite direction, increasing the homogeneity of incomes across states rather than reducing them.

Indeed, there is some tentative evidence that the difference in the bottom of the distribution between the EU and the US is due to a higher mobility and more flexible labour market institutions in the US as compared to the EU. The evidence comes from personal incomes. For in terms of the personal income distribution European countries are more homogeneous than the US.[29] Though average personal disposable income in PPP was 39 per cent higher on average in the US than in the EU (1990), most of the indicators point towards the dispersion of personal incomes being lower within the EU than within the US (Atkinson (1996: 22)).[30,31] The Gini coefficient for the US, for instance, is with 0.341 approx. 0.05 points higher than the EU-wide coefficient. In particular, the bottom of the US distribution was less well off than the bottom in the EU was. The share of

---

[29] However, the spread of Gini coefficients across individual countries within the EU is higher than between the EU average and the US (not adjusted for PP). In particular, the periphery of the EU (Spain, Portugal and Ireland) shows an exceptionally high decile ratio (that is the ratio of the top decile to the bottom decile of the personal income distribution) See Atkinson (1996: Figure 1/2, 18) (Atkinson gives no numbers for Greece). The Hasse diagram for the 1980s displaying the cases of Lorenz-curve superiority give additional evidence that the personal income distribution is less skewed in the centre than in the periphery (Atkinson (1996: 21)).

[30] On the evolution of the personal income distribution in the US see Danziger and Gottshalk (1994) and Burkhauser and Poupore (1997). However, though aggregates might differ, the US have not been as unique as far as the recent rise in income inequality is concerned. See Jenkins (1996) on the UK.

[31] Personal income distribution in the EU and the US: Shares of total income in the late 1980s

| Region | Share of decile group | | | | | | | | |
	10	20	30	40	50	60	70	80	90
United States	1.9	5.7	11.2	18.0	26.2	35.7	46.9	60.2	76.3
Europe-wide (referring to 14 countries)	2.9	7.9	14.1	21.3	29.5	39.0	49.8	62.3	77.2

Source: Atkinson (1996: Table 3, 26), and sources cited therein.

the lowest quintile in overall disposable income in the US was 5.7 per cent in the late 1980s while it reached more than 8 per cent in the EU (except for Spain, the UK and Ireland with 7.4, 7.5 and 7.1 respectively).

Clearly, during the 1980s the personal income distribution widened within the EU as well, in particular in the UK (Atkinson (1996: 23); Economic Report of the President (1994: 25)). Yet, as far as ranking is possible according to Lorenz-curve dominance, the personal income distribution in the US was characterised by larger disparities than in most of the EU countries in the 1980s.

In so far as calculations for comparison draw only upon a certain point in time it is not clear whether the future dispersion in the EU will reflect more closely the one currently observed in the US or whether national income gaps will become even bigger in size. But the same objection can be raised with regard to any extrapolations of historical data into the future. At any rate, a historical US-EU comparison supplies no indication that integration is inevitably associated with income-divergence, that is a more pronounced centre-periphery pattern.

III. Heterogeneity in macroperformance

Drawing on GDP data there is hardly any overall trend towards an increase in dispersion of per capita incomes across EU member states. Rather, there has been a decline in income disparities from the very beginning of European economic integration, with the decline losing its force somewhat recently. As far as the more recent evolution is concerned, that is since the early 1980s, the dynamics of the overall trend was considerably shaped by a decline in the dispersion between EU countries, that is the between-set dispersion, while dispersion on the NUTS II level, the so-called within-set dispersion, stagnated.

Neither has there been a move towards a more definite centre-periphery pattern in the course of European economic integration. The period from the mid-1960s to the mid-1970s with Spain, Portugal and Greece becoming much more outward-oriented than previously was characterised by these countries substantially catching up vis-à-vis the major European countries. The period of a minor increase in dispersion with the dispersion stagnating subsequently (1975-84) was also a period of political shocks (and a major recession) and not a period of unfettered market forces at work. Except for Greece, relative income growth picked up again after the second enlargement of the EU. Nor is there evidence from US data that a single market per se is associated with a more pronounced centre-periphery pattern.

There are differences with regard to particular experiences though. In particular Ireland enjoyed well above-average income growth rates. The Iberian countries experienced a development push upon joining the EU. Greece, however, failed to enter the convergence club. The variety in performance points more towards the role of particular circumstances in economic performance rather than the starting position in the income distribution being responsible for catching up or falling behind.

Being left with some doubts whether disparities widen because of integration, we will take a closer look at the reasons why the pattern, according to the new approach to economic integration, might be shaped by centripetal forces.

3. Centripetal Forces Dominating: the Home Market Effect

I. Economies of scale on the demand side and the proliferation effect of integration

This chapter will provide an overview of the driving forces of recent theory in support of the centripetal hypothesis. Basically, the outcome is due to two ingredients: technology and distance to the market. This section will be about the first of the ingredients, namely technology. In particular, economies of scale are alleged to give rise to a regionally skewed income pattern emerging endogenously in the course of integration.

Technology also provides one of the major differences between the early economic geography and the new approach. That the integrated economy might be characterised by a regionally uneven income distribution is not a fundamentally new issue. Centre-periphery models have a long tradition in economic theory (see von Thünen (1990 (1818-42)); Weber (1909); Christaller (1933) to mention only some of the most prominent ones; Martin (1997) provides an overview how early contributions to the field are related to the new economic geography). However, according to the new view, in these early models agglomeration was merely assumed. It was taken as the point of departure for analysing the regional impact of integration. Rather than being endogenous, the centre-bias of economic activity was exogenous to the model. The division of labour was still subject to strong centrifugal forces because of the assumption of constant returns to scale technologies. With some factors of production being in fixed supply, in particular land, congestion provided for an incentive to move further away from the centre. Technology thus led to a more even allocation of production in space rather than a more skewed one. Centripetal forces were not due to technology but arose from the market value of the product and the distance to the market. As the value of the product declined with distance to the market, distance and technology were in fact opposing forces, one pulling the industry regionally together (distance) and the other pushing industry regionally apart (technology).

Because of focusing on the location of industries where the regional pattern is already characterised by agglomeration from the onset, the 'new' economic geography criticised early theories for putting the cart before the horse. The 'old' economic geography provides a 'description rather than (an) explanation' (Krugman (1996a: 15)) of the forces at work in economic integration. In contrast, the new approach claims to go one step back.

Instead of taking agglomeration as given, it aims at deriving the pattern from economic reasoning. Basically, it is the assumption about technology that makes for the difference. Models from the new strand try to capture the dynamics of the pattern by incorporating the fact that frequently scale matters for a firm's competitiveness. In fact, in models from the new strand technology is alleged to reinforce the impact of distance on the regional pattern. Starting with a homogenous surface, they claim to show that a pattern emerges from this flat earth economy, and investigate what the pattern looks like if scale matters (Krugman (1995a)). However, Lösch (1943: 72) and Giersch (1949) already had pointed out that economies of scale are at the heart of the explanation of agglomeration, though not by use of a formalised model.

In analysing the forces of self-organisation of industry in space the 'new' economic geography, too, makes a couple of assumptions which make life easier. Though convenient, some of these assumptions are far from realistic, limiting the explanatory power of the theory as regards the evolutions actually observed. One of these assumptions is the assumption about the technology being employed and its evolution, both in transportation and in production. In particular, technology is considered exogenous. Note that by taking a certain kind of technology as given, the new models assume a point of departure quite similar to the old strand. This section will nevertheless be about the most stripped down version of the model for emphasising what actually drives these models. The presentation paves the way for two tasks: First, it enables us better to contrast the prediction of the models with current developments in the world economy and in the European economies in particular. Second, it shows where theory can best be modified to capture the difference.

Following Hooverian (1948) tradition, one can basically distinguish three levels on which economies of scale might occur (see also Fujita and Thisse (1996) or Stahl (1997) for a more recent classification), namely

(1) economies of scale within a firm,
(2) localisation economies due to industry specific externalities,
(3) urbanisation economies, which means economy-wide externalities.

The following analysis will be dealing with the first level, namely economies of scale internal to the firm. The subadditivity of the cost function of an individual producer can have several economic reasons: it can be due to indivisibilities, such as in case of networks, specialisation and so on, simply any kind of lumpiness. Or it can be due to the so-called two-thirds rule which applies to production processes in which the elasticity of the costs with regard to output is two-thirds. Pipelines are one example where this relationship is supposed to hold, shipping is another. In both cases output is a matter of carrying capacity as measured by volume while costs are related to the surface of the object being handled, thus making for an output-cost ratio of 3:2. A third driving force can be the law of large numbers in case of stochastic demand as far as bundling allows to economise on costs.

However, as made explicit by much of the new trade theory (e.g. Krugman (1980; 1995d); Ethier (1982); Helpman (1984); Helpman and Krugman (1985: Chs 6-9)) it does not necessarily follow from economies of scale internal to the firm that the location of firms in space, though probably regionally skewed, leads to an uneven regional income distribution.

In focusing on the impact of technology and the cost structure in the division of labour the new approach to integration has some affinity with the discussion on competitiveness. In the discussion about competitiveness, as well, economies of scale are considered to shape the performance of whole nations. This kind of reasoning is for instance implicit in much of the literature on market share analysis (Dluhosch, Freytag and Krüger (1996: 77 et seq.)). Exactly because of technology, standard comparative advantage reasoning is said no longer to apply (e.g. Tyson (1992); Scherer (1992); and, for a more policy-oriented view Seitz (1991)). Instead, there would be a considerable first-mover advantage with regard to market share translating into higher incomes for whoever comes first. The Boeing-Airbus example is the most widely appreciated industry where this is supposed to hold. In fact, it became established in textbooks (e.g. Krugman and Obstfeld (1994: 284-7)).

Though the notion of a particular specialisation pattern being associated with higher incomes is not especially new (see the discussion in development economics, on which Krueger (1997) provides an overview), it gained prominence again as markets became more international and the number of actual competitors declined (thus 'strategic trade policy' became fashionable; for a selection of papers see Helpman (1992: Chs 6-10))[1]. However, as can be shown in a simple trade-theoretic framework, without

---

[1] Strategic trade policy is associated with work by Brander and Spencer (1981; 1984; 1985); and Krugman (1984). See also the overview in Krugman (1990). Again, the underlying reasoning is not particularly new but can be traced back to Stackelberg's (1934) duopoly model. Assumptions, results and policy conclusions of these models are not undisputed. On the main weaknesses in the argument see, for instance, Stegemann (1988); Siebert (1988); and, with particular emphasis on the assumptions and implications concerning competition von Weizsäcker and Waldenberger (1992) and Donges (1994). Empirical evidence seems to be poor as well, even in industries where the theory is frequently considered to apply. See Grossman (1990); Bletschacher and Klodt (1992); Monopolkommission (1992).

any further refinement, there is not much to this argument. In fact, though being considered a driving force in association with distance, economies of scale per se do not necessarily give rise to centripetal forces.[2]

The analysis starts by assuming an integrated economy, that is an economy with perfect regional and sectoral mobility of factors of production. There is one factor of production in the economy, namely labour L (see Krugman (1980) for a one-factor one-sector model along these lines). The one-factor assumption ensures that the result is not influenced by differences in factor proportions, but it is not crucial for results to hold (see for instance Helpman (1981) for a 2×2×2 model). Actually, the model abstracts from any sort of cost differences and comparative advantage of the ordinary kind, focusing only on how economies of scale might matter for the allocation of industries and the income distribution. Analysing what the integrated economy would look like provides some kind of reference with regard to the evolution after opening up national markets. For tracing the impact of trade on regional incomes Samuelson's Angel (Samuelson (1949/1987: 14)) will be invoked who splits the integrated economy into two countries, Home H and Foreign F, so that the 1×1 model becomes a 2×1 model. This approach allows to check whether the integrated economy can nevertheless be reproduced.[3] The major difference between the integrated economy and the 2×1 model naturally lies in the mobility of the factors of production. Under the assumption of perfect mobility between sectors in the integrated economy wage differences (which in this one-factor model amount to income differences[4]) are not persistent. In case of factors being immobile, as in the 2x1 model, it is less obvious whether the outcome is the same or whether the cross-national income distribution is skewed. However, as theory has shown, the difference need not matter.

The integrated economy is assumed to consist of two industries: Industry x is characterised by monopolistic competition à la Chamberlin, while industry y exhibits constant returns to scale. The demand side is based on a utility function of the Cobb-Douglas type, which means that a constant share of income is spent on both types of goods, x and y. The good y serves as numeraire. In specifying the demand for the good produced under

---

[2]   Neither does the number of actual local competitors allow for any conclusions about the intensity of competition which in turn might have consequences for the distribution of incomes (Baumol, Panzar and Willig (1982)). A lack in numbers may be actually due to low earnings in an industry (Dluhosch, Freytag and Krüger (1996)).

[3]   The concept of the integrated economy was first introduced by Samuelson (1949).

[4]   In a 2×2 model with either factor accumulation or international factor mobility the distributional impact may be substantially different from that. Per capita income also differs in case of different capital-labour ratios. See Slaughter (1997) for two back-of-the-envelope examples.

monopolistic competition the model draws upon Dixit and Stiglitz (1977) which is based on the assumption of a representative consumer and a constant elasticity of substitution (CES) between a large number of differentiated products. All consumers are supposed to have the same utility function which is of the love of variety kind which means that the utility increases with the number of varieties available.

Though each differentiated good is produced under an increasing returns to scale technology, economies of scale actually result from the utility function in this framework. Due to the CES assumption all goods are demanded in a certain proportion. Given the elasticity, utility is higher the more varieties are available. Instead of exploiting economies of scale further by increasing individual output, it is the number of varieties offered that climbs as market size increases. Individual output, instead, stays the same. This feature of the utility function is interpreted as some kind of economies of scale: the higher the elasticity of substitution, the lower the economies of scale and vice versa. Thus, in this set-up the demand side is the driving force of the model.

However, the driving force need not necessarily originate from consumption. As for instance in the case of Ethier's (1982) model, it might well be due to producers gaining from being able to choose from a larger array of components instead of having to rely on a single source. In case of the latter, economies of scale are basically Marshallian (1919) in nature.[5] The reasoning is the same though (see, however, Markusen's (1990) refinement).

In any case, qua assumption, market size only has a proliferation effect and no effect on cost competition. Given fixed and variable costs, the taste for variety pins down the number of firms and thereby the output of each individual firm. Excluding any pro-competitive effect of market size is a rather peculiar feature of the model which will be discussed in more detail in Chapter 4.

At any rate, demand of a representative consumer is derived from a Cobb-Douglas utility function with constant shares of spending μ, 1-μ on the class of goods x and y respectively.

$$U = x^\mu y^{1-\mu} \tag{3.1}$$

---

[5] Marshallian externalities are usually associated with externalities working through the factor market. See, for instance David and Rosenbloom (1990); von Hagen and Hammond (1994). However, the reasoning is basically the same as in case of externalities arising through intermediates.

The consumption of x is a CES-aggregate of expenditures on the varieties of x; the number of varieties is n, the constant elasticity of substitution between the varieties is σ which may have any value between 1 to ∞. As σ tends to ∞, the closer the goods are substitutes. Hence, the gain in utility from the number of goods is decreasing as σ increases. As regards the various varieties consumers are assumed to have the following sub-utility function:

$$x = \left[\sum_{i=1}^{n} x_i^{\frac{\sigma-1}{\sigma}} \right]^{\frac{\sigma}{\sigma-1}}, \qquad 1 < \sigma < \infty \tag{3.2}$$

Expenditures are allocated in a two-stage optimisation process (Helpman and Krugman (1985: 122 et seq.)). The first step involves the allocation of expenditures between the varieties $x_1, \ldots, x_i, \ldots, x_n$ taken as a bundle, that is x, on the one hand and y on the other hand, subject to the budget constraint $E = y + qx$

$$L = U\left(x(x_1, \ldots, x_n), y\right) - \lambda(y + qx - E) \tag{3.3}$$

where q denotes the price index of the bundle in terms of the numeraire y while E denotes total expenditures.

In a second step, the expenditure for the bundle x, i.e. $(E-y)$, is allocated among the varieties of x, with p_i being the (relative) price for the good x_i.

$$L_i = U\left(x(x_1, \ldots, x_n), y\right) - \lambda\left(\sum_{i=1}^{n} p_i x_i - (E - y)\right) \tag{3.4}$$

Setting the first derivative of (3.4) with respect to x (y) to zero gives the optimal allocation of expenditures between the bundle x and y:

$$\frac{\partial L}{\partial x} = \frac{\partial U}{\partial x} - \lambda q = 0 \quad \Rightarrow \quad \frac{\partial U}{\partial x} = \lambda q$$

and

$$\frac{\partial L}{\partial y} = \frac{\partial U}{\partial y} - \lambda = 0 \quad \Rightarrow \quad \frac{\partial U}{\partial y} = \lambda \tag{3.5}$$

Inserting (3.5) into the first derivative of (3.4) with respect to x_i yields:

$$\frac{\partial L}{\partial x_i} = \frac{\partial U}{\partial x} \frac{\partial x}{\partial x_i} =$$

$$\lambda q \frac{\sigma}{\sigma-1} \left[\sum_{i=1}^{n} x_i^{(\sigma-1)/\sigma} \right]^{1/(\sigma-1)} \frac{\sigma-1}{\sigma} x_i^{-1/\sigma} - \lambda p_i = 0 \qquad \forall i = 1,...,n$$

(3.6)

Hence, one obtains the demand for the differentiated good and its varieties as a function of relative prices:

$$\frac{p_i}{q} = \left(\frac{x}{x_i} \right)^{1/\sigma} \quad \Rightarrow \quad x_i = x \left(\frac{q}{p_i} \right)^{\sigma}$$

(3.7)

$$\Rightarrow x = x_i q^{-\sigma} p_i^{\sigma} \qquad \forall i = 1,...,n$$

Due to the budget constraint, expenditures on x must equal income received in producing x. Hence, the volume of x bought times the implicit price index q for the bundle of x, that is qx, has to be smaller or (as shall be assumed here since the model does not contain capital) equal to income. Income is determined by the wage rate times the labour supply multiplied with the share of expenditures μ spent on the bundle x.

$$xq = \sum_{i=1}^{n} x_i p_i^{\sigma} q^{1-\sigma} \le \mu w_x L$$

(3.8)

On the supply side each differentiated good is produced by a single firm with fixed costs F and variable costs v. Fixed and variable costs in this framework are considered to be the same across all firms and total costs in the production of a single variety amount to $w_{x_i} L_{x_i} = F + v x_i$. Costs across all firms are:

$$\sum_{i=1}^{n} w_{x_i} L_{x_i} = \sum_{i=1}^{n} (F + v x_i)$$

(3.9)

Good y is produced according to a Leontief production function with constant returns to scale:

$$w_y L_y = y$$

(3.10)

Full employment is ensured as prices are assumed to be flexible and labour is considered to be mobile between sectors. Thus, the labour market is cleared:

$$\Sigma_{i=1}^{n} L_{x_i} + L_y = L \tag{3.11}$$

Under the assumption of free market entry, profits are driven down until the break-even point is just reached. With a constant elasticity of demand price setting is characterised by a constant mark up on variable costs.[6] With these assumptions one can calculate prices p_i, individual output x_i and the number of firms n in the x sector. Individual prices and output can be derived from the first order condition for a profit maximum and the zero profit condition:

$$\pi_{x_i} = p_i x_i - v x_i - F \tag{3.12}$$

$$\frac{\partial \pi}{\partial x_i} = p_i + \frac{\partial p_i}{\partial x_i} x_i - v = 0 \quad \Rightarrow \quad p_i = \frac{\sigma}{\sigma - 1} v \tag{3.13}$$

$$(p_i - v)x_i = F \quad \Rightarrow \quad x_i = \frac{F}{v}(\sigma - 1) \tag{3.14}$$

Due to free entry and the symmetry assumption all prices and quantities are identical $p_i = p$ and $x_1 = ... = x_i = ... = x_n$ for all $i = 1,...,n$ in equilibrium. Since profits are zero ($\pi = 0$) and nominal wages are the same in all sectors of the economy, $w_{x_1} = ... = w_{x_i} = ... = w_{x_n} = w_y = w$, total employment in the monopolistic industry is determined by μL: Demand (3.8) has to be equal to supply (3.9) in the x industry $\mu w_x L = n w_{x_i} L_{x_i}$, from which follows that employment in the x sector is μL, if wages are the same across all sectors. Total employment in the x sector divided by the output of each firm gives the number of goods produced which is identical to the number of firms in the x sector:

$$n = \frac{\mu L}{L_{x_i}} = \frac{\mu w L}{F + v x_i} = \frac{\mu w L}{F + v((\sigma - 1)F/v)} = \frac{\mu w L}{F\sigma} \tag{3.15}$$

Due to the utility function, welfare of a representative consumer increases with the size of the economy since the number of differentiated

---

goods is a function of total employment, and utility depends on the number of varieties n produced:

$$n \approx L, \quad U = f(n) \tag{3.16}$$

$$U = \left[\sum_{i=1}^{n} x_i^{(\sigma-1)/\sigma} \right]^{\sigma/(\sigma-1)} = \left[n \left(\frac{w}{p} L_{x_i} \right)^{(\sigma-1)/\sigma} \right]^{\sigma/(\sigma-1)} \tag{3.17}$$

Now imagine that Samuelson's Angel comes down and the integrated economy is separated, forming from now on two countries Home (H) and Foreign (F) with factor endowments L^H and L^F respectively.

$$L = L^H + L^F \tag{3.18}$$

Despite monopolistic competition prevailing in the x sector, the integrated economy can still be reproduced so that the real and the nominal wage rates are the same in Home and in Foreign. This means that there are situations in which the (real) bundle of goods consumed by the representative individual is the same as well no matter where he is located.

In particular, residents are assumed to have the same preferences so that the share of expenditures spent on the various x goods on the one hand and the share spent on y is the same in both countries. Due to the assumption that each variety of the x good is produced by a single firm both countries are producing disjoint sets of goods n^H, n^F. However, the allocation of firms need not matter for the regional distribution of incomes.

The production of different sets of varieties while consumers wish to consume from each variety provides an incentive for international trade. If the integrated economy is reproduced by trade, the two sets must add up to a total of n varieties available for consumption in the world economy:

$$n^H + n^F = n \tag{3.19}$$

The condition that the numbers have to add up to the number of varieties produced in the integrated economy is sufficient to show that the integrated economy is reproduced since all of the varieties are produced with the same cost function which essentially means that individual output and prices are the same.

Similarly, the joint production of y in F and H must reach the amount of the integrated economy:

$$y^H + y^F = y \tag{3.20}$$

However, by Walras' law one can concentrate on the x sector. For real incomes not being regionally skewed because of the production pattern, the nominal wage rate must be the same in both of the economies and in all of the four sectors, as in the integrated economy. Since due to perfect mobility wages are the same in each sector of the economy ($w_x^H = w_y^H$ and $w_x^F = w_y^F$), the proof reduces to showing that

$$w^H = w^F = w \tag{3.21}$$

That this condition holds can be inferred from the conditions for market clearing. For market clearing to take place, the value of the bundle produced must buy the value consumed. This must hold for three markets in the x sector: (1) the market for x varieties produced in Home, (2) the market for x varieties produced in Foreign and, finally, (3) the international market. With CES preferences residents of Home spent a share of their income proportional to the share of x varieties produced in Foreign in the total number of varieties on Foreign varieties and vice versa.

Market clearing for x varieties produced in Home thus occurs if:

$$\frac{n^H}{n^H + n^F}\left(w^H L^H + w^F L^F\right) = w^H L^H \tag{3.22}$$

Similarly, market clearing for x varieties produced in Foreign requires supply and demand to be balanced:

$$\frac{n^F}{n^H + n^F}\left(w^H L^H + w^F L^F\right) = w^F L^F \tag{3.23}$$

Finally, trade is balanced if the value of Home's imports is equal to the value of its exports:

$$w^H L^H\left(\frac{n^F}{n^F + n^H}\right) = w^F L^F\left(\frac{n^H}{n^F + n^H}\right) \tag{3.24}$$

Since we know from (3.15) that n^F, n^H are proportional to L^F, L^H, equation (3.24) can be stated in terms of labour forces:

$$w^H L^H \left(\frac{L^F}{L^F + L^H} \right) = w^F L^F \left(\frac{L^H}{L^F + L^H} \right) \tag{3.25}$$

Equation (3.25) holds if nominal wages w^H, w^F are the same in Home and in Foreign. Since due to the symmetry assumption and the no-costs of trade assumption prices are the same as well, real income per worker is equally distributed between Home and Foreign. Hence, we are left with two equations (3.22), (3.23), and two unknowns, which can be solved for n^F, n^H, given L^F and L^H.

Summing up, imperfect competition per se does not yet imply that some countries benefit from integration at the expense of others. Theoretically, the integrated economy can still be reproduced and factor price equalisation can still occur, even if some industries are characterised by economies of scale. As long as there are no transportation costs it does not matter for local well being (that is real income) whether particular industries are located in Home or in Foreign. Instead, by adding to the variety of goods available for consumption trade raises welfare in Home and in Foreign. Actually, due to the love of variety assumption, residents of the smaller country gain the more the larger the trading partner country (see Lawrence and Spiller (1983: 64) in a two-factor framework).

Drawing upon a sample of 43 countries, Maddison (1994: 50 et seq.) indeed found no empirical evidence that national GDP is a function of the size of the local economy, suggesting that there is no presumption that it is only the economy attracting a particular industry characterised by economies of scale that benefits from being able to exploit them. Maddison concludes from this that either small economies can share in the benefits of scale via international trade or economies of scale are far less important than usually assumed.[7] Though the second conclusion is not necessarily warranted, the first might well hold as theory has shown.

Hence, economies of scale per se need not imply a regionally skewed income pattern. Theoretically, they can though, as for instance Baumol (1993) has pointed out. One such case which might give rise to a skewed income distribution is 'lumpiness', that is if economies of scale are not exploited relative to demand (see also Courant and Deardorff (1992) for a two-factor model of this sort; whether there are still gains from trade to be expected is discussed in Deardorff (1994)). However, if technology is

---

[7]   However, one has to keep in mind that his measure of economies of scale is employees per establishment, which might be misleading. At the same time he criticises Chandler (1990) for not being more precise (Maddison (1994: 53)) in disentangling economies of scale from other forces driving US manufacturing growth.

considered as given and the exploitation of economies of scale is not limited by demand, this result need not materialise.

In the most stripped down version of the basic model, both imperfect competition and transportation costs are needed for persistent differences in real incomes despite free trade. If trade is costly, economies of scale are considered to cause local externalities because of the impact on *local* demand. Actually, due to their impact on demand, the difference between pecuniary and technological externalities[8] becomes blurred. How the relationship between economies of scale and distance to the market gives rise to locational externalities will be explored in further detail in the next section.

II.   Costs of distance and local demand

According to the new perspective on integration the picture becomes different if there are translocation costs.[9] Together with economies of scale, costs of shipping goods to their market give rise to centripetal forces.[10] Costs of distance other than the transportation of goods are neglected. In particular, the models abstract from costs of communication and information-related services. By doing so, they rest on two premises. First, they refer to a narrowly defined set of goods, namely bulky goods which reach their point of consumption via railroad, air or road transportation. Implicitly, they assume that these are the only kind of goods produced and consumed in the economy. Second, they assume that the evolution of the division of labour within trading blocs (as the EU) is actually driven by a change in the costs of transportation related to these goods, that is, in the costs per railroad, air or road mile.

Both of these premises miss one central aspect of current developments. First, intra-EU trade, as international trade in general, is not confined to goods which need to be shipped on the road, railroad or aircraft for getting

---

[8]   Since Scitovsky (1954) these two concepts have been considered as being fundamentally different in nature. However, that they become blurred in case of economies of scale and transportation costs becomes clear if the partial equilibrium and the general equilibrium perspective are being compared. The difference of these two perspectives in judging pecuniary externalities has been pointed out by Shubik (1971).

[9]   Of course, in a more realistic framework, the demand producers face may not only depend on the costs of transportation (given similar costs of production). Rather, the place of production in itself may be a characteristic by which consumers evaluate goods. However, this implies leaving the Dixit-Stiglitz framework. See Armington (1969) for an investigation of this issue.

[10]   The fact that in reality there is a capitalisation of locational advantages because of factors being in fixed supply like land (see the literature on local public goods and the Henry George Theorem, e.g. Scotchmer and Thisse (1992)) is no contradiction. Keep in mind that capitalisation is already the *outcome* of centripetal forces (i.e. just like the adjustment of the exchange rate in response to a local change in productivity).

to the consumer or (in case of intermediate goods) to the producer.[11] Recently, there has been a secular shift in all major industrialised economies towards services (in terms of both employment and nominal GDP; see Klodt, Maurer and Schimmelpfennig (1997: Table 1); DIW (1997c)). Second, most of the change in the costs of transportation related to bulky goods took place by the end of the nineteenth century. Most recently, costs of distance have plummeted because of dramatically diminishing costs of communication (see Table 3.1),[12] which in many respects differ from the former.

In particular due to the economic features of information, these costs of distance are different in character from the costs of shipping a good to its point of consumption. As will be pointed out in more detail in Chapter 4, costs of communication are more of a fixed cost character with respect to output. Costs of transporting goods on the road, by railroad or by aircraft, in contrast, are more of the variable kind: they come up with each piece carried. The difference matters. In fact, as we will see shortly, it is crucial for a centre bias in development to materialise.

Despite these shortcomings, the new economic geography claims to provide a reference model for the development of the intra-European division of labour. According to these models centripetal forces arising from a change in the costs of shipping goods to their market are not only responsible for the location of industries to become probably regionally quite skewed. In addition, their location would also affect the income distribution. If, for instance, Home were bigger in market size as measured by labour consumers it is assumed to attract all of the industry exhibiting economies of scale as soon as a critical size in terms of local demand is reached. The turning point of the allocation of industries depends on three parameters: preferences as regards product variety in the sector which exhibits economies of scale, translocation costs and relative market size in Home and in Foreign. Actually, according to the new perspective, costs of

---

[11] Recall also the famous example of the clothing industry. Dresses are designed in Paris, Milan or New York with 'blueprints' sent to South-east Asia where the clothes are manufactured. See also Morawetz (1981) on the issue: Though Columbia enjoyed a comparative advantage in manufacturing US-designed clothes because of being closer to the market, US industries nevertheless moved their production to East Asia. For a more recent study focusing on the Mexican apparel industry with the design and marketing coming from the US and Hong Kong and production taking place in Mexico see Hanson (1996). For a broader view underlining the trend towards the globalisation of production see, for instance, Nunnenkamp, Gundlach and Agarwal (1994). See also DIW (1997b) and Rodrik (1997) for an evaluation.

[12] Williamson, J.G. (1996: 286), for instance, reports that the price of grain in Liverpool exceeded Chicago prices by approximately 60 per cent around 1870 while around 1912 the difference was already less than 15 per cent. On the role of communication costs in accelerating the globalisation of production see Harris (1993: 766-8; 1995).

distance do not have an unambiguous impact on the localisation of industry. Rather, the regional distribution of industries and GDP might twist the further transportation costs move into one or the other direction. However, the interesting thing to note is that a decline in the costs of transportation might push the regional location of firms more towards agglomeration instead of a more regionally even distribution.

Due to the costs of shipping, the regional bias in the location of industries has consequences for the regional distribution of incomes (measured in any common good). Thus there might emerge a persistent gap of real incomes between regions (or countries for that matter) in the course of integration (e.g. Krugman and Venables (1990) with reference to the EU). This seems all plausible though: if there are costs of distance, the location of industries matters for local well-being. Per capita income is higher in real terms in whichever market is bigger in size.

Table 3.1: Costs of air transportation, telephone calls, and computer price deflator

Year	Average air transportation revenue[a] per passenger mile	Cost of a three-minute call, New York to London	US Department of Commerce computer price deflator (1990 = 1000)
1930	0.68	244.65	
1940	0.46	188.51	
1950	0.30	53.20	
1960	0.24	45.86	125000
1970	0.16	31.58	19474
1980	0.10	4.80	3620
1990	0.11	3.32	1000

In 1990 US dollars unless otherwise indicated; [a] since no numbers of costs are available revenues serve as a proxy.
Source: Herring and Litan (1995: 14). Figure 7.1 (p. 51) in the 1995 development report of the World Bank displays a similar development. For additional evidence see also Baldwin and Martin (1999).

The basic reasoning behind these models can be shown following essentially Krugman (1980; 1991a) and Krugman and Venables (1995).[13] Consider the following extension of the model of the first section of this

---

[13] The number of studies into the new economic geography has mushroomed recently. However, they differ only slightly with regard to some details. See, for instance, Brakman and Garretsen (1993); Martin and Ottaviano (1995); Brülhart and Torstensson (1996); Feix (1996); Junius (1996); Puga and Venables (1996); Venables (1997); Letzner (1997); Ottaviano and Puga (1997) and Ottaviano and Thisse (1998).

chapter. There are two countries, Home H and Foreign F, each having pre-integration two sectors x and y. The x sector, again, is characterised by monopolistic competition whereas the production of y is subject to constant returns to scale. Qua assumption, y is produced in both of the countries. Incomplete specialisation in y ensures that the nominal wage rate is the same in both countries $w^H=w^F=w$. For this to hold, μ, must not be too big. For ease of exposition it will again be assumed that there is only one factor of production, labour L, with L^H, L^F denoting labour endowment of Home and of Foreign, respectively.

In addition, costs of distance will be introduced which provide the driving force in all models from the new geography strand. Usually, costs of distance are considered to be costs of transportation (see Chapter 4 for a critical appraisal). These costs are assumed to be of the iceberg-type as introduced by Samuelson (1954). Iceberg transportation costs means that only a fraction $1/t$ of each unit shipped arrives at its destination, with $t > 1$. Without loss of generality (due to the specification of the utility function) only the differentiated good x is assumed to be subject to transportation costs. n^H is the number of differentiated goods produced in Home, n^F the number produced in Foreign. n^H and n^F are endogenous to the model. In effect, their evolution makes for the impact of integration on the distribution of incomes between Home and Foreign. In what follows we will thus derive the post-integration allocation n^H, n^F in Home and in Foreign. p_i^H and p_j^F denote the price of one unit of a differentiated good in Home and in Foreign respectively. x_i^H, x_j^F are the quantities purchased. The budget restriction requires that expenditures gross of transportation on the bundle x, that is E_x, equal income. Knowing that because of the utility function residents in Home and in Foreign want to consume from all of the goods, x_i^H and x_j^F, the budget restriction of a consumer in Home and in Foreign (with respect to his consumption of x) can be written as:

$$\Sigma_{i=1}^{n^H} p_i^H x_i^H + \Sigma_{j=1}^{n^F} p_j^F t x_j^F = \mu w L^H = E_x^H \qquad (3.26)$$

$$\Sigma_{i=1}^{n^H} p_i^H t x_i^H + \Sigma_{j=1}^{n^F} p_j^F x_j^F = \mu w L^F = E_x^F \qquad (3.27)$$

Consumers in Home, again, allocate their total expenditures $E^H = E_x^H + E_y^H$ $= \mu w L^H + (1 - \mu)w L^H$ [in Foreign $E^F = E_x^F + E_y^F = \mu w L^F + (1 - \mu)w L^F$] in a two-stage process, first between bundles x and y, and second, between the varieties x_i^H, x_j^F with $i=1,...,n^H$ and $j=1,...;n^F$. The second stage differs depending upon whether the individual resides in Home (3.29) or in Foreign (3.30). This is because, depending upon residency, different goods have to be shipped. Thus, the price index q which is a weighted mean of all of the goods purchased is a different one for residents in Home (q^H) and in Foreign (q^F) as well:

$$L^{H,F} = U(x, y) - \lambda \left(q^{H,F} x + y - E^{H,F} \right)$$ (3.28)

$$L^H_{x_{i,j}} = U\left(x_i^H, x_j^F \right) - \lambda \left(\sum_{i=1}^{n^H} p_i^H x_i^H + \sum_{j=1}^{n^F} t x_j^F - E_x^H \right)$$ (3.29)

$$L^F_{x_{i,j}} = U\left(x_i^H, x_j^F \right) - \lambda \left(\sum_{i=1}^{n^H} p_i^H t x_i^H + \sum_{j=1}^{n^F} x_j^F - E_x^F \right)$$ (3.30)

The following analysis concentrates on the basic calculus of a representative individual residing in Home. For an individual located in Foreign the same reasoning applies as a mirror image. Similarly to (3.5) one can derive the demand for each category of goods from the first order conditions for a utility maximum:

$$\frac{\partial L^H}{\partial x} = \frac{\partial U}{\partial x} = \lambda q^H$$ (3.31)

$$\frac{\partial L^H}{\partial x_i^H} = \frac{\partial U}{\partial x} \frac{\partial x}{\partial x_i^H} = \lambda p_i^H \qquad \forall\, i = 1, \dots, n^H$$ (3.32)

$$\frac{\partial L^H}{\partial x_j^F} = \frac{\partial U}{\partial x} \frac{\partial x}{\partial x_j^F} = \lambda t p_j^F \qquad \forall\, j = 1, \dots, n^F$$ (3.33)

Inserting equation (3.31) into equations (3.32) and (3.33) gives

$$q^H x^{1/\sigma} \left(x_i^H \right)^{-1/\sigma} = p_i^H$$ (3.34)

$$q^H x^{1/\sigma} \left(x_j^F \right)^{-1/\sigma} = t p_j^F$$ (3.35)

By dividing the last two equations, one obtains the relative demand for varieties produced in Home x_i^H and in Foreign x_j^F:

$$\left(\frac{x_i^H}{x_j^F}\right)^{-1/\sigma} = \frac{p_i^H}{tp_j^F} \quad \Rightarrow \quad \frac{x_i^H}{x_j^F} = \left(\frac{tp_j^F}{p_i^H}\right)^{\sigma} \tag{3.36}$$

Rearranging equations (3.34) and (3.35) yields the demand of a representative consumer located in Home as a function of relative prices:

$$x_i^H = \left(q^H\right)^{\sigma}\left(p_i^H\right)^{-\sigma} x \tag{3.37}$$

$$x_j^F = \left(q^H\right)^{\sigma}\left(tp_j^F\right)^{-\sigma} x \tag{3.38}$$

The price index q^H for the bundle of goods x (as seen from the perspective of Home's residents) can be derived by inserting the last two expressions, (3.37) and (3.38), into the budget restriction of the representative consumer (3.26):

$$n^H p^H \left(q^H\right)^{\sigma}\left(p^H\right)^{-\sigma} x + n^F p^F t \left(q^H\right)^{\sigma}\left(tp^F\right)^{-\sigma} x = q^H x \tag{3.39}$$

$$q^H = \left[n^H \left(p^H\right)^{1-\sigma} + n^F \left(tp^F\right)^{1-\sigma}\right]^{1/(1-\sigma)} \tag{3.40}$$

Now define

$$\left(q^H\right)^{1-\sigma} \equiv Q^H \tag{3.41}$$

so that equation (3.40) can be rewritten as:

$$Q^H = n^H \left(p^H\right)^{1-\sigma} + n^F \left(tp^F\right)^{1-\sigma} \tag{3.42}$$

From the perspective of Foreign's residents the price index is

$$Q^F = n^H \left(tp^H\right)^{1-\sigma} + n^F \left(p^F\right)^{1-\sigma} \tag{3.43}$$

Total demand by Home's residents for locally produced goods x_i^H (with $i=1,...,n^H$) thus amounts to:

$$x_i^{H,H} = \frac{E_x^H}{Q^H}\left(p_i^H\right)^{-\sigma} \tag{3.44}$$

Similarly, one can calculate Home's residents' total demand for goods produced abroad x_j^F (with $j=1,...,n^F$):

$$x_j^{H,F} = \frac{E_x^H}{Q^H}\left(p_j^F t\right)^{-\sigma} \tag{3.45}$$

In principle, the same applies with regard to Foreign's residents for goods produced in Home:

$$x_i^{F,H} = \frac{E_x^F}{Q^F}\left(p_i^H t\right)^{-\sigma} \tag{3.46}$$

and in Foreign:

$$x_j^{F,F} = \frac{E_x^F}{Q^F}\left(p_j^F\right)^{-\sigma} \tag{3.47}$$

Due to the symmetry of the model, total demand, D^H, for goods produced in Home can be derived from adding equations (3.44) and (3.46) across all n^H sectors of the economy:

$$D^H = n^H\left(x^{H,H} + tx^{F,H}\right) = n^H x^H = n^H\left(\frac{E_x^H}{Q^H}\left(p^H\right)^{-\sigma} + t\frac{E_x^H}{Q^F}\left(tp^H\right)^{-\sigma}\right) \tag{3.48}$$

Total demand in Foreign, D^F, can be calculated in the same manner:

$$D^F = n^F\left(tx^{H,F} + x^{F,F}\right) = n^F x^F = n^F\left(t\frac{E_x^H}{Q^H}\left(tp^F\right)^{-\sigma} + \frac{E_x^F}{Q^F}\left(p^F\right)p^{-\sigma}\right) \tag{3.49}$$

$p^{H,F}$ can be eliminated from the two terms on the RHS of (3.48) and (3.49) by setting $p=1$. This leaves us with the following expressions for the demand an individual producer faces in Home (3.50) and in Foreign (3.51):

$$x^H = \frac{E_x^H}{n^H + n^F t^{1-\sigma}} + \frac{t^{1-\sigma}E_x^F}{t^{1-\sigma}n^H + n^F} \tag{3.50}$$

$$x^F = \frac{E_x^H t^{1-\sigma}}{n^H + n^F t^{1-\sigma}} + \frac{E_x^F}{t^{1-\sigma} n^H + n^F} \tag{3.51}$$

From these expressions, one can derive three hypothetical equilibria. Which of the three equilibria is being realised depends upon the parameters of the model, that is E_x^H, E_x^F, t, and σ. The first equilibrium is characterised by all production taking place in Foreign, $n^H = 0$. If there is no production in Home, it follows from equation (3.51) that the number of firms in Foreign amounts to:

$$n^F = \frac{E_x^H + E_x^F}{x^F} \tag{3.52}$$

Similarly, the second equilibrium can be calculated. If $n^F = 0$, the number of Firms in Home is:

$$n^H = \frac{E_x^H + E_x^F}{x^H} \tag{3.53}$$

Third, by drawing upon equations (3.50) and (3.51), a non-specialised equilibrium can be derived. Multiplying equation (3.51) with $t^{1-\sigma}$ yields:

$$t^{1-\sigma} x^F = \frac{t^{2(1-\sigma)} E_x^H}{n^H + n^F t^{1-\sigma}} + \frac{t^{1-\sigma} E_x^F}{n^H t^{1-\sigma} + n^F} \tag{3.54}$$

Solving (3.50) for $t^{1-\sigma} E_x^F / (n^H t^{1-\sigma} + n^F)$ and inserting the expression into (3.54) one obtains:

$$x^F t^{1-\sigma} = \frac{E_x^H \left(t^{2(1-\sigma)} - 1 \right)}{n^H + n^F t^{1-\sigma}} + x^H \tag{3.55}$$

Keeping in mind that the quantity supplied by each producer is the same no matter whether he is located in Home or Foreign, $x^H = x^F = x_i$, (this emanates from the assumption of a constant elasticity of substitution) one obtains by rearranging and solving for n^H:

$$n^H = \frac{E_x^H \left(t^{2(1-\sigma)} - 1 \right)}{x_i \left(t^{(1-\sigma)} - 1 \right)} - n^F t^{(1-\sigma)} \tag{3.56}$$

Similarly, multiplying equation (3.50) with $t^{1-\sigma}$ yields:

$$t^{1-\sigma}x_H = \frac{t^{1-\sigma}E_{x,H}}{n_H + n_F t^{1-\sigma}} + \frac{t^{2(1-\sigma)}E_{x,F}}{n_H t^{1-\sigma} + n_H} \tag{3.57}$$

Using (3.51) and rearranging one obtains the number of firms in Foreign:

$$n^F = \frac{E_x^F\left(t^{2(1-\sigma)} - 1\right)}{x_i\left(t^{(1-\sigma)} - 1\right)} - n^H t^{(1-\sigma)} \tag{3.58}$$

Inserting equation (3.56) into equation (3.58), (3.58) can be solved for the equilibrium number of firms in Foreign n^F in case of non-specialisation:

$$n^F = \frac{t^{(1-\sigma)}E_x^H - E_x^F}{x_i\left(t^{(1-\sigma)} - 1\right)} \tag{3.59}$$

Similar reasoning gives the number of firms in Home:

$$n^H = \frac{t^{(1-\sigma)}E_x^F - E_x^H}{x_i\left(t^{(1-\sigma)} - 1\right)} \tag{3.60}$$

It follows directly from (3.59) and (3.60) that the larger country will be a net exporter in the differentiated good since $n^H > n^F$ if $E_x^H > E_x^F$ (and vice versa). The result gives support to the notion put forward by Burenstam Linder (1961) that countries tend to export those goods where they themselves have the larger market.

There are also conditions under which all of the production of x takes place in Home (or in Foreign). Given the elasticity of substitution and transportation costs, full specialisation occurs if either

$$\frac{E_x^H}{E_x^F} > \frac{1}{t^{(1-\sigma)}} \tag{3.61}$$

or

$$\frac{E_x^H}{E_x^F} < t^{(1-\sigma)} \tag{3.62}$$

that is, if the size of the local market reaches a certain threshold when compared to the market abroad.[14] Both conditions follow from equations (3.59) and (3.60). In the first case, (3.61), all firms of the x industry will locate in Home, while in the second case the reverse holds true. The impact of a change in the costs of transportation can be seen from equation (3.61) while holding everything else constant. Since the elasticity of substitution is at least unity, the right hand side of equation (3.61) is positive; it shrinks though as transportation costs decline. Thus, given a certain relation between the size of the market in Home and in Foreign, the inequality might suddenly be satisfied as transportation becomes cheaper, thus fostering the agglomeration of industry.

If the allocation of industries is biased towards one or the other market, the distribution of real incomes is biased as well. As long as both countries are incompletely specialised with respect to the y sector, nominal wages are the same for Home's and Foreign's residents $w^H = w^F$. However, real wages differ. The relative real wage ω is:

$$\omega = \frac{w^H/q^H}{w^F/q^F} = \frac{q^F}{q^H} = \frac{\left[\left(t^{(1-\sigma)}E_x^F - E_x^H\right)t^{(1-\sigma)} + t^{(1-\sigma)}E_x^H - E_x^F\right]^{1/(1-\sigma)}}{\left[t^{(1-\sigma)}E_x^F - E_x^H + t^{(1-\sigma)}\left(t^{(1-\sigma)}E_x^H - E_x^F\right)\right]^{1/(1-\sigma)}} \quad (3.63)$$

From equation (3.63) follows that the relative real wage is larger (smaller) than unity if Home (Foreign) is the larger market. The gap in real incomes reaches its maximum in case of full specialisation, in case of which it is t.

If, in addition to trade, there is also factor mobility between countries (or regions for that matter) agglomeration is reinforced: the higher real wage in the country specialised in x attracts workers which add to market size. The increase in market size via labour mobility makes it even more attractive for producers in the x industry to locate close to the market. Thus integration triggers a process which is cumulative in character, favouring the centre at the expense of the periphery. If these conditions prevail indeed, it is divergence rather than convergence in the pattern of production and in per capita incomes which is to be expected as markets are opened. Or to put it differently: history might well be destiny. Whichever country manages to have a lead may well enjoy a persistent locational advantage.[15] If this holds

---

[14] The fact that the degree of heterogeneity is an important factor in driving the regional pattern of economic activity is also stressed by Scotchmer and Thisse (1992: 13). Notably, the home market effect resembles the allocative impact of the provision of public goods (Scotchmer and Thisse (1992)).

[15] Based upon simulation studies Martin and Ottaviano (1995) reach a different conclusion. They claim that in case of mobility of factors a postponement of EU membership for countries being relatively backwards in terms of per capita income might not be warranted whereas in

true, the periphery, because of being smaller in market size as measured by effective demand, will be relegated to the lame track.

The model was recently refined in a number of ways. Production, for instance, is assumed to take place in different stages, so that the final product is assembled from intermediates. If the production of the final good is subject to economies of scale because of a love of variety with respect to intermediates, these models arrive at a production structure with forward and backward linkages. The input-output linkages can tie the whole production to a particular region (e.g. Venables (1996; 1998b)). As in the case of a change in the costs of transportation in the purely horizontal model, the evolution after integration need not be linear. Rather, there may be sudden changes in the spatial distribution of industries whenever a critical mass is being reached. As the authors do not fail to point out, rather than the outcome of local economic policy or other changes in the data (Puga and Venables (1996)), these changes in the allocation of industries are endogenous to the process of integration.

However, from a theoretical point of view, the models have a couple of unsatisfactory features: only three issues shall be mentioned here in short, namely (1) explanatory power, (2) economies of dispersion and (3) comparative advantage. Two others, even more substantial ones, namely technology and the special kind of distance costs assumed, will be dealt with in detail in Chapter 4.

(1) Explanatory power: as far as explanatory power is concerned, the model is unsatisfactory because implicitly the landscape is considered to be already scattered with centres at the beginning. That is, theory does not explain how they develop in the first place; the theories have somewhat the characteristic of being 'physical social science'. The starting point of the evolution is not derived from an individual calculus. Instead, the way the individual actions are coordinated at the very start remains largely a black box. But, like the case of driving on the left or the right of the street (e.g. Schelling (1978); David (1985); Sugden (1986); and the papers by Arthur (1994)), which might be considered as equivalent ex ante, the question arises why the former is chosen rather than the latter. This question is all

---

case of factor immobility it might well be. This is because in case of postponing the incentive for mobility might even be increased.

Even if observed, divergence need not be due to economies of scale, as Blanchard and Katz (1992) have shown. Divergence can also be due to regional shocks having a permanent impact on regional employment and incomes. For if wage flexibility is not sufficient to absorb the unemployed, adjustment takes place via mobility even with constant returns to scale, thus leaving probably permanent traces in the regional pattern of industries and GDP per capita.

the more pressing since there seems to be no case that Pareto-superior outcomes will prevail.[16]

To be sure, if by accident, or 'luck and randomness' as Crafts (1985) put it, one set is bigger in size than the other (either those driving on the left or those driving on the right), it forms a basin of attraction. Once a critical mass is reached, there is a strong incentive for switching to the set already bigger in number which increases as differences in size become larger. Yet, merely invoking accident is quite unsatisfactory a solution. For the question of why there is more than one centre still remains to be answered.[17] The latter obviously requires a closer look at the forces which make for regional concentration. Thus it seems as though we are back to our initial question without having gained many more insights.

Certainly, if it is assumed that the landscape is inhomogeneous, providing some places with a natural locational advantage (even though this is explicitly excluded in these models), the presumption of an uneven regional distribution of economic activity seems not that farfetched and therefore might well be accepted. Furthermore, from the perspective of European economic integration, the question of how centres start up from scratch might be considered irrelevant, since it is already a bygone fact for EU integration. Yet, a considerable discomfort remains with regard to the model's explanatory power. This is particularly disappointing from an economic policy perspective. On the one hand, these models nurture the expectation that a policy of actively promoting industries and fuelling local demand provide for a development push, that they might even be a sine qua non for getting development processes started. On the other hand, they are in several respects weak in explanatory power, leaving the question as to what matters for economies to manage the take off basically unanswered. Accordingly, policy recommendations based on these models lose credibility.

---

[16] Coordination games of the sort described (like in the driving example) and the regional evolutions traced by the new economic geography differ in so far as in case of the former the equilibrium selection has no distributional impact, so that the Pareto principle can be applied. In case of the new economic geography, in contrast, the change cannot be evaluated by drawing upon Pareto. However, if factors were perfectly mobile and there were no locally scarce resources in fixed supply, Pareto would again be applicable.

[17] Starting with Christaller (1933) there is a rich literature though on city systems, the size distribution of cities and edge city dynamics. See, for instance, Allen and Sanglier (1979); Allen (1982); Henderson (1988: 45 et seq.); Fujita (1989: 155 et seq.); Störmann (1993), Krugman (1993; 1994); and Arthur (1994), to mention only a few. Much of the recent literature shares aspects with the theory of coordination games (sorting and mixing equilibria) where multiple co-existing equilibria had been found possible (Schelling (1978: 180 et seq.) and Sugden (1995)) and the theory of self-organisation developed in the natural sciences (e.g. Prigogine and Stengers (1984) and Kauffman (1993)).

(2) Economies of dispersion: another aspect that is missing in the analysis is what Melvin (1991: 738 et seq.) labelled 'economies of dispersion'. This is because there is no explicit treatment of the market for transportation or services to overcome the distance constraint. Rather, transportation remains primitively modelled in the form of the iceberg assumption. Neither does the theory take account of the fact that costs of communication diminished dramatically in recent times, the implications of which will be analysed in detail in Section IV of Chapter 4. Nor do the authors acknowledge the nature of the market for transportation. However, the nature of the market for services to overcome the distance constraint matters.

What matters in particular is whether the market clears or not. Suppose for instance that a good x_k is being shipped from H to F[18] and suppose that demand is quite inelastic so that consumers demand the same amount gross of transportation as net of transportation. For this consideration to hold, it is not important that the assumption of an inelastic demand is only valid in a partial equilibrium framework but cannot occur in general equilibrium where consumers face a budget restriction. The point is: what about back hauling?

Obviously, having shipped something in one direction, there is an excess supply in the market for transportation.[19] This means that goods into the other direction can almost be shipped for free or at least at a very low marginal cost. Thus there are economies of dispersion, that is economies in offering transportation services in both directions. That there might be costs involved in shipping the y good does not prove the opposite, namely that there is no excess supply.[20]

Of course, having an excess capacity might well be efficient. However, this is different from the assumption implicit in iceberg costs that *any*

---

[18] Naturally, whether something is being shipped or not also depends on whether the local market offers close substitutes or not. Yet, differences in substitutability between goods are eliminated by the assumption of Dixit-Stiglitz preferences. We will deal more explicitly with these issues in Section I of Chapter 4.

[19] In some cases the notion of iceberg costs might in fact apply. One obvious case is in services which require the coincidence of production and consumption such as haircuts. In this case either consumers move towards the location of production or the other way round. Now, if all consumers face the same costs of mobility, land is in fixed supply and there is perfect competition, the Henry George Theorem applies: the costs of mobility are in fact a percentage of the price of the service.

[20] For a historical assessment with reference to Canada see Innis (1936/1956). According to Innis outbound cargo was much more bulky during Canadian history than inbound cargo so that there was excess capacity in shipping from the old to the new world. This excess capacity lowered mobility costs for people. The transportation of immigrants in turn fuelled the Canadian market.

excess capacity is an equilibrium. To sum up: if there are economies of dispersion, centripetal forces due to local market size are being curbed.

(3) Comparative advantage: neither the model of Section I nor the model of Section II of this chapter allowed for regional differences in production functions or other kinds of costs of production. Rather, the surprising thing is that a spatial pattern of industries and per capita incomes emerges even if there is no such structure. However, what amounts to a nice feature of the model from a theoretical perspective is a drawback when it comes to explain regional development in reality – or the role of economic policy. Next, we will therefore investigate the consequences for the pattern of industries and incomes if labour in efficiency units differs across countries in the context of the basic model.

III. Cost differences in production

In Sections I and II of this chapter we have assumed that every producer, no matter where located, employs the same technology and operates under the same costs of production. The lack of structure in the regional costs of production proper immediately gives rise to the question of whether demand-side effects due to both economies of scale and costs of distance can be counterbalanced by supply-side effects due to differences in the costs of production.

In fact, comparative advantage in the presence of costs of distance has long been with trade theory, in particular with Ricardian trade theory (see Haberler (1933: 107-10); Samuelson (1954); Dornbusch, Fischer and Samuelson (1977); Melvin (1985a,b)). Transportation costs served to endogenously determine the range of commodities which are non-tradables. However, traditional Ricardian trade theory assumes that production takes place under constant returns to scale. In addition, it differs from models with increasing returns in so far as the latter are usually based on Dixit-Stiglitz preferences in which all goods are being traded.

There are a couple of studies though focusing on what comparative advantage does to the regional pattern of industries and trade if production is subject to economies of scale (e.g. Helpman (1981; 1984); see also Krugman (1995d: 1245-51) for a summary). Usually, in these models comparative advantage is not of the Ricardian type but of the Heckscher-Ohlin-Samuelson type: differences in factor endowment make for differences in the relative costs of production across industries. According to these comparative advantage cum economies of scale studies, trade provides two independent ways to reproduce the integrated economy. Part of the trade in goods is explained by factors being relatively abundant in one country as compared to the other, while the other part is being traced back to the advantages of economies of scale. Inter-industry trade is associated with the former, intra-industry trade with the latter. However, usually they abstract from issues raised by the costs of distance.

In contrast, what is interesting from our perspective is the relationship between economies of scale *and* local differences in the costs of production *and* the costs of distance. Rauch (1991) is one study aiming at such a unified view with the help of a Ricardian model with a continuum of goods. Venables (1987) and Ricci (1996) do so in a two-sector and three-sector increasing returns framework respectively. Both of the studies focus on the question whether in contrast to the standard Ricardian case imperfect competition may lead to incomplete specialisation. Rauch, in addition, tries to derive the volume of trade in particular goods by adding a spatial context to the basic Ricardian framework.

However, for reasons of comparability we will stay for another moment with the basic model of Sections I and II of Chapter 3. Another reason is that we are interested in grasping the main consequences of local differences in production costs of the Ricardian type rather than in analysing the features of any special model. Supply-side effects can be captured in this framework even if one sticks to the CES-type utility function as introduced by Dixit and Stiglitz.

As usual, it will be assumed that there are two countries Home and Foreign, each with two sectors, a monopolistically competitive x sector and a constant returns to scale y sector. As before, it will also be assumed that there is only one factor of production, namely labour L. Home's (Foreign's) endowment shall again be denoted by L^H (L^F). The endowments can be of the same size but they need not. The basic difference compared to former models is that cost differences along the lines of Ricardo are introduced. Suppose that Foreign enjoys a comparative advantage in the production of x while Home enjoys a comparative advantage in the production of y.[21] More precisely, marginal labour unit requirements (v_i) in the x industry shall be smaller in Foreign than in Home by a factor χ: $v_i^H / v_j^F = \chi > 1$. If Foreign is the smaller of both countries, one would thus expect that the home-market effect works against Foreign while the supply-side effect improves Foreign's terms of trade. The reason to expect that this is the case is that the higher productivity in Foreign with respect to x is in effect factor

---

Torstensson (1997), in contrast, sees comparative advantage on the one hand and economies of scale and distance on the other hand as *two competing hypotheses* for explaining the trade pattern actually observed. However, what we are interested in is their relationship, that is, how they work *together*.

augmenting. This means that the size of the economy is larger in terms of efficiency adjusted labour units than in terms of pure labour endowment.

The consequences of regional differences in marginal production costs can be worked out in more detail by first modifying the supply side. By analogy to equations (3.12) and (3.13) profits and price setting behaviour can be described by the following equations in Home and in Foreign:

$$\pi_{x_i}^H = p_i^H x_i^H - v_i^H x_i^H - F_i \quad ; \quad p_i^H = \frac{\sigma}{\sigma-1} v_i^H \tag{3.64}$$

$$\pi_{x_j}^F = p_j^F x_j^F - v_j^F x_j^H - F_j \quad ; \quad p_j^F = \frac{\sigma}{\sigma-1} v_j^F \tag{3.65}$$

Recalling equation (3.13), relative prices f.o.b. reflect relative marginal production costs:

$$\frac{p_i^H}{p_j^F} = \frac{v_i^H}{v_j^F} = \chi > 1 \tag{3.66}$$

With fixed costs F_i and F_j being identical, and the zero profit condition satisfied, relative supply is determined by the inverse of marginal production costs:

$$\frac{x_i^H}{x_j^F} = \frac{v_j^F}{v_i^H} = \frac{1}{\chi} < 1 \tag{3.67}$$

The demand side stays the same as sketched out in equations (3.26) to (3.49). However, in contrast to Sections I and II of Chapter 3 the analysis must now differentiate between the price f.o.b. in Home and in Foreign, p_i^H, p_j^F, and the quantities supplied in Home and in Foreign, x_i^H, x_j^F. Choosing $p^H = 1$, yields $p^F = 1/\chi < 1$. Hence, the demand an individual producer in Home faces amounts to:

$$x^H = \frac{E_x^H}{n^H + n^F (t/\chi)^{1-\sigma}} + \frac{E_x^F t^{1-\sigma}}{n^H t^{1-\sigma} + n^F (1/\chi)^{1-\sigma}} \tag{3.68}$$

Similarly, demand in Foreign is:

$$x^F = \frac{E_x^H t^{1-\sigma} (1/\chi)^{-\sigma}}{n^H + n^F (t/\chi)^{1-\sigma}} + \frac{E_x^F (1/\chi)^{-\sigma}}{n^H t^{1-\sigma} + n^F (1/\chi)^{1-\sigma}} \tag{3.69}$$

The modified equilibria can be derived by setting $n^H = 0$, so that

$$n^F = \frac{\chi \left(E_x^H + E_x^F \right)}{x^F} \tag{3.70}$$

and setting $n^F = 0$

$$n^H = \frac{E_x^H + E_x^F}{x^H} \tag{3.71}$$

Since it is known from (3.68) that individual supply in Foreign is larger by a factor χ than in Home one obtains the same number of firms in Foreign as in the model without comparative advantage, given that all production takes place in Foreign:

$$n^F = \frac{E_x^H + E_x^F}{x^H} \tag{3.70'}$$

The mixed equilibrium is

$$n^H = \frac{E_x^H (1/\chi)^{-\sigma} \left(t^{2(1-\sigma)} - 1 \right)}{x^H \left(\chi t^{(1-\sigma)} - (1/\chi)^{-\sigma} \right)} - n^F (t/\chi)^{1-\sigma} \tag{3.72}$$

$$n^F = \frac{E_x^F \left(t^{2(1-\sigma)} - 1 \right)}{x^H \left(t^{(1-\sigma)} (1/\chi)^{-\sigma} - \chi \right)} - n^H \frac{t^{1-\sigma}}{(1/\chi)^{1-\sigma}} \tag{3.73}$$

By inserting (3.73) into (3.72) one obtains

$$n^H = \left[\frac{(t/\chi)^{(1-\sigma)} E_x^F}{x^H \left(t^{(1-\sigma)} (1/\chi)^{-\sigma} - \chi \right)} - \frac{(1/\chi)^{-\sigma} E_x^H}{x^H \left(\chi t^{(1-\sigma)} - (1/\chi)^{-\sigma} \right)} \right] \tag{3.74}$$

and

$$n^F = \left[\frac{E_x^H t^{1-\sigma}}{x^H \left(\chi t^{(1-\sigma)} - (1/\chi)^{-\sigma} \right)} - \frac{E_x^F}{x^H \left(t^{(1-\sigma)} (1/\chi)^{-\sigma} - \chi \right)} \right]. \tag{3.75}$$

With these expressions at hand, one can calculate the critical size of Home relative to Foreign which leads to full specialisation with regard to the two sectors x and y. This result can then be compared to the one obtained without differences in the costs of production. Let us consider first the critical size of Home relative to Foreign for the balance to tip towards Foreign completely specialising in the production of x:

$$\frac{E_x^H}{E_x^F} < t^{(1-\sigma)} \frac{\left[t^{(1-\sigma)} - (1/\chi)^{(1-\sigma)}\right]}{\left[t^{(1-\sigma)}(1/\chi) - \chi\right]} = t^{(1-\sigma)} A \qquad (3.76)$$

This critical relative size can be compared to the one without Foreign enjoying lower production costs in x. In case of the latter A is unity (see inequality (3.62)). For the balance to tip sooner towards Foreign, A has to be larger than unity. Solving A for numerical examples shows that this indeed is the case.

Second, one can calculate the critical relative size for the equilibrium to turn into the other direction, namely favouring Home as the location for the x industry:

$$\frac{E_x^H}{E_x^F} > \frac{1}{t^{(1-\sigma)}} \frac{\left[\chi t^{(1-\sigma)} - (1/\chi)^{-\sigma}\right]}{\left[t^{(1-\sigma)}(1/\chi)^{-\sigma} - \chi\right]} = \frac{1}{t^{(1-\sigma)}} B \qquad (3.77)$$

Comparing inequality (3.77) with the case in which marginal production costs in Home and in Foreign are the same (that is inequality (3.61)), shows that with marginal production costs lower in Foreign than in Home, the relative size of Home must be larger for the balance to tip towards Home. This is because the RHS of equation (3.61) is now scaled by a factor B. With B being larger than 1, however, Home has to be larger as well for the inequality to hold.

In fact, local differences in the costs of production in the x industry either curb or strengthen the locational advantage enjoyed by the larger market depending on whether the smaller or the larger market has lower marginal costs. In this section it was assumed that the supply-side effect is on the side of Foreign while the home market effect is on the side of Home. In this case Home has to be larger for complete specialisation in the x industry to occur than would be the case if there was no supply-side effect.

According to the new view countries can be expected to share the same fate in case of either being equally remote from the centre or being equally behind in terms of per capita income. The fact of local markets being initially smaller should retard development in both cases. However, in reality, no such homogeneity can be observed (recall results of the empirical analysis in Chapter 2). Rather, the actual picture observed is characterised by two developments:

(1) On average, there seems to be a process of catching up of the laggards after markets have been opened. (2) Within the set of those behind as well as within the set of those ahead there has been a diversity in experiences among those seemingly similar in their starting position in terms of remoteness or per capita income. This is particularly obvious with regard to the economic success of the Newly Industrialising Countries (NICs) on the one hand and the economic malaise of most of the rest of the non-OECD countries on the other hand. But one need not go that far. The picture is also diverse within Europe. The Iberian countries improved their relative income position while Greece even fell behind since joining the EU. The newcoming Scandinavian countries enjoy above average per capita incomes despite not being close to the EU market in terms of distance and so on. Yet, it is hard to explain on the basis of either the canonical approach to integration or the new view why on an overall scale there has been a trend towards higher real incomes in countries being initially lagging. And it is equally hard to discriminate with the theories at hand among those which managed to make it and those which did not.

To fill the gap between the theoretical framework and the actual observation we aim at a refined perspective. In what follows we will concentrate our efforts on both of the driving forces of the new view, thus actually re-examining them. The first issue we are going to focus on is technology and the division of labour. In fact, a second look at the basic framework reveals that due to the assumptions about technology, a particular kind of the division of labour is captured.

In the basic model, regional developments are driven by a constant (that is exogenous) elasticity of substitution. But what does this actually mean? It means that cost competition does not become any more intense, even if the extent of the market becomes larger. However, this is not only counterintuitive. It also seems to contradict current developments. Otherwise, one should not observe that industries come under pressure even in those countries which form quite big a market before integration takes place. Neither would we observe any talk about labour market problems stemming from low-wage competitors. There should be no German jobs at stake, for instance, because of markets becoming more open, as a substantial part of what is considered the European centre of economic activity lies within Germany. In addition, it is frequently the centre which is reluctant in promoting integration. This is particularly evident in case of EU enlargement. However, on the basis of the new theory, one would expect the periphery rather than the centre to raise complaints about low-cost competitors.

To put it differently: though in theory there seems to be a clear geographical dividing line between who is to win and who is to lose in relative terms, the actual debate is hot on these topics, no matter whether industries are located closer to the centre or closer to the periphery. The current debate on these issues raises the question whether one can adapt the framework so that it is more in line with the real world situation as regards competition and the evolution of the division of labour currently under way, even if this means sacrificing elegance for relevance.

The pressure for structural change shows that obviously there is no such thing as a constant elasticity of substitution. Rather, there are two things concerning competition to note: First, cost competition becomes more intense if markets are opened. The increase in cost competition implies that the elasticity of substitution between *similar* goods increases with the extent of the market. Second, due to cost competition being intensified, the various *dissimilar* components a particular good is built from become increasingly specialised. In any case, the elasticity of substitution is endogenous to the market and the processes triggered by integration. Thus, for capturing the consequences, one has to endogenise technology choice and the evolution of the division of labour as the environment becomes more competitive in the course of integration.

The second issue we are about to reinvestigate apart from competition is the role of the distance to the market for the intra-European division of labour (Section IV of Chapter 4). In the new approach to integration distance is associated with transportation costs. Recall, however, that the most important changes in the costs of transportation of commodities occurred in the last century. That being so, the evolution they triggered can be basically regarded as being completed. What the world has witnessed recently is a substantial change in the costs of information across space, in particular due to the pioneering developments in telecommunications. Yet, as will be pointed out in more detail in Section IV of Chapter 4, these costs differ in their nature from transportation costs. However, first we will focus more closely on the role of competition in the division of labour.

4. Centrifugal Forces Dominating: the Foreign Market Effect

This chapter on competition and the division of labour is in five sections. First we will take a closer look at the nature of the division of labour as modelled by the new approach to economic integration (Section I). Second, we will present some scattered evidence from EU-US economic history on the evolution of the division of labour in response to market size and compare it to the division of labour as sketched out by the new approach to economic integration (Section II). The historical digression will pave the way to Section III. In this section we will try to capture the difference between the historical evidence and the basic model of the new economic geography as regards the relationship between the division of labour and integration in a more theoretical manner. Having done so, in Section IV we will refine the theoretical framework into a direction which is more in line with the stylised facts on the actual evolution of the division of labour as triggered by integration. Notwithstanding that there might be something like the home market effect at work, our model stresses the point that frequently there is also a strong 'foreign market effect' present. The key to the foreign market effect lies in the fact that the liberalisation of markets fosters cost competition. The cost competition induces a change in the mode of production: The larger the market, the more are variable costs traded off against fixed costs. One way to economise on variable costs is via outsourcing and thus slicing the value added chain. This is the reason why production tends to become more internationalised as the integration of markets is pushed forward. In fact, acknowledging the impact of a more competitive environment on the division of labour enables us to be more optimistic concerning the economic prospects of the periphery. The optimistic view at least applies to the forces which are related to being peripheral per se. Putting cost competition into perspective thus shows that integration also provides a centrifugal momentum. Finally, we will draw in Section V some policy conclusions from our investigation into the foreign market effect.

II.   Two views on the division of labour: the horizontal versus the vertical perspective

A.   The horizontal perspective and the focus on the proliferation effect of integration

In the previous models competition was modelled in a rather rudimentary way. In fact, the integration of markets had no impact on costs and prices. The sectoral and regional pattern of industries was determined by demand, not by supply. Due to the assumption of a constant elasticity of demand firms chose individual output and mill prices independent of both the number of actual competitors and the evolution of overall market size. Integration basically triggered a proliferation effect: each consumer (or producer) asked for more varieties (intermediates) while purchasing less of each variety offered. Whenever the ratio of individual output to the size of the market grew by integration, it did so by opening just another niche. The dynamics of integration did not go beyond the mere reallocation of all the already existing firms in an infinite space of niches and varieties.

Notably, the refined varieties appearing on the market were produced and supplied in the same manner under autarky as under free trade. Producers were in effect sheltered from international competition, no matter how open the economy. They found a new niche, and even the reallocation frequently was considered to take place without any friction. In this theoretical world the only competition came from the budget restriction (that is demand side), not from the supply side of the economy.

The composition of demand changed.[1] Due to the change in demand, the division of labour became finer, but in a rather peculiar way: the shelf from which the consumer (or in case of intermediates the producer) could choose was extended. And the consumer-producer took less of everything while demanding it all. Note that qua assumption all the goods were considered to be substitutes. But, even though similar, the representative consumer-producer liked to have something of all of them. Or to put it more strongly by use of an example: instead of consuming four kinds of cornflakes the representative consumer bought eight or whatever. The division of labour thus primarily worked on a horizontal basis.

The horizontal differentiation of the product space only had a vertical impact on production or consumption insofar as either productivity or utility was increased the more open the economy and the greater the number of

---

[1]   See also the short remarks by Buchanan and Yoon (1995) in their review of Arthur (1994) on the various sorts of the division of labour based on increasing returns and their normative implications concerning the deregulation and liberalisation of markets.

similar goods which were on the shelf. This is the approach to the division of labour taken in Chapter 3 and this is the approach underlying, for instance, the economics of integration in Romer (1987); Grossman and Helpman (1991/1995); Krugman and Venables (1995); and Venables (1996; 1998b) as they focus on the evolution of the pattern of trade and growth, and more generally, the regional clustering of economic activity. This is because most of these models are driven by a Dixit-Stiglitz utility or production function (Dixit and Stiglitz (1977)) which has the feature of a constant elasticity of substitution making for a love of variety. However, though important, the proliferation effect is just one effect probably triggered by integration. And it is not necessarily the most important one.

B.   *The vertical perspective and the focus on the pro-competitive effect of integration*

Following Dixit and Stiglitz, market size seems to be irrelevant for production. Yet, the notion that the size of the market does not matter is already in contrast to antitrust experience. Take for instance the case of IBM in the late 1970s. According to its position in the US and a narrow definition of the relevant market, IBM enjoyed a monopolistic position. IBM was even alleged by US antitrust authorities to exploit its outstanding position. A wide definition of the market revealed, however, that IBM's position was subject to considerable cost competition and in case of exploitation in danger to be challenged (see Fisher, McGowan and Greenwood (1985) for details). Indeed, the difference as concerns the relevant market turned out to be of considerable importance: in the 1980s, IBM's market share plummeted within a very short time span – a development nobody expected if judged by its former position in the US market alone. That the *economically* relevant market was not confined to the US but was in fact international thus made for a crucial difference.[2] Obviously, openness – and therefore market size – matters for competition. The antitrust experience suggests that a considerable part of the impact of integration on the division of labour will be missed if the analysis is built on the assumption of a constant elasticity to scale. Rather, the elasticity of substitution is endogenous to the market. As such it is subject to change whenever barriers to trade are removed. Presumably, integration does have a pro-competitive effect. This pro-competitive effect is, as we will see shortly, somewhat orthogonal to the proliferation effect as it actually curbs

---

[2]   In the meantime, it has in fact become common practice in antitrust proceedings to take the international market into account in any examination of market power.

the latter.[3] The fact that integration has a pro-competitive impact is more in line with the evolution of the division of labour classical economists such as for instance Adam Smith (1776) and Charles Babbage (1832) had in mind.[4] Because of the role they ascribed to competition, they associated the evolution of the division of labour much closer with the range of different tasks carried out by a unit of production in manufacturing.[5] But exactly because of fostering competition, integration in their framework triggers a process of specialisation very different from the opening of just another niche. Because of intensifying cost competition, integration in their framework actually has two supply-side consequences. One of the consequences affects the horizontal division of labour, the other works with regard to its vertical dimension (thus it shares aspects with Austrian capital theory; see Hicks (1973)).[6] Both of the effects feed into the extent with which economies of scale are in effect exploited – and both have an impact on the prospects of the periphery in participating in the (intra-European) division of labour.

The horizontal effect operates with regard to final products. Notably, the elasticity of substitution between final products is considered to be a function of the size of the market: the more open the economy, the tougher competition will be. Consequently, the perceived demand curve faced by a single producer becomes more elastic. Mark ups become smaller and the average quantity sold by producers surviving in the market increases.[7] Hence, the first source of economies of scale stems from an *increase* in *individual output* under a given technology.

Because the average scale of operation climbs, the horizontal impact of integration in turn triggers a change in the mode of organisation and in the technology employed, that is, it has a vertical effect. Notably, the number

---

[3]   On the relationship between both, the pro-competitive and the proliferation effect in a purely horizontal framework (that is without considering the vertical evolution of the division of labour) see Anderson (1991).

[4]   See also Corsi (1991: 9-31) and Rosenberg (1994a) on the notion of classical economists about the division of labour.

[5]   In the pure proliferation case tasks only become narrower in the sense that the size of the firm becomes smaller relative to the economy as markets become more open.

[6]   That both are frequently fudged (and wrongly so) is a major critique of Stigler (1951); for a discussion akin to Stigler but with an international perspective see Jones and Kierzkowski (1990); for a recent discussion from an IO perspective see, for instance, Elberfeld (1997).

[7]   In constructing a computable general equilibrium model of the Canadian economy, Cox and Harris (1985) showed that benefits from trade liberalisation are considerably higher than usually estimated by conventional general equilibrium analysis. As the authors point out, this is because trade liberalisation results in intra-industry rationalisation which is associated with a lengthening of production runs and a lowering of mark ups. Because of inducing producers to rationalise production, trade liberalisation is accompanied by an increase in factor productivity.

and characteristics of the components the final product is made from is subject to modification. The vertical division of labour which is fostered by the horizontal impact of integration is characterised by a process of specialisation showing three important features:

- Final products tend to be made from a *larger number* of components so that the range of tasks necessary for manufacturing a particular component *narrows*.
- In the process of reorganising and switching technology, the components of a particular product become increasingly *dissimilar* while *complementarities* amongst them are strengthened.
- At the same time, components become more *specific* with regard to a particular product.

The reason for changing the mode of production is that with sales being larger either other techniques or another type of organisation becomes profitable.[8] Usually, the new technique or organisation entails a finer division of labour: As the production run becomes longer with competition being intensified it allows for splitting the production process into different stages or production blocs. Factors of production can concentrate their efforts on a particular production bloc thus sharing in the benefits of vertical specialisation, namely an increase in productivity. With economies of scope lacking, the production process thus disintegrates into *different* specialised undertakings (rather than *similar* undertakings). Because of being different, the range of tasks carried out by each unit of production becomes more limited. Probably the most straightforward example of the kind of process is provided by Smith's (1776: 15) famous pin-making example.[9]

As the range of tasks becomes smaller within each stage of production, there is more room for rationalisation and mechanisation. Actually, the vertical division of labour requires standardisation (see also Rosenberg (1981/1994), and Romer (1996) who investigate the issue in historical perspective) to make sure that the various components fit together. The necessary standardisation is usually achieved by rationalising and mechanising the process of production. Refining the process of production in this manner tends to have two side-effects. The first effect is with regard to the characteristics of components. As they are carefully matched and

---

[8]   Note also that there is substantial evidence on (skill-biased) technological change as markets become more integrated recently. See, for instance, the empirical study by Berman, Bound and Machin (1998).

[9]   See also Pratten (1980), who picked up the issue again, focusing on the long-term productivity changes in the manufacturing of pins since the time of Adam Smith.

designed with regard to a particular product they tend to become more specific and more dissimilar. In fact, complementarities are strengthened. The second effect is with regard to the cost structure. The change in technology towards rationalisation and mechanisation is for the most part associated with higher fixed cost and lower marginal costs.[10] Hence, because of triggering a fragmentation of production into different activities, neither *fixed* nor *marginal* costs of production are given in the classical case, but are in fact being driven by *competition* influencing the *output* of individual firms.

C. Two views compared: the fundamental differences

Note how the pro-competitive effect of integration differs from the source of economies of scale and the assumption of a constant elasticity of substitution in models based on a division of labour along the lines of Dixit and Stiglitz. Apparently, in both cases, the Dixit-Stiglitz division of labour and the classical, economies of scale seem to emerge from a production technology involving fixed and variable costs. However, in models from the Dixit-Stiglitz strand the extent of economies of scale on the level of the firm is being taken as given. Neither *fixed* nor *marginal* costs are subject to any change. *Individual output*, as well, *stays the same*, no matter how large the economy.

Actually, in the division of labour along the lines of Dixit and Stiglitz the source of economies of scale is not on the supply side at all, that is technology or the organisation of the production process, but in fact on the demand side: it enters the analysis solely via the love of variety. Economies of scale in this framework are in fact a matter of (exogenous) preferences. As traditionally in most of economic theory, preferences are taken as given and are not subject to change.

The constant elasticity of substitution turns out to be crucial for the evolution of the regional pattern of industries in Dixit-Stiglitz models as it provides for regional linkages tying several firms to the same location: due to the love of variety the representative consumer splits his expenditures among *all* of the goods becoming available by integration. Being fairly similar, f.o.b. prices of all commodities are considered to be the same.

---

[10] The process of fragmentation *itself* is not necessarily accompanied by an increase of the share of fixed costs in the overall costs of production. Rearranging different tasks into several production blocs can even save on machinery and tools being otherwise partly idle, that is on fixed costs (Leijonhufvud (1986: 210)). The fact that the division of labour can be capital and skill saving actually provided a concern for classical economists (see Rosenberg (1965)). However, the concern primarily is due to neglecting the incentive to accumulate and employ more *specialised* capital which arises from output being larger.

Differences in sales are thus solely due to prices c.i.f. and local expenditures. Because of the spending pattern, the demand each producer faces individually reflects the overall expenditure pattern (Home plus Foreign). Since due to this feature of demand all of the producers of the differentiated good make most of their sales in the larger market, demand provides an incentive for all of them to locate close to it. The constant elasticity thus gives rise to a special kind of economies of scale which strengthens centripetal forces. Naturally, these economies of scale are stronger the lower the exogenous elasticity of substitution and vice versa (recall that according to equation (3.61) the critical value of relative expenditures at which the larger market attracts all of the business $E_x^H / E_x^F > 1/t^{(1-\sigma)}$ is lower the smaller the elasticity of substitution).

Contrary to the classical division of labour, technology and organisation in this setting are both being taken as given.[11] Production is characterised by what Leijonhufvud (1986: 203) labelled the 'bouillabaisse approach' to production: the factors of production (in this case a certain amount of workers L) 'are dumped in a pot ,..., heated up, $f(\cdot)$, and the output, X, is ready'. Production takes place in one step. There is no structure of the production process to be arranged in one way or another, no sequence of operations which can be deliberately ordered depending upon output (for a critique of the 'production-function approach' to the division of labour see also Williamson (1980: 6 et seq.) and Georgescu-Roegen (1972/76)).

Thus, the sources of economies of scale differ in the division of labour along classical lines as opposed to Dixit and Stiglitz. Since they are not a supply-side phenomenon in the division of labour along Dixit-Stiglitz lines, market size has no impact on either the organisation of production and/or the technology employed. Lower barriers to trade only have an impact on the *composition* of demand an individual producer faces.

In the division of labour akin to the classical notion economies of scale are a supply-side phenomenon indeed. They are a matter of both technology and the organisation of production. In the classical case the process of production is to be organised and the organisation of economic activity is considered a variable rather than a constant. Actually, both technology and the organisation of production are a function of the size of the market. Thus, they cannot be treated as exogenous (as preferences usually are treated in economic analysis) but must be endogenous to any analysis of the impact of the integration of markets. To be more precise, they tend to increase with market size as the range of choices becomes larger for the consumer-

---

[11] In models featuring (substitutable) intermediates economies of scale evolve at least in the production of the final good. However, the evolution is driven by the assumption of a love of variety in *similar* and *substitutable* components.

producer. Note that because of the elasticity of substitution tending to become larger economies of scale of the Dixit-Stiglitz sort are actually being curbed.

Admittedly, if the evolution of the division of labour proceeds along Dixit-Stiglitz lines, final products might, as in the classical case, be made from a larger number of components after integration took place (just substitute the demand of a representative consumer for various final commodities by the demand of a representative producer for various intermediates). However, there is a substantial difference: this effect is due to the love of variety. That being so, integration has no impact on the specification of the components. After integration, components are still characterised by being similar and substitutable with regard to each other, whereas in the classical case they tend to be *dissimilar* and more *specialised* so that substitution amongst them becomes increasingly *difficult*. Since this latter change in the production process is the result of a change in individual output it is lacking in models from the Dixit-Stiglitz strand in which integration has no impact on individual output.[12]

We can thus identify three main differences between a division of labour à la Dixit and Stiglitz (DS) and a division of labour akin to classical lines:

- In the division of labour along DS lines the representative producer buys *any* component available on the market. In the classical case the producer asks for a *particular* component which fits *his* product.
- In the division of labour along DS lines, the components of a *particular* commodity remain *similar*. In the classical case they become more *dissimilar*.
- Taken together, these differences give rise to a third one: in the division of labour along DS lines the range of tasks carried out by a unit of production stays the *same*; in the classical case the range of tasks *narrows* within each production bloc, that is the production of each component.

Figure 4.1 summarises the main differences in the pattern of the division of labour.

---

[12] As a matter of fact the share of intermediates in the total volume of trade is on the rise (see Section IV of this chapter).

Figure 4.1:   The evolution of the division of labour: two different views

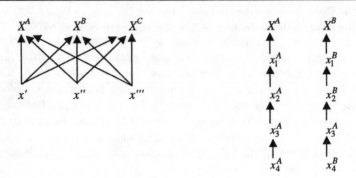

The production mode on the LHS illustrates the division of labour along DS lines. All three producers of final goods A, B, C assemble the final goods from the same three (similar) components. The division of labour on the RHS reflects the classical case. Producer C drops out of the market, while the production run of producers A, B become longer. Both products (X^A, X^B) are made from a larger number of components (for example four instead of three). Each component of product X^A (X^B) is dissimilar if compared to other components of X^A (X^B), that is component x_1^A is not basically the same as component x_2^A etc. In addition, each product is made from a set of components being specific with regard to this particular product (and costs being lower).

D.   Implications of the pro-competitive effect for post-integration patterns of production

The three differences suggest that the evolution of the post-integration pattern of industries differs in both cases as well. First, in the division of labour along classical lines each producer develops a demand for components with specific characteristics instead of components fitting into a broad variety of similar intermediates.[13] Already upon designing a product its components are carefully matched in several dimensions: quantity, quality, location, and time. That being so, the more extensive vertical division of labour triggered by integration brings about a delinking of demand patterns. Referring again to Figure 4.1, the demand pattern of producer A is described by the quadruple ($x_1^A, x_2^A, x_3^A, x_4^A$) which is disjunct to

---

[13] This frequently applies both with respect to the various components of a single commodity as well as with respect to components of different commodities.

the demand pattern of producer B ($x_1^B, x_2^B, x_3^B, x_4^B$). In models resting on a DS framework the linkages between demand patterns (recall that producers A and B share the same demand pattern in the DS case in Figure 4.1) are inter alia responsible for centripetal forces in economic integration.

Figure 4.2: Integration, cost competition and fragmentation: an example

$$\frac{a^F(x_1; x_2)}{a^H(x_1; x_2)} > \frac{w^H}{w^F} \tag{4.1}$$

$$\frac{a^F(x_1'; 0)}{a^H(x_1'; 0)} > \frac{a^F(x_1; x_2)}{a^H(x_1; x_2)} > \frac{w^H}{w^F} > \frac{a^F(0, x_2')}{a^H(0, x_2')} \tag{4.2}$$

$$a^F(x_1'; 0) + a^H(0; x_2') + \delta_{ex} < a^{H,F}(x_1; x_2; \delta_{in}) \tag{4.3}$$

a^H, a^F (w^H, w^F) denote unit labour costs (wages) in Home (H) and Foreign (F) respectively. x_1, x_2 (x'_1, x'_2) stand for two activities necessary in producing a unit of commodity x if trade is costly (if trade becomes cheaper). $a^F(x_1; x_2)/a^H(x_1; x_2)$ thus indicate relative unit labour costs if the production takes place in one stage. The first inequality assumes that Home has a comparative advantage in this case. $a^F(x_1; 0)/a^H(x_1; 0)$ and $a^F(0; x_2)/a^H(0; x_2)$ indicate relative unit labour costs as sales become larger and a vertically disintegrated production becomes sustainable. Inequality (4.2) shows that there might be situations in which the stages become regionally scattered. As shown, Home (Foreign) specialises in activity x_1 (x_2). Inequality (4.3) takes into account that there are coordination costs between both activities which may differ depending on whether production is regionally scattered (δ_{ex}) or not (δ_{in}).

Second, recall that in the classical case components become more dissimilar with regard to each other as the various activities become increasingly disentangled. Various stages of production emerge. Production at these stages is confined to carrying out specific activities. The capabilities needed become limited to specific tasks within each stage of production. Being dissimilar means that the activities necessary for producing these components demand different capabilities. This enables producers to allocate the various activities involved in the production of a particular good much better according to absolute and comparative advantage (that absolute advantage might matter as well has been pointed out by Jones (1980)).[14]

---

[14] Principally, this kind of functional differentiation and its relation to comparative advantage was already envisioned by Babagge (1832: 175 et seq.): 'That the master manufacturer, by dividing the work to be executed into different processes, each requiring different degrees of skill or of force, can purchase exactly that precise quantity of both which is necessary for each

Figure 4.2 provides an example for the process thus triggered as barriers to trade are removed.

Since there is good reason to assume that the variety of skills, knowledge and so on is greater across countries rather than within a single country, there is an incentive to exploit specific locational differences. The result is an increase in the entropy of activities because of a finer geographical division of labour.[15] Or to put it differently, the value added chain tends to be sliced in the process of integration with the pieces becoming more regionally scattered. In the standard Dixit-Stiglitz case there is no such *built-in* incentive to exploit comparative advantage as the market becomes larger (though cost differences might matter, as shown in Section III of Chapter 3).

At first glance, economies of scale might give rise to the expectation that comparative advantage in the narrow Ricardian sense becomes less important as a driving force of the regional pattern of specialisation, that they might even work against comparative advantage (see Baumol (1993); Baumol and Gomory (1996)). From the classical perspective, exactly the opposite seems to hold true. Due to the process of fragmentation comparative advantage becomes more rather than less important as barriers to trade and mobility are increasingly removed. For becoming competitive on an international scale within a sector producers need not be competitive on an overall basis, that is comprising all the activities necessary for supplying a particular good. Instead, they can enter the market within a smaller segment in which they enjoy a comparative advantage. Hence, for the individual producer or region a larger market requires *less* of a *variety* in skills. This makes it considerably easier for peripheral regions to compete themselves into the market. Thus, as trade becomes less costly by integration, it in fact induces a change in technology and organisation which establishes a 'foreign market effect'. This kind of division of labour promoted by integration escapes if the focus is only on the horizontal division of labour.[16] Naturally, Say's Law ensures that there will always be

---

process; whereas, if the whole work were executed by one workman, that person must possess sufficient strength to execute the most laborious of the operations into which the art is divided.' In addition, economies of scale changing endogenously with the extent of the market crowd out other economic activity. As output expands different activities compete for locally scarce resources thus reducing the extent to which economies of scale can be exploited in other stages of production if taking place at the same location (Dluhosch, Freytag and Krüger (1996)). Hence, the expansion of one sector comes at the expense of another sector.

[15] On measuring the division of labour by use of the concept of entropy see Theil (1967) and von Weizsäcker (1991).

[16] There are refinements of horizontal models which incorporate a vertical perspective. However, the division of labour does not evolve in the sense that different undertakings emerge.

some[17] industries in Home and in Foreign which are internationally competitive (Baumol (1977); Van Suntum (1986); Dluhosch (1995)). Given flexible labour markets, relative wages w^H/w^F will adjust for balance of payments equilibrium to be achieved. However, absolute welfare and the terms of trade will usually differ depending upon whether the induced fragmentation is modelled or not. And this is what the issue of centrifugal versus centripetal forces is all about.

There is some sort of tension though which provides for linkages even if the classical case applies. The tension arises because components are complementary while at the same time being dissimilar. As is known since Coase (1937) and Williamson (1980) (and more recently Williamson, O.E. (1996) and Becker and Murphy (1992)) there are costs involved in coordinating economic activities if they are complementary. And depending on the particular economic activity there may in addition be costs of transportation. If space matters for the costs of coordination, these costs might tie several stages of production locally.[18] However, the fact that complementarities require coordination does not yet imply that distance determines the regional allocation of production (as it does together with the special kind of economies of scale in the new economic geography; see Chapter 3). First, there might be substitutes for proximity which stabilise the relationship and which safeguard specific investments. Second, costs associated with coordinating a vertically disintegrated production process are more easily sustained the larger the market. Third, as far as communication is concerned, costs are currently declining substantially (for details see Section IV of this chapter). At any rate, there is an opposing force emerging *endogenously* as the size of the market becomes larger (which is lacking if the division of labour is confined to DS lines), namely the fact that in the course of integration economic activities at the various stages of production become more specific. Therefore, the value added chain tends to be sliced more extensively.

To sum up: in the classical case, the division of labour is driven by fundamentally different forces than in the love of variety case. The sectoral and regional pattern of industries is governed by supply, that is cost

---

[17] Notably, the EU white paper (CEC (1994: Chapter 2A)) considers 'global competitiveness' a goal.

[18] Thus, the question of regional dispersion versus regional concentration has some affinity to the theory of the firm and vertical integration. It is interesting to note that the fact that some activities are complementary to each other is in case of the theory of the firm neither necessary nor sufficient for the activities to be carried out under the same roof (see for instance Klein and Leffler (1981)). This applies even if there are economies of scope (see Teece (1980)). Richardson (1972: 891) therefore distinguishes between complementarities and close complementarities and considers only the latter to give rise to vertical integration.

competition, rather than demand. Integration truly results in structural change on the supply side (rather than only on the demand side). Some firms of those already established drop out of the market. Those remaining rearrange their scope and mode of organisation. The difference in driving forces raises the question as to whether the proliferation effect and the pro-competitive effect also differ with respect to whether centripetal or centrifugal forces dominate. In fact, the pro-competitive effect suggests that centripetal forces are reduced. This issue will be examined in more detail in Section IV of this chapter. However, before proceeding to the theoretical analysis of Sections III and IV, we will present in the next section some scattered historical evidence in support of the division of labour along classical lines.

By switching perspective to the pro-competitive effect of integration we do not claim that there is no such thing as a love of variety. Consumers quite clearly prefer to have a choice from a whole set of differentiated products. Producers may face lower costs of production if there is a range of substitutable intermediates supplied by different producers among which they are able to choose. This might have a favourable impact on costs because of two effects. First, the risk of depending on a particular source of supply may be reduced for downstream firms (see also the literature on Marshallian pooling equilibria, e.g. David and Rosenbloom (1990); Krugman (1991a: 38-49); Townsend (1993)). Second, upstream firms may be able to benefit from the insurance effect a larger market provides. Due to the law of large numbers and the pooling of different demand patterns aggregate demand can become more stable as markets are opened. This insurance effect might provide for an incentive to serve several markets rather than only a particular market (Richardson (1972)).[19] Pooling may in turn be responsible for so-called forward and backward linkages in regional development. They may tie production locally because all of the consumer-producers ask for all of the varieties actually produced. Under these circumstances it is indeed reasonable for producers to locate where they expect demand to concentrate. By doing so, they add to local demand, thereby attracting even more firms. Differences in local market size are thus reinforced. However, the linkages are due to the constant elasticity of substitution. The kind of division of labour induced thereby may work in addition to the division of labour promoted by competition, but certainly not in lieu of them.

---

[19]   In this case the specificity of demand is a necessary condition for the insurance effect of a larger market to work. Whether the fluctuations in the various demands actually cancel out is a matter of the degree of specificity of the capital stock in the production of the particular component (that is the sufficient condition; see also Richardson (1972)).

II.   Digression on systems of production in economic history

For assessing the impact of market size on production methods and the supply side, we will make a short digression into US-European economic history. Notably, differences in nineteenth century US and British manufacturing suggest that integration induces a technological change. Early industrialisation provides particularly illustrative material since high distance costs as compared to nowadays between European and North-American markets implied that producers in the US and Europe operated in different environments with respect to market size.

The difference was not so much with regard to the overall size of the economy. Rather, the difference was due to the local characteristics of demand. Because of these differences, the US and Europe differed fundamentally in terms of market size for particular products. As it turns out, these differences in market size are mirrored by differences in production methods.

The differences in production methods between the new and the old world were so significant that the British coined the phrase of the 'American System of Manufactures'. US manufacturing became subject to close examination by the British, as summarised in the reports by Wallis, Whitworth, and Anderson on the machinery of the United States which were prepared right after the Crystal Palace Exhibition of 1851 (see Rosenberg (1969)). In particular, the American systems of production was characterised by (Rosenberg (1981/1994: 110-12)):

- having longer production runs,
- standardised products being assembled from interchangeable parts,
- employing highly specialised machinery.

In contrast, British production was much more geared towards local markets; production methods were frequently characterised by

- small, parallel, production runs,
- parts of the goods, and sometimes even the goods themselves, being individually fitted,
- a pre-dominance of crafts production and general purpose machinery.

Thus, compared to European technology, US production processes were arranged in such a way as to exploit economies of scale to a much greater extent. Note that this is exactly what classical economists thought would happen in response to a widening of markets. On average, individual output expands and the vertical division of labour becomes subtler as tasks become increasingly divided and differentiated. In a Dixit-Stiglitz framework one would not necessarily expect differences in the organisation of industry for reasons of market size alone. However, that the degree with which markets are integrated makes for a difference on the supply side will become evident as we go into some details of US and European production in historical perspective. Even though structural change in response to diminishing barriers to trade will materialise differently nowadays when compared to historical times, nevertheless some basic principles along which the organisation of industry changes can be identified. In fact, there seems to be a general law which links market size to market structure because of some economic features of production methods.

Though the actual extent of economies of scale is hard to measure in any exact manner, some differences still apply to the US economy and the European economies nowadays:[20] firms within the same category of industries, for instance, attain on average a larger size in the US than elsewhere (Chandler (1977; 1990)); products are much more standardised as certainly every visitor to the US notes: no matter whether door frames, salad dressing, fast food or motel chains, they are to a great deal the same across the US; franchising is widespread in use, providing a standardised concept with the product, the equipment, the furnishing and so on all being pre-set.

Though the choice of technology is to a great deal governed by local factor endowments (see Rosenberg (1977) with special reference to the US and Williamson (1960) on the relationship between mass production and endowment during early US industrialisation),[21] there is also evidence that the special characteristics of the US system of production can partly be traced back to a Smithian process driven by the expansion of markets: in particular the local composition of demand in the US and in Europe made for differences with regard to the size of markets. Complementary to market size, the nineteenth-century US system of production was characterised by a different kind of organisation entailing in effect a finer intra-firm and inter-firm division of labour if compared to the European.

There surely is disagreement among economic historians about the actual weights of both exogenous and endogenous factors in shaping the US

---

[20] See also Rosenberg (1977: 26). Sokoloff (1992: 357), in trying to explain the persistent regional differences in the rates of productivity change within the US, considers it likely that there is some kind of path dependence prevailing. If this held true, the early Smithian process would have made for a long-lasting difference in growth rates surviving even the decline in the costs of transportation since the mid nineteenth century.

[21] On the theory of factor bias in technological change see Kennedy (1964) and Samuelson (1965). The basic idea can be traced back to Hicks (1932). Critical on induced technological change is David (1975) in examining the factor bias in US economic history.

systems of production (e.g. Abramovitz and David (1995: 21-3)). The discussion about the two views is also known as the supply-side versus demand-side controversy (e.g. Mokyr (1990); Rosenberg (1981/1994); Rothenberg (1992)). Supply-siders are said to be those who think of the US systems of production as being primarily the outcome of macroinventions driven by human ingenuity, chance and randomness, that is factors which are mostly exogenous to any economic explanation. Demand-siders, instead, consider US production methods to be mostly endogenous, that is being driven by a Smithian process of adjustment to circumstances, in particular to demand. The term 'supply-side' is thus somewhat misleading in this context in so far as supply-side policy nowadays is usually known to have a special focus on individual incentives. However, this kind of classification has become practice among economic historians.[22]

Mokyr (1977; 1990), for instance, being in the supply-side camp, considers the distinguished US production methods as being mostly due to radical innovations and major technological breakthroughs rather than the outcome of individual incentives for fine-tuning the process of production according to circumstances. Rosenberg (1981/1994), on the contrary, having studied the economic circumstances and the history of production methods in various US industries, is convinced that the American way of production is a supply-and-demand phenomenon.[23] Supporting basically the Smithian perspective, Sokoloff (1992: 354, 363) notes that the special features of American manufacturing during early industrialisation were not confined to only a number of industries. If they were primarily observable in some industries while in others not the pattern would clearly be suggestive of them being due to the emergence of macroinventions. Yet, in the first half of the nineteenth century differences applied to a whole range of industries and they appeared even before the macroinventions diffused and were put into widespread use. The fact that differences were pervasive is an indication of them being induced by something which was shared by almost all of the industries. This is where market size and a gradualist adjustment to economic circumstances enters the picture. In addition, inventive activity concentrated according to Sokoloff (1988; 1992) much more on the organisation of production rather than on macroinventions. This provides another piece of evidence that Smithian processes played a substantial role in shaping the US methods of production emerging in the

---

[22] As Rosenberg (1981/1994) rightly remarks, both determinants, supply-side and demand-side elements, are in any case difficult to disentangle.

[23] In contrast to Mokyr (1990), Rosenberg (1977; 1981/1994) considers the supply-side influence on US technology much more due to relative factor abundance and an induced factor saving bias.

mid nineteenth century. Evidently, it is worthwhile to take a short look at US-European economic history through Smithian glasses.

A.   Market size, cost competition, and production methods

In the mid nineteenth century entrepreneurs essentially faced different environments in the United States and in Europe. As a matter of fact, the composition of demand in the United States and in Europe differed substantially. Compared to its European counterparts most of the markets in the US were already much broader in size by the first half of the nineteenth century. The difference in size was due to a couple of structural reasons. One of the major differences was the consumption pattern of private households making for a difference in the composition of overall demand. In particular, the average American pattern was relatively uniform if measured against the European.

Three of the major reasons for the uniformity of the US consumption pattern as compared to the European shall be mentioned here: (1) relative prices, (2) distributional aspects, and (3) living conditions. First, because of the abundance of fertile land relative prices of foodstuffs were significantly lower in the US than in Europe. Consequently, for any given income level a larger fraction of income was available for spending on manufactures and non-food items in general in the US (Rothenberg (1979); Rosenberg (1981/1994: 114)). Fishlow (1973: 77) indeed finds evidence that Americans spent less for food in the late nineteenth century than Europeans did. Since relative food prices in the US were even more favourable in the early nineteenth century, the evidence suggests that US-European differences in the share of food expenditures in total expenditures were even more pronounced at that time.

The second difference is with regard to the income distribution. Measured on an overall scale, the personal income distribution in the US was less skewed than the one in Europe. Except for the southern part of the US, the majority of people was living under quite similar economic circumstances. On the contrary, the inequality in Europe accounted for a rather diverse composition of expenditures. Large parts of the European population received only low incomes, while those few on top of the income scale made for a much more individualistic demand. Due to the diversity in tastes products were catered to local markets if not even to individual tastes. The European demand for standardised products thus was relatively thin. This was very different from the American case.

Third, living conditions were much more homogeneous in the US than in Europe. In 1810 approximately 80 per cent of the whole US population was engaged in agriculture and even by 1870 it was still more than half of the total population (that is 51.3 per cent; see Rosenberg (1981/1994: 114) for numbers). That being so, people living in rural areas accounted for approximately three quarters of total expenditures (Rosenberg (1981/1994: 115)). Facing more or less equal living conditions, expenditure patterns were pretty much alike as well. Being spread out in the countryside most of the consumers were in favour of goods made in a simple fashion. The severity in design had the considerable advantage of the goods being easy to handle without depending either on special skills, personnel or services. In general, for a number of economic, social and cultural reasons the US market was (and still is) much more ready to absorb commodities with a high degree of standardisation (Abramovitz and David (1995: 15-7)).

Because of the structure of demand markets for particular manufactured commodities were substantially larger if compared to corresponding markets in Europe. Moreover, US markets at that time could even be expected to grow above world average as the growth rate of the population in the US outpaced those experienced elsewhere, in particular the one in Europe. Partly due to the abundance of fertile land, American population growth (natural plus immigrated) attained almost 3 per cent annually in the period from 1790 to 1860, while European numbers were hovering around half the size in percentage points (Rosenberg (1994b); Engerman and Sokoloff (1994)). The high rate of US population growth fed into a high rate of US market growth: measured on an overall scale, demand in the mid nineteenth century surely still was smaller in the United States if compared to Europe. In terms of relative GNP in US dollars at 1985 relative US prices (adjusted for differences in PPP) the US market reached a mere 35.2 per cent of the British market by 1820. However, in 1870, the US already had overtaken the UK by attaining 113.9 per cent of the British GNP (see Maddison (1991: Table A2, 198, for data). Yet, the more homogeneous structure of demand and its growth implied that US markets on average were already larger in size than the British in the first half of the nineteenth century, even though American GNP was still lagging at that time. In addition, US market size was fostered stronger than the British in the first half of the nineteenth century by canal building and the development of a railroad grid linking the major markets.

The larger size of particular markets overseas promoted a supply of standardised goods. The distinctive features of the American products in the nineteenth century are vividly described by the reports on the Crystal Palace Exhibition of 1851 and the subsequent investigation into American production methods during early industrialisation, gathered together by

Rosenberg (1969). As one of the reports on the American exhibition of 1851 notes:

> Certainly a visitor who came to the American exhibit to gratify his aestetic sensibilities was wasting his time. It was severe and utilitarian in nature, and the visitor beheld a profusion of objects, most of which possessed no ornamental value whatever, but where contrived to cater to some specific human need. (p. 7).

B.   Evidence on integration and induced technological change from nineteenth century US and Europe

The differences in the pattern of demand and the size of the market between the US and Europe were accompanied by remarkable differences in the organisation of production. The distinguishing characteristics between the US systems of production and the British are remarkable for two reasons (Rosenberg (1981/1994: 112). First, in the mid nineteenth century Britain can still be considered to have held the technological leadership as much of US technology was borrowed from Britain (however, not without being modified and adapted to the US environment). Second, a considerable part of production methods employed in the US was invented in Europe, but not put to use there (obviously due to a lack in demand). Both aspects highlight that the differences in US and British technology deserve explanation. Market size induced organisational and technological change is one kind of explanation.

Corresponding to the heterogeneous structure of demand, European production methods differed quite sharply from their American counterparts: the diversity was in conflict with production processes geared towards the exploitation of economies of scale. Instead, low-scale production, technical skills and crafts production were rated much higher; and general purpose machinery dominated the overall picture of production methods. Due to the organisation of production, goods were by and large produced in one piece rather than by use of standardised interchangeable parts. The British tradition of pre-industrial crafts production even retarded the emergence of a specialised production on a high scale later on as markets expanded (Rosenberg (1969: 68)). As Rosenberg (1977: 25) notes, the diversity in demand also proved to be somewhat destructive to technological creativity, honouring a more or less passive adjustment to customer wishes.

Due to the homogeneity of US demand, economies of scale on the level of the firm could be exploited to a much greater extent in the US by reorganising and restructuring the mode of production in an appropriate manner. For exploiting economies of scale, production was grouped in sequences of similar tasks rather than into sequences of different tasks, as traditionally in crafts production. At each stage of production a different component was manufactured. The vertical division of labour was thus considerably finer. Rather than made one piece after the other, commodities were more frequently composed of interchangeable parts. With individual output at each stage being larger and the tasks being narrower, a strategy of employing more specialised machinery was sustainable as the employment of highly specialised machinery only pays under the expectation of demand being quite stable and a limited taste for variety. The mechanisation of production and the use of specialised machinery was also due to the fact that a finer division of labour requires that each part of the product is manufactured in such a way as to fit to the other. Specialised machinery with a limited tolerance was thus necessary for the products to be assembled from several components rather than fitted together manually. The standardisation of the different parts of production not only increased the intra-firm division of labour, it also promoted inter-firm specialisation as it made quality control considerably easier. On the contrary, quality control in British production with a low degree of standardisation provided a strong incentive for in-house production as in case of the latter monitoring was frequently easier (Rosenberg (1977: 26)). Pushed consequently forward, the US production mode led to the development of the assembly line. Mass production evolved.

One of the first industries employing the new production methods was the firearms industry. In particular the British were so impressed by US gun making from interchangeable parts that they launched an investigation of the firearms industry (Rosenberg (1969)). However, the distinctive production methods were not limited to the firearms industry. From there, mass production began soon to spread to a broad range of other industries in the United States, such as for instance the watch, clock and lock-making business, and the production of hardware, office machinery and automobiles. The chain from metallurgy and metal using industries to food processing, to packing and to canning provides a typical example of the American road towards mass production (Mowery and Rosenberg (1989: Ch. 3)). Yet, mass production was not confined to (either durable or non-durable) consumer goods. Instead, it had a general impact on the organisation of US industry. Via a feedback effect the standardised production of commodities for final use also shaped the production of the machinery and the US capital stock in general. The characteristics of demand in the mid nineteenth century thus paved the way to distinguished methods of production with an extensive vertical division of labour

(Rosenberg (1969; 1981/1994); Chandler (1990); Sokoloff (1986; 1988)). Indirectly, the distinctive features of the American goods and the American system of production also fostered interregional mobility in the United States. By lowering the costs of getting informed and adjusted in different regions, it eased the frictions in getting started elsewhere.

The theory of technological change as induced by a homogeneous structure of demand is supported by data on US labour productivity. Simple growth accounting back-of-the-envelope calculations along Solow lines show that US labour productivity took over European labour productivity in the late 1870s.[24] The same holds for total factor productivity. The very fact that differences in labour productivity were accompanied by differences in total factor productivity provides additional evidence that the distinct characteristics of the American system of production are primarily due to technological change rather than differences in capital intensity, that is endowment (see Broadberry 1993: 788; 1994) and Sokoloff (1992: 360 et seq.) for data).[25]

Sokoloff (1992: 358) also lends support to the notion that US production processes were frequently distinct from the European in the organisation of production rather than in differences of factor proportions. Referring to differences within the US, he points out that average firm size correlated strongly with market size. Nevertheless, manufactories in larger markets basically worked with the same capital to labour ratios as those being smaller and more remote. Indeed, even in applying simple growth accounting to different industries in the US, capital deepening explains little. Except for the 1850s, labour productivity growth is mainly associated

---

[24] Naturally, data quality and conceptual problems in measuring productivity growth require careful interpretation of results. One of the conceptual problems arising is the well-known fact that growth accounting which takes a residual approach to TFP growth (as it usually does) neglects the technological change embodied in capital stock increases. Instead, it rests on the assumption that inputs (labour, capital, and technology) contribute independently to the growth rate of the economy. To what extent TFP growth is underrated thereby is open to dispute. In addition, data quality for the nineteenth century only allows for rough estimates of productivity. For instance, precise knowledge on operating times of firms is lacking, as is knowledge on the amount prices of firms differed purely because of transportation costs. In both cases differences imply that productivity data is distorted. For details about data quality and measurement of the sources of growth and their rates in early industrialisation see Sokoloff (1992: 348-50). Nonetheless, and interestingly to note, all indicators show a marked difference between the US economy and the European economies in the nineteenth century.

[25] Further historical evidence on the evolution of productivity in the major industrialised countries is provided by Baumol, Blackman and Wolff (1991), and more recently, by Maddison (1994). For conceptual issues of international productivity comparisons see Dollar and Wolff (1993) and Jorgenson (1995). Broadberry (1993: 787) argues that US labour productivity was already ahead of Britain's in the mid nineteenth century as population was smaller in the US than in Britain. However, this argument misses the point that it is not only the overall volume of market size that matters for effective demand, but its structure as well.

with TFP growth in all of the industries no matter whether mechanised, less- or non-mechanised, capital intensive or labour intensive (see Table 4.1). One of the main distinguishing characteristics, however, was the finer division of labour and the standardisation of output.

Table 4.1: Growth rates in labour productivity and total factor productivity in urban firms^a with different capital to labour ratios US 1820-60 (in per cent)

	Mechanised Industries		Less or non-mechanised industries		Capital-intensive industries		Labour-intensive Industries	
	LP	TFP	LP	TFP	LP	TFP	LP	TFP
1820-50	2.8	2.2	0.5	0.8	2.3	1.8	0.7	1.0
1850-60	2.0	2.2	3.7	2.0	1.8	1.9	4.4	2.5

With LP (TFP) denoting labour productivity (total factor productivity).
^{a} In the light of Smithian processes it is interesting to note that less or non-mechanised firms and labour intensive firms in rural areas both experienced higher TFP growth than their urban counterparts during 1820-50 (as transportation costs declined significantly) (Sokoloff (1992, 361)).
Source: Sokoloff (1992: Table 8.3, 360).

Thus, market-led organisation indeed seemed to have played a significant role. In later periods Smithian growth fed into a more capital intensive production (Sokoloff (1992: 354)). Yet, this development is basically in line with the evolution sketched out in the first section of this chapter.

Capital deepening is certainly only one aspect how factor endowment might feed into the methods of production. Natural resources which are not considered in a two-factor framework of growth accounting are another issue shaping production. And there is no doubt that the development towards mass production in the US was reinforced because of natural resources being relatively abundant and human capital relatively scarce (Williamson (1960); David (1975)). As Rosenberg (1977: 23) points out, on its direction towards accommodating the special pattern of US demand US technology strongly benefited from relative factor abundance, in particular of natural resources. According to his studies much of the early machinery employed was characterised by being resource consumptive. Scarcities in Europe, on the contrary, were much less conducive for a push towards mechanisation and standardisation in so far as it was consumptive in natural resources. This is most evident in the case of wood-processing and wood-working (Rosenberg (1981/1994: 116)).[26]

Nevertheless, differences in endowment are by no means the whole story. The fact that supply was not only governed by endowment but also by the growth and the pattern of demand also becomes obvious in comparing the economies from Northern and Latin America. Though most of Latin America was also well endowed with natural resources, it took a rather different path than Northern America.[27] Hence, given endowment, demand did play a critical role. Notwithstanding the fact that the US and Europe differed in many respects, in particular in endowment, a demand-side perspective has thus its merits. And in fact, as already pointed out, there is considerable evidence that the US and Europe differed in effective market size in the nineteenth century.

The historical evolution within the States also suggests that market size not only shapes the direction of technological change but in addition speeds up its rate. Market size thus exerts an impact on technology via two channels, an intratemporal and an intertemporal one. As far as the intertemporal part is concerned, the rate of change is spurred as the fixed costs incurred by inventive activity are more easily sustained the larger subsequently expected sales.[28] However, regarding US technology during early industrialisation it also has to be noted (as Rosenberg (1981/1994: 112) points out) that the direction into which the search for improvements of production methods was guided because of market size proved to be quite fertile a ground. In any case, drawing upon patent records as an indicator for the speed of technological change, Sokoloff (1988; 1992) found evidence that the integration of markets and the expectation of an increase in demand spurred technological change during the early phase of industrialisation in the US from 1790 to 1846.[29] The overall number of patents issued per annum and per million of residents exhibited two peaks, one in 1796-1812 and another one in 1820-36, with the former being

---

[26] On historical evidence of a labour-saving bias in technological choice in the US see Habbakkuk (1962); Rosenberg (1982: 15 et seq.); Saul (1970); Temin (1971); and Broadberry (1994). David (1975: Ch. 1) added a localised learning by doing argument to the factor bias.

[27] Engerman and Sokoloff (1994) show that Latin America already started with a more unequal income distribution due to land use grants. In trying to preserve the status quo, inequality was coercively maintained by barriers to entry. The rise of a manufacturing sector was thus hampered by the structure of purchasing power being rather skewed. Because of differences in tastes between the bulk of middle income earners in Northern America and high income earners in Latin America, markets for standardised products were much smaller in the latter.

[28] Sokoloff (1992: 362) obviously fails to acknowledge this relationship as he considers the surge in inventive activity not to be explained by economies of scale.

[29] See also the *Historical Statistics of the United States, Colonial Times to 1970*, Washington DC, 1975, Series W-99 published by the US Department of Commerce (1975).

slowed down by trade disruptions[30] and the latter being choked off by changes in the procedure of granting patents and an economic contraction. As Sokoloff himself remarks (1992: 355), issued patents are known to be a very rough indicator for inventive activity, yet, there is no other source providing more reliable information concerning inventive activity in the antebellum period. Moreover, according to econometric studies by Sokoloff (1992: Tables 8.4 and 8.5, 364, 365, 369), the correlation between patenting and firm productivity proves to be quite robust for the antebellum period.

Of particular interest are the regional disparities in inventive activity during the two periods. The issue of patents recorded a strong increase as from 1799 in Southern New England and New York, both of which outpaced the rest of the Northeast and the US by far, namely by a factor of 4 and 20 respectively (Sokoloff (1992: 352)).[31] By running regressions on regional characteristics Sokoloff (1988) factored out the costs of distance with a statistically significant coefficient: navigable waterways by which significantly more markets were in reach turned out to be statistically significant. The level of inventive activity within the region under consideration was more than 50 per cent higher in the case of proximity of navigable waterways, even in cases where the data was adjusted for the sectoral composition of the labour force, and even though transportation is only one factor in determining market size.[32] With infrastructure as the leading variable, his numbers supply evidence that demand provided a considerable engine for technological change thereby shaping the US systems of production.

To sum up, US-European economic history suggests that the integration of markets shapes the direction as well as the rate of technological change and thereby the structure and methods of production: market size seems to give technological change a specific direction, thereby shaping the regional pattern of production. As the US pattern of demand in the nineteenth

---

[30] According to Sokoloff (1992: 373) the pro-cyclical pattern of patent activity is also indicative of inventive activity driven by market size.

[31] The patent rate per million residents in Southern New England climbed from 7.2 in the 1790s to 65.2 in the first years of the nineteenth century, while plummeting to 55.4 in the 1810s and rising again to 106.4 in the first half of the 1830s. The numbers for New York are 10.9, 62.0, 49.9 and 95.6 per million residents respectively. In contrast, the overall level of inventive activity in the US was much lower and exhibited a less pronounced pattern with 5.2, 23.9, 22.9 and 41.8 patents per million residents (Sokoloff (1988: Table 1, 824-25; 1992: Table 8.1, 353)).

[32] The correlation is especially pronounced in case of the construction of the Erie canal which sparked a boost in inventive activity as of 1825 along its route (Tryon (1917); Sokoloff (1988: 842, and Tables 5 and 6)). In a similar manner, the surge in inventive activity within Northern New England in 1805-11 and 1830-36 can be traced back to the Conneticut and Merrimack rivers and the linking of the Lake Champlain to the Hudson.

century displayed a much greater uniformity than the European, the US market proved to be more absorptive for standardised products. The demand for standardised products is reflected in US methods of production having comparatively long production runs, employing highly specialised machinery and in the commodities being made from interchangeable parts. The European diversity instead was much less conducive for these methods. Instead, European markets promoted production on a small scale with general purpose machinery and a considerable share of crafts production. Commodities tended to be manufactured piece after piece rather than in parallel production runs. Generally, US production methods displayed a much finer vertical division of labour. Hence, there is considerable evidence that the larger size of local markets (with regard to certain classes of commodities) in the US induced a special kind of technological change which differed substantially from the one induced in Europe.

The differences in production methods raise the question whether, because of the vertical division of labour induced by market size, integration triggers a process different from the regional concentration of production. For answering the question we will try to capture the forces provided by market size in a more theoretical manner by developing a model of market size and induced technological change in the next two sections. With the help of this model we will show that integration indeed can strengthen rather than weaken the process of development in peripheral countries.

III. A unifying approach to the division of labour

This section is devoted to an investigation in the impact of intensifying competition due to the opening up of markets with the help of a multi-stage framework. Some firms will not manage to survive in the new environment whereas those succeeding can expand their business. The rise in the scale of operation lays the foundation for a vertical division of labour which will be examined in more detail in Section IV of this chapter. The vertical impact of competition will be crucial for the question whether centripetal or centrifugal forces dominate in economic integration.

Recall that in the standard Dixit-Stiglitz (1977) case competition does not intensify in the sense that there is a pressure on mark ups which requires firms to reduce prices for staying in business. Rather, in the standard case, they manage to survive by sticking to their former, pre-integration, policy.

In exploring the horizontal consequences of integration in this section we will sketch out a unifying model of the division of labour sharing some aspects with Lancaster's approach (1979; 1996) to consumer choice.[33] The model shows how due to cost competition the horizontal division of labour evolves as national markets are opened up. As it turns out, the framework outlined in this section also incorporates the standard Dixit-Stiglitz consequences of integration as a *special case*.

The analysis is based on the decision of a representative consumer about the allocation of his expenditures.[34] Theoretically, the decision can be split into three levels. On the first level the consumer allocates his expenditures between a numeraire and a bundle of other goods; on the second he decides about how to spent his income on the various characteristics the goods may have; and on the third he chooses the goods themselves which can carry various characteristics. This approach differs from the basic model used in the first section of the third chapter by introducing characteristics of goods. In contrast, the framework presented in the first section of the third chapter was a hypothetical two-step procedure of allocating expenditures: the first decision concerned the numeraire and a CES aggregate of expenditures on a bundle of monopolistically supplied goods, while the second concentrated on the demand for various goods.

By introducing explicitly the notion of characteristics which goods may share or not it becomes clear that the proliferation effect which basically replicates the pre-integration pattern in the post-integration division of labour is likely to be the exception rather than the rule. Generally, the division of labour post-integration will not be a mere replication of the situation which prevailed before integration. Rather, it will be different.

The first decision is about allocating the expenditures between a $(M \times 1)$ vector of characteristics c and another good y which serves as numeraire. Similar to models in the first part of the third chapter, we retain the assumption of a utility function of the two-stage Cobb-Douglas CES type on this juncture.

$$\underset{c,y}{\text{Max}} \quad U(c,y) = \left[\left(\sum_{m=1}^{M} c_m^{(\sigma-1)/\sigma} \right)^{\sigma/(\sigma-1)} \right]^{\mu} y^{1-\mu} \qquad (4.4)$$

The choice is subject to the following budget constraint:

---

[33] For the economics of multi-stage optimisation we will employ see Greene (1964). The multi-stage approach to demand functions focusing on characteristics has in particular been recently employed in finance theory with regard to the characteristics of various assets. See Magill and Quinzii (1996), for example.

[34] Hence, each individual in the economy is assumed to allocate his income in the same manner so that the economy-wide budget restriction can be derived from a representative household by mere aggregation over all the individuals in the economy.

$$\mathbf{q_c c} + y = wL \tag{4.5}$$

where $\mathbf{q_c}$ is a $(1 \times M)$ price vector of characteristics; w denotes wages and L stands for labour force so that wL amounts to total income of worker-consumers.

By employing the Lagrange method to (4.4) and (4.5) one obtains the demand for the bundle of characteristics $\mathbf{c}$ on the one hand and the numeraire y on the other hand as a function of relative prices:

$$L = U(\mathbf{c}, y) + \lambda(wL - \mathbf{q_c c} - y) \tag{4.6}$$

$$\frac{\partial U/\partial c}{\partial U/\partial y} = \frac{\mu}{(1-\mu)} \frac{y}{c} = q_c \tag{4.7}$$

In equation (4.7) q_c is the price index of characteristics while c is the CES aggregate of characteristics. Equation (4.7) reveals that, due to the Cobb-Douglas assumption, a constant share (μ and $1-\mu$ respectively) of income wL is spent on the bundle of characteristics on the one hand and the numeraire on the other hand.

$$q_c c = \mu wL \quad \text{and} \quad y = (1-\mu)wL \tag{4.8}$$

The second stage refers to the demand for each of the various characteristics. The characteristics of the goods will be denoted by c_m. Assuming that there are M characteristics, the space spanned by the characteristics is $\mathbb{R}_+^M$. It will be assumed that they feed into utility according to a CES function as usually employed in trade and agglomeration models (see also Section I of Chapter 3) with constant elasticity σ.

$$\underset{c_m}{\text{Max}} \quad U[c(c_m)] = \left(\sum_{m=1}^{M} c_m^{(\sigma-1)/\sigma} \right)^{\sigma/(\sigma-1)}, \qquad m = 1,...,M \tag{4.9}$$

From (4.8) it follows that the choice of characteristics is subject to the following budget constraint:

$$q_c c = \mu wL = \sum_{m=1}^{M} q_m c_m \tag{4.10}$$

With q_m denoting the price of characteristic c_m, the sum of expenditures on the various characteristics has to equal the price index of characteristics times the CES aggregate of characteristics or (which amounts to the same) the (constant) share of income spent on the whole bundle of characteristics. For maximising utility the first derivative of the Lagrangian with respect to the various characteristics c_m is considered:

$$L = U[c(c_m)] + \lambda\left(\mu wL - \sum_{m=1}^{M} q_m c_m\right) \qquad (4.11)$$

$$\frac{\partial L}{\partial c_m} = \frac{\partial U}{\partial c}\frac{\partial c}{\partial c_m} - \lambda q_m = q_c\left[\sum_{m=1}^{M} c_m^{(\sigma-1)/\sigma}\right]^{1/(\sigma-1)} c_m^{-1/\sigma} - q_m = 0 \qquad (4.12)$$

Condition (4.12) can be solved for the price of a particular characteristic c_m:

$$q_m = q_c\left(\frac{c}{c_m}\right)^{\frac{1}{\sigma}} \qquad (4.13)$$

By rearranging (4.13) and substituting $q_c c$ by μwL (that is equation (4.10)), one arrives at an expression which can be solved for c_m thus giving the demand for a particular characteristic as a function of prices and income:

$$c_m = \frac{q_c^{\sigma-1}}{q_m^{\sigma}}\mu wL \qquad (4.14)$$

Drawing again on (4.10), the aggregate price index for characteristics can be eliminated from (4.14). By inserting (4.14) into (4.10), solving for $q_c^{\sigma-1}$ and substituting again into (4.14), one obtains the following functions for the demand for individual characteristics:

$$c_m = \frac{q_m^{-\sigma}}{\sum_{m=1}^{M} q_m^{1-\sigma}}\mu wL \qquad (4.15)$$

On the third stage goods $(x_1...x_n) \in \mathrm{IR}_+^n$ are being chosen, depending upon prices and characteristics they carry. Consider **x** to be a $(n \times 1)$ vector of the goods x_i $i=1,...,n$. Given the decision about characteristics, the representative consumer chooses his optimal basket of goods by minimising his expenditures:

$$\mathbf{q_c c} := \min \mathbf{px} \qquad (4.16)$$

The characteristics of each good x_i are displayed by a $(M \times 1)$-vector $\mathbf{a_i}$. The matrix A then describes the characteristics of all goods on offer, with the various characteristics of each good being arranged in columns and the same characteristics of various goods in rows. With n goods and M characteristics A is a $(M \times n)$ matrix.

$$\mathbf{c} = \mathbf{Ax} \tag{4.17}$$

$$\begin{bmatrix} c_1 \\ \vdots \\ c_m \\ \vdots \\ c_M \end{bmatrix} = \begin{bmatrix} \sum_{i=1}^{n} a_{1i}x_i \\ \vdots \\ \sum_{i=1}^{n} a_{mi}x_i \\ \vdots \\ \sum_{i=1}^{n} a_{Mi}x_i \end{bmatrix} = \begin{bmatrix} a_{1,1} & \cdots & a_{1,i} & \cdots & a_{1,n} \\ \vdots & \ddots & & & \vdots \\ a_{m,1} & & a_{m,i} & & a_{m,n} \\ \vdots & & & \ddots & \vdots \\ a_{M,1} & \cdots & a_{M,i} & \cdots & a_{M,n} \end{bmatrix} \begin{bmatrix} x_1 \\ \vdots \\ x_i \\ \vdots \\ x_n \end{bmatrix} \tag{4.17'}$$

In case of $n=M$ solving (4.17) for the demand for goods x_i is straightforward. Recalling (4.15), one can write the demand as a function of the prices of characteristics:

$$\mathbf{x} = \mathbf{A}^{-1}\mathbf{c} = \mathbf{A}^{-1} \begin{bmatrix} \dfrac{q_1^{-\sigma}}{\sum_{m=1}^{M} q_m^{1-\sigma}} \\ \vdots \\ \dfrac{q_m^{-\sigma}}{\sum_{m=1}^{M} q_m^{1-\sigma}} \\ \vdots \\ \dfrac{q_M^{-\sigma}}{\sum_{m=1}^{M} q_m^{1-\sigma}} \end{bmatrix} \mu w L \tag{4.18}$$

Prices of goods are related to the characteristics they carry and their prices according to the following equation:

$$\mathbf{p'} = \mathbf{q_c' A} \qquad \text{or} \qquad \mathbf{A' q_c} = \mathbf{p} \tag{4.19}$$

or, in explicit notation,

$$\begin{bmatrix} p_1 \\ \vdots \\ p_i \\ \vdots \\ p_n \end{bmatrix} = \begin{bmatrix} a_{1,1} & \cdots & a_{m,1} & \cdots & a_{M,1} \\ \vdots & \ddots & & & \vdots \\ a_{1,i} & & a_{m,i} & & a_{M,i} \\ \vdots & & & \ddots & \vdots \\ a_{1,n} & \cdots & a_{m,n} & \cdots & a_{M,n} \end{bmatrix} \begin{bmatrix} q_1 \\ \vdots \\ q_m \\ \vdots \\ q_M \end{bmatrix} \tag{4.19'}$$

In the case of a particular good x_i we thus have $p_i = \sum_{m=1}^{M} a_{m,i} q_m$. As will be seen shortly, the way in which the division of labour evolves in case of an enlargement of the market crucially depends on the matrix A, in particular on its rank. The rank of the matrix A is determined by the number of goods or the number of characteristics, depending upon which of both is smaller, that is $rk(A) \leq \min(M, n)$.

Considering matrix A, two major cases can be distinguished. Case (1) prevails if there are more characteristics than goods $(M > n)$. In this case the rank of A is n:

Case (1) $$rk(A) = n \qquad (4.20)$$

With n being equal to M, we actually have the special case of a constant elasticity of demand for various goods as frequently employed in standard trade models with imperfect competition based on Dixit-Stiglitz preferences. Each good x_i exactly carries one characteristic a_{ij}. Or in formal terms: vectors a_i indicating the characteristics of a particular good x_i are identity vectors and the matrix A describing the characteristics of all goods on offer is the identity matrix:

$$A = Id = \begin{bmatrix} 1 & 0 & 0 & 0 & 0 \\ 0 & \ddots & 0 & 0 & 0 \\ 0 & 0 & 1 & 0 & 0 \\ 0 & 0 & 0 & \ddots & 0 \\ 0 & 0 & 0 & 0 & 1 \end{bmatrix} \qquad (4.21)$$

Furthermore, it is assumed that pre-integration countries H and F produce non-overlapping sets of goods. If, for instance, country H produces the range of goods with characteristics $i = 1, ..., M/2$ while country F produces the goods with characteristics $j = M/2, ..., M$, one obtains the standard Dixit-Stiglitz case of the division of labour. Upon removing barriers to trade, the autarky equilibrium expands in a trivial way to equilibrium with trade. Basically, specialisation is already the point of departure.

The liberalisation of markets had no consequences on cost competition so far. Only the number of goods supplied expanded in proportion to the size of the overall economy. This is the proliferation effect: there is a pure replication of the pre-integration pattern. Nota bene, post-integration, producers offer the same goods in the same manner as pre-integration. In particular, the individual scale of operation remains the same, no matter how large the economy and no matter whether liberalisation takes place or not. Contrary to experience with integration, trade liberalisation in this framework does not trigger any structural change on the supply side (as it does in the classical case of the first section of this chapter). What changes is the composition of demand each producer faces. Pre-integration consumer choice is restricted to domestically produced goods. Consumers spread their income on these goods according to equations (4.15) and (4.17). After integration, they will distribute their buys on the larger set of goods then available, imported goods included. Compared to the situation before integration took place each consumer buys less from each particular producer. This is why the composition of demand changes. However, without introducing any additional assumptions (such as distance to the market and so on) this is the only modification in the division of labour that happens as market size expands upon integration. While theoretically convenient, this is not the world we are living in.

In the second case (which will be considered as the ordinary case), there are more goods than characteristics ($n > M$) so that all characteristics are within reach and the rank of the matrix A is M.

Case (2) $$\mathrm{rk}\,(A) = M \tag{4.22}$$

Now consider again what happens in case barriers to trade are removed. As all the characteristics were already in reach with the goods pre-integration, liberalisation means that there are $(n - M)$ goods redundant. The bundle of characteristics they represent can be realised by a combination of the other M goods, namely $(n - M)$ a_i vectors are collinear. Since demand is perfectly price-elastic (goods sharing characteristics completely can be considered perfect substitutes), costs alone decide which of the producers drop out of the market in case of integration and which are able to survive.[35] Compared to the autarky equilibrium the price elasticity of demand is higher and producers operate on a larger scale post-integration. Due to cost competition, the supply side in a more liberalised environment thus differs fundamentally from the supply-side prevailing before liberalisation took place.

Note the difference to case (1): in case (1) overall market size has no impact on competition. Producers stick to their pre-integration policy. Mark ups stay the same and so does the scale of operation. In case (2), however,

---

[35] Goods dropping out of the market have a shadow price of $p_j = \sum_{m=1}^{M} a_{m,j} q_m$. But, since the demand for these goods is zero, they are not produced according to $p_i = F_i/x_i + v_i$. Consequently, in this case we have $\sum_{m=1}^{M} a_{m,j} q_m \geq F_i/x_i(p) + v_i$. The expression on the right hand side therefore only holds iff $x_i > 0$.

cost competition increases, urging producers to reconsider their former, pre-integration, strategy. Mark ups become smaller and the scale of operation increases. Because of intensifying competition, market size has an impact on production and production processes in particular. Via its horizontal impact integration provides the foundation for a finer vertical division of labour which will be considered in more detail in the next section.

However, before entering the vertical perspective, the second special case which marks the opposite of the standard Dixit-Stiglitz case shall be shortly noted. This case occurs if before integration both sets of the good's attributes, those in Home and those in Foreign, are identical:

$$\mathbf{A}^H = \mathbf{A}^F .$$ (4.23)

If both sets are identical and the number of goods in principle is already larger than the number of characteristics before integration, the removal of barriers to trade does not trigger a proliferation effect but a pro-competitive effect.

Summarising, it can be said that a situation in which integration has no substantial impact on the supply side is a special (theoretical) case. In the more general case the price elasticity of demand increases and competition intensifies so that integration will change the situation each producer faces, one of the results being that on average the individual scale of operation climbs. The multi-stage framework showed that the price elasticity of demand faced by a single producer only stays constant despite the market becoming larger in one particular case: if each good exactly carries one characteristic and if in addition the number of goods is always larger than the number of characteristics. However, the case of a constant elasticity of substitution between goods is a rather peculiar case if one thinks of characteristics such as transportation, shelter, food and so on. Any of these services can be provided to a greater or smaller extent and in different combinations by a number of goods. Hence, there is good reason to assume that there is some overlapping in the characteristics of goods in case of integration so that in general elasticity climbs with overall market size and so does individual output. Because of this horizontal impact of an increase in market size on the division of labour a finer vertical division of labour becomes sustainable. As it turns out, the consequences of market enlargement for the vertical division of labour are of particular importance for the issue of centripetal versus centrifugal forces in economic integration.

The impact of integration on the vertical division of labour will be analysed in detail in the next section by comparing the optimal production mode of individual producers before and after integration. In this section it will be shown how, because of competition being intensified as barriers to trade are removed, the production mode and therefore cost structures are endogenous to the size of the market. In particular, producers tend to employ a production mode which involves a higher share of outsourcing in gross product as the size of the market becomes larger. This is because the cost structure that goes along with more steps of production and a more extensive slicing of the value added chain proves to be advantageous in the new, more competitive, environment a larger market brings about.

IV. Integration cost competition, and induced technological change: a detailed treatise

This section will analyse more explicitly the impact of integration on the supply side with a particular focus on the vertical division of labour as triggered by integration.[36] The vertical consequences of integration will be captured by comparing the cost function of individual producers before and after liberalising international transactions to a greater extent. Since trade is based on individual transactions, the focus on an individual producer and how he modifies the mode of production in response to an increase in openness is warranted.[37] This perspective shows how – because of cost competition intensifying as barriers to trade are removed – cost structures are endogenous to the size of the market.

The economic reason for the endogeneity is that with competition being tougher post-integration, producers are forced to economise on production costs. Yet, not all kinds of costs shape individual competitiveness in the same manner. Rather their impact depends upon the size of the market. In particular, the share of variable costs in total costs climbs as the market becomes larger. Henceforth, the higher scale of operation provides an incentive to economise on variable costs.[38] As will be seen shortly, economising on variable costs is achieved by

---

[36] Kelly (1997) has outlined a model which is Smithian in spirit but in which market size is driven by the investment of individual firms in boosting sales. Though an interesting variant, in our case, market size is due to political decisions about liberalising economic transactions.

[37] As pointed out by Lösch as early as 1938, Ricardian comparative advantage actually applies to individuals. Or to put it differently: the macro-pattern of specialisation and its evolution must have its ultimate foundation in the deliberate actions of individual producers and consumers.

[38] The basic calculus affecting the choice of technology employed here rests on similar reasoning as considerations about the factor bias of technological change being driven by the factors' shares in the total costs of production. On the latter see Hicks (1932); Kennedy (1964); and Samuelson (1965).

(a) rearranging production processes in such a way that they involve more different steps of production, each displaying a greater homogeneity in tasks;

(b) outsourcing a larger share of production in gross output;

(c) dividing the value added chain into even 'thinner' slices (that is more narrowly defined activities) than in case of a purely local production (= case a) for better exploiting the cost advantages outsourcing provides.

In case of cost competition integration does not necessarily imply a geographical concentration of economic activity and a bias in the regional income distribution as economies of scale working on the demand side only would suggest. Rather, there is a centrifugal force emerging endogenously as the size of the market becomes larger. If the components entering a product become more narrowly defined as sales grow, producers of intermediates can specialise in specific advantages they enjoy. A productivity gain arises which can be divided among the parties involved. This gain is out of reach when sales are smaller and each component requires a broader range of capabilities. In this case, costs for some parts of the work may wipe out cost advantages possessed in other parts. If the productivity gain integration allows for is mostly on the side of producers in lagging regions, one not only observes a rise in real wages. But, there is also, as in fact frequently in EU history, a convergence in real wage rates because less of a price change (or less of a change in the exchange rate) is needed to achieve equilibrium in the trade balance.[39] This effect working in favour of a finer vertical division of labour will be dubbed 'foreign market effect' as opposed to the notion of integration inducing a 'home market effect' in the manner described in Chapter 3.

The vertical dimension of production and trade has been largely neglected with the upsurge of intra-industry models of trade in the 1980s and 1990s. The latter were primarily focusing on horizontal specialisation. Feenstra and Hanson (1996a: 240) are therefore right in remarking: 'this feature of globalisation – the fragmentation of production into discrete activities which are then allocated across countries – has received little attention in the literature'.[40]

---

[39] Recall from the first section of Chapter 3 that price adjustments and exchange rate changes are required if the *y* sector is too small to equilibrate real wages regionally. In fact, for instance, the peseta even appreciated while Spain was catching up in the second half of the 1980s.

[40] However, Feenstra and Hanson (1996a) in their work are more interested in empirically estimating the impact of outsourcing on the relative scarcity of skilled versus unskilled labour

There are few investigations into trade and the fragmentation of production, despite the contributions by Stigler (1951) and Ippolito (1977) to the theory of the firm which suggest that firms tend to vertically disintegrate into different activities as markets expand. Sanyal and Jones (1982); Slaughter (1995); Jones (1996); Ishii and Yi (1997) are studies which do take account of the fact that the international division of labour has a vertical dimension as well. However, they take the number of production blocs engaged in the production of final goods as given (usually two). The assumption of a given number of production blocs has the advantage that the authors are able to exactly determine the pattern of production. But since the fragmentation of production itself is not subject to analysis, they fail to capture how the organisation of production – in particular with regard to the fragmentation into different activities – changes because of the integration of markets.

Sanyal (1983) and Feenstra and Hanson (1996b) developed a model with a vertical dimension involving a continuum of tasks which are to be allocated between countries. However, since their analysis rests on purely Ricardian differences in production functions (Feenstra and Hanson (1996b) add differences in factors endowments), it primarily transposes the horizontal model of Dornbusch, Fischer and Samuelson (1977) into a vertical model. Thus, they do not answer the question of how and to what extent integration induces a fragmentation of production into different undertakings.

There are a number of studies in which productivity depends on the number of components and in which goods for end use are made from a larger array of components after integration than before. Trade models by Ethier (1982); Feenstra, Markusen and Zeile (1992); Feenstra and Markusen (1994); Yang and Shi (1992) and Matusz (1996), for instance, display this feature, as do growth models by Romer (1987) and Grossman and Helpman (1991/1995). But, these models are driven by the preference for variety as described in Chapter 3. The preference for variety is either on the side of the downstream firm for which variety raises productivity or on the side of the consumer for whom it increases utility. A larger market improves either productivity or utility because it sustains a greater variety of intermediates or goods for consumption. A higher scale of production can be the *result* of the productivity thus increased. The same holds true (as shown in Chapter 3) for some contributions to the new economic geography with a vertical dimension, of which Venables (1996; 1998b) is just one example and

---

in the US (on this issue see also the work by Slaughter (1995)) rather than in the process of induced change in particular, as we are.

Krugman and Venables (1995) is another one. However, as already pointed out in Sections I and II of this chapter, this notion of the evolution of the division of labour contrasts substantially with ours.

In our case, the driving force is a fundamentally different one: instead of the scale of operation being the *result* of a greater variety of components in a larger market, it is the change in the scale of operation a larger market brings about which due to cost competition *induces* a process of fragmentation and outsourcing. The difference matters. As noted in the first section of this chapter, in models driven by the preference for variety, only the number of components changes, but not the way they are produced. Hence, these models do not display the phenomenon of fragmentation in which components become more specific in the sense that they require less of a range of tasks. Moreover, in reality, a downstream producer does not demand all components on the market. Rather, components of a product are carefully matched in several dimensions (quantity, quality, location and time) upon the products' design. The goods are thus made of specific intermediates. In particular, concerning quality, they are characterised by being dissimilar with regard to other components and to other products' components while at the same time being complementary to each other.

This process of fragmentation with the contribution of each part of the whole chain becoming more narrowly defined is much more in line with thoughts of Jones and Kierzkowski (1990), though they did not employ a formalised model. Since the specificity of components suggests that inter alia coordination costs play an important role in the fragmentation of production and its international dispersion, the following analysis is also related to the work of Coase (1937), Williamson, O.E. (1980; 1996), Becker and Murphy (1992), Yang and Ng (1993) and de Groot (1997).

A.   *Evidence on the trend towards fragmentation*

The vertical dimension of integration which will be investigated in more detail in what follows is backed by empirical evidence on increasing vertical specialisation-based international trade (no matter whether it takes place within firms via foreign direct investment or whether it is market-mediated).[41] Naturally, empirical evidence on vertical specialisation is suggestive since data quality is poor. Trade data, for instance, has two major shortcomings.[42] First, trade volumes have to be adjusted for re-

---

[41] They are also in line with empirical findings of Cortes and Jean (1997) who relate higher import penetration rates in a given industry to factor productivity growth. See also Isçan (1998) with reference to Mexican manufacturing.

[42] For instance, Kol and Rayment (1989) try to infer the evolution of imported inputs from trade data.

exports. Re-exports are imports which are only subject to insignificant changes before being exported again. To the extent that re-exporting takes place, numbers being based on overall exports and imports are inflated (see also Campa and Goldberg (1997: 60) on this problem). Second, intermediates in trade statistics are classified differently from national income accounts. Sometimes they are classified as being for end use though in fact they are inputs subject to further treatment. So far, trade statistics underestimate the extent of vertical specialisation in the world economy.

National income accounts, however, frequently provide no meaningful time series for the evolution of the share of imported purchases in total figures either; and input-output tables which theoretically should allow for a more disaggregated perspective than national income accounts are published infrequently. This has the drawback that numbers are distorted by particular events and that they are not available up-to-the-minute. Moreover, input-output data is sometimes not based on actual numbers but on estimates. German input-output data, for instance, assumes that the structure of imported inputs across industries is the same as in the case of domestic inputs. Similarly, no reliable data exists on the evolution of the fraction of imported intermediate inputs in exports nor is there a possibility to derive exact numbers from the raw data. Hence, numbers do not provide exact quantities on the evolution of the share of domestic value added in total value added of exports. There is only data available on the amount of imported intermediate inputs entering production in general, no matter whether final products are destined for the international or the domestic market. Hence, the fact that the data shows weaknesses has to be kept in mind when interpreting the evolution of imported inputs.

Nevertheless there is substantial indication that (measured in constant prices) purchases of intermediates from other firms climbed as barriers to trade and mobility have melted down during the last twenty-five years. Instead of being exported only once, one and the same good is frequently exported several times before it arrives at the point of consumption.

One indicator for measuring the fragmentation of production is the coefficient of value added (for details on how to measure international inter-industry linkages see, for instance, Kubo (1985)). Given everything else, an increase in the 'intermediate-intensity' should show up in a lower coefficient of value added. The coefficient of value added is defined as the ratio of value added at a particular stage of production to the value of intermediates used for manufacturing the output of this stage. From the perspective of the economics of integration it is natural to calculate an economy-wide coefficient of value added rather than focusing on a particular stage. However, since it is hard to infer the value added coefficient from macro-data, the GDP to export ratio shall serve as a first proxy.

Table 4.2 shows the inverse of the corresponding coefficient for selected years and countries in real terms, that is deflated with the appropriate price index, the export deflator and the GDP deflator.[43] Since it shows the inverse, an increase of the slicing of the value added chain should also show up as an increase in the ratio.

Table 4.2: Real export to value added ratios for selected years and countries

	Year					
Country	1970	1975	1980	1985	1990	1995
France	12.7	16.1	19.1	20.6	22.6	25.9
Germany	18.1	21.1	23.1	27.8	27.9	26.9
United Kingdom	18.0	20.1	22.5	23.5	24.4	28.8
Belgium	46.6	49.6	57.5	62.8	73.1	85.8
Netherlands	35.4	40.9	44.0	48.7	54.2	60.8
Portugal	22.5	17.5	21.5	27.8	34.3	42.0
Spain	9.5	10.3	13.2	17.6	17.1	25.4
EU-15	17.7	20.1	22.8	25.8	27.4	32.0
United States	5.5	6.9	8.1	6.8	10.0	12.8
Japan	6.0	7.4	9.5	11.5	10.7	12.3
Singapore	n.a.	n.a.	129.6	102.1	140.6	155.1[a]

Export values and GDPs are deflated with their respective price indices; [a]refers to 1994.
Source: OECD (1997a); IMF (1996); own calculations.

The actual level of the ratio indicates that even internationally the vertical division of labour is of considerable importance nowadays. With usually more than half of the GDP originating from the non-tradable sector currently, export to GDP ratios exceeding a third of GDP suggest that only small value is added in exports over imported inputs (see also Krugman (1995c) on this issue). This is the case in many of the major industrialised economies. It applies in particular to countries like Singapore and Hong Kong whose value of exports by now exceeds the value added in the export industry by far: in these cases export values reach more than 150 per cent of the value added of the total economy (World Bank (1995: Table 9, 179);

---

[43] In choosing real numbers we take account of the Samuelson-Balassa effect, that is the fact that the increase in the price of services usually exceeds the price increase in manufactures. The export-GDP ratio has the advantage of being free from changes in the costs of transportation since exports are registered f.o.b. in trade statistics, whereas imports are noted c.i.f. On the distorting impact of the Samuelson-Balassa effect in measuring globalisation see Irwin (1996) and Van Bergeijk and Mensink (1997).

IMF (1996)). However, even in European countries, on which this study focuses in particular, the chain of value added is being sliced remarkably.

In fact, in 1995, the EU reached on average a value of exports to GDP ratio of 32 per cent. A couple of European countries are well ahead of these 32 per cent: take for instance Belgium, Ireland or the Netherlands with real export to total value added ratios hovering around 50-85 per cent in the early 1990s (OECD (1997a), see also Table 4.2). Though in smaller countries higher ratios are in general to be expected, volumes on that high a scale are informative as regards the nature and the dynamics of the vertical division of labour triggered by the process of integration. The numbers indicate that vertical linkages across different countries are all but negligible.

From our perspective, the evolution of the ratio is of even greater interest than the level and, indeed, export to GDP ratios were on the rise throughout the period under consideration.[44] EU-wide, they climbed continuously in the last twenty-five years. Exceptions are few. In addition, they are related to particular events: Germany in the aftermath of unification, Portugal as the political climate changed in the mid-1970s, Spain during the economic slump of the early 1990s, the United States during the surge in net capital imports and the real appreciation of the US currency in the mid-1980s and so on. Thus, the overall impression one gets from the data is that of a trend towards higher export to GDP ratios the more barriers to trade are removed. And there can be no doubt that the world economy has experienced a considerable integration of markets over the last decades, even though governments now and then raised non-tariff barriers to trade. Outsourcing triggered by a growth in market size, that is an induced vertical division of labour, could provide an explanation for the trend towards higher export to GDP ratios.

More precise numbers are difficult to obtain, however. For example, measured in current prices, the German economy shows no clear movement in the fraction of imported inputs in total inputs since the late 1970s – despite the fact that the German automobile industry for instance is known to be affected strongly.[45] However, the lack in movement does not

---

[44] This is all the more remarkable since one factor influencing the extent of outsourcing is the relative price of intermediates at home and abroad. The numbers suggest that the elasticity of outsourcing with respect to cost savings is larger than one. However, the chain of value added can be sliced finer without the ratio necessarily climbing. This has to be kept in mind when interpreting value added coefficients. These indicators contrast with findings by Molle (1997) who claims that European regions tended to de-specialise in the period of 1950 to 1990.

[45] See also the reports on the structure of the German economy, most recently, Klodt, Maurer and Schimmelpfennig (1997). However, Fels and Schmidt (1980: 31ff.) already arrived at similar results.

necessarily run counter to the fragmentation hypothesis as there might be an increase in the overall input intensity due to openness. The general increase in competitive pressure a larger market brings about can also imply a rise in imports of final goods which triggers a process of outsourcing within the German industry. Therefore, the impact of openness on production need not necessarily show up in a higher ratio of foreign inputs. In fact, German income accounts display an increase in the overall input intensity of the German economy over the last twenty-five years (that is from 1970 to 1995) if measured in 1991 prices.[46] In total, purchases climbed by some 6.7 percentage points, reaching an all time high of 63.7 per cent of gross production in 1995 (all data taken from the 1996 edition of the German Statistical Office Data Tape).[47] Manufacturing itself still added some 5.5 percentage points in purchases, with the fraction of intermediates in gross output amounting to 64.57 per cent in 1995.[48]

The overall extent of outsourcing has climbed in line with openness when measured as the ratio of two price indices, those of imports and those of final goods.[49] A decline of the ratio can be interpreted as indicating that competition from foreign sources has intensified. In particular since the

---

[46] In nominal terms, however, there is hardly any indication of a significant change in the share of imported inputs in total inputs. Rather, the increase is confined to some industries.

[47] The only years providing for an exception from the trend are 1977, 1981 and 1983.

[48] Outsourcing is even on the rise in parts of the economy which compared to other sectors traditionally had much in-house production: in the construction business purchases grew by some 8.5 percentage points (from 46.2 to 54.74 per cent), in the banking and insurance industry by more than 7 percentage points (from 28.16 to 35.59 per cent of gross output) and even in services they climbed by some 5 percentage points (from 30.41 to 35.53 per cent of gross output). Exceptions from the trend towards a significantly higher share of outsourcing are confined to three sectors: retailing stagnated at an already high level of 85.7 per cent in gross output. Government, non-profit organisations, private households and agriculture even curbed the share of intermediates bought in gross output. However, sectors having curbed their share are either in one way or the other exempted from competition or they face, as private households do, an increasing burden of taxation from which vertical integration provides a route of escape. Private households can either evade taxation by doing it themselves or by taking resort to the underground economy. The first case shows up as a decline in outsourcing, the second at least provides for wrong numbers as the actual division of labour is underrated by official statistics. And as far as the public sector itself is concerned it is well known from the theory of bureaucracy that the incentives are biased towards increasing the range of activities rather than concentrating on those carried out efficiently. In agriculture, where the CAP is known to promote the horizontal and vertical concentration, numbers deviate the strongest from the general trend.

[49] Usually, trade volumes are used for measuring openness. However, frequently trade is not balanced. Major swings in the magnitude and direction of net capital flows thus have an impact on the indicator without being necessarily associated with a change in the extent the national economy is exposed to foreign competition. Rather than a change in openness, these movements indicate a change in relative capital scarcity. Of course it is openness vis-à-vis foreign goods and services which actually allows the exploitation of international differences in real interest rates. In any case, this shortcoming has to be kept in mind when drawing conclusions based on this indicator.

1980s there has been an inverse relationship between outsourcing and relative price movements: outsourcing was by and large on the rise while import prices rose by less than prices of manufactured goods in Germany.[50]

However, there are clear signs that the ratio is affected by exchange rate movements which spoil the trend. In the first half of the 1980s the relative price index shows a strong impact of the rise in the US dollar as the US on balance increased its capital demand. Shortly thereafter the growth in purchases flattened out. The strong real appreciation of the US currency obviously deterred German producers from buying more foreign made inputs. However, by the mid-1980s the relative price index deteriorated and with a slight lag, outsourcing took off again, moving almost in line with prices during 1985-94.

Campa and Goldberg (1997) also provide evidence in favour of a finer vertical division of labour in a case of four countries by using input-output data of a single year as a benchmark.[51] In doing so they keep the structure of production constant while measuring the evolution of import penetration with regard to intermediates. Results are based on twenty industries on the 2-digit level of the Standard Industrial Classification system for the UK, the US, Canada and Japan (see also Feenstra and Hanson (1996a); as well as Slaughter (1995) on the measurement of import penetration). They found that between 1975 and 1995 the imported input share (in total inputs) was on the rise – except for Japan (Campa and Goldberg (1997: Tables 1, 3 and 5)). In US manufacturing it increased from 4.1 per cent to 8.2 per cent with most of the increase taking place in the production of leather and leather products (5.6-20.5), in the production of industrial machinery and equipment (4.5-11.6), and in transportation equipment (6.4-15.7). Similarly, in Canada the share climbed from 6.4 per cent in 1974 to 15.7 percent in 1993, again with reference to total manufacturing. In the case of Canada the machinery industry (17.7-26.6), transportation equipment (29.1-49.7) and electrical machinery products (13.2-30.9) were particularly affected. Finally, Campa and Goldberg (1997) found that in the United Kingdom the share rose from 13.4 (1974) to 21.7 per cent (1993), however, with the increase being much more equally distributed across industries than in the US or in Canada.

Since input-output tables do not distinguish between inputs used for domestic markets and those entering exports, Ishii and Yi (1997) present

---

[50] During the 1970s the relationship was somewhat looser as prices for manufactures in general were affected by the first oil crisis and industry was reluctant to increase its purchases of inputs. Even in the 1970s, however, the trend is in line with the expected relationship.

[51] See also the evidence cited in Hummels, Rapoport and Yi (1997) and Irwin (1996) with the latter being based on the increase of capital goods in US trade in particular.

case studies which allow for a more detailed tracing of the uses.[52] Studying the US-Canada Auto Part Pact of 1965, US-Mexican maquiladoras trade, recent Japan-Asia electronics trade and GM's expansion into Spain in the early 1980s, they found evidence in support of a slicing of the value added chain and a trend towards an international specialisation in particular stages of production.[53] For instance, after the US-Canadian Auto Part Pact went into effect, vertical specialisation climbed to 20 per cent of total US-Canadian auto trade, with current numbers reaching more than 40 per cent (p. 13). Similarly, they came up with an increase of 31 per cent in vertical trade in the US-Mexican maquiladoras trade for the period 1979-89 (p. 15).[54] Referring to the European Union, they cite GM's production in Spain showing a fivefold increase in vertical specialisation based trade in US dollars between 1983 and 1995 (p. 17).[55]

In the theoretical section on fragmentation we propose a simple framework for understanding how the value added chain tends to be sliced more extensively the more open the economy. It consists of three subsections. In this we essentially follow the list of features of the process of fragmentation, (a) to (c), as outlined in the introduction to this section, namely in that we first investigate how production is organised, (given that production takes place locally); second, how different steps in the production process are internationally allocated; and third, how the allocation has a feedback-effect on the organisation of production. Finally, we will draw some policy conclusions emanating from the theoretical analysis.

B. Integration and the fragmentation of production into complementary production blocs

The three-stage budgeting process of Section III of Chapter 4 showed that, on average, individual output is positively related to the integration of

---

[52] See also the case studies focusing on particular industries and regions by Amsden (1985) and Kubo (1985) as well as the spatial distribution of component-sourcing within Europe presented in Dicken (1986: 304) who draws on the example of the Ford Escort.

[53] Ishii and Yi (1997) also aim at capturing the trend towards slicing the value added chain by developing a Ricardian model of trade in intermediates and final goods. However, in contrast to the model presented in Section IV.B. of this chapter in which the number of stages of production is determined endogenously, they start from the assumption of production taking place in two stages (p. 3). For a two-stage approach see also Sanyal and Jones (1982).

[54] Parts used in the so-called maquiladoras trade which originate from the country of destination to which the final product is being shipped are not subject to tariffs by the country of destination.

[55] Referring to the Spanish automobile industry, Lagendijk (1993) provides an interesting description of organisational changes, in particular those affecting the governance structure during internationalisation.

markets if the number of characteristics, (M), is smaller upon integration than the number of goods, (n). In this case, which we assume prevails, a larger market provides more opportunities for consumers to switch between different sources of supply for goods with similar characteristics so that the price elasticity of demand increases upon integration. Standard reasoning then tells us that profit maximisation under monopolistic competition implies that the average mark up of prices over unit costs becomes smaller. With prices being lower the higher the elasticity, and with free entry, the optimal individual scale of operation, x_i, is larger in a more liberalised environment, so that the scale of operation can be written as a function of the economy-wide number of goods and the number of characteristics as markets are opened:[56,57]

$$x_i = f(n, M) \tag{4.24}$$

The function $f(\cdot)$, evaluated at a particular constellation $(\tilde{n}', \tilde{M}')$ as trade becomes more liberalised, can thus be considered as providing some measure of the competitive climate post-integration. The higher its value, the more competitive the environment. In effect, integration not only has an impact on the location of the demand function faced by any producer in the economy but also on its slope.

With sales being larger, production can be rationalised. Rationalisation can be achieved by dividing the process of production into more production blocs. This is because changing the mode of production so that it involves more different stages allows to save on switching costs as the range of activities performed within each production bloc becomes more homogeneous. Crafts production, to mention the other extreme, in which the products are more or less made piece after piece, requires not only a broad variety of skills from the craftsmen but also a frequent switching between different tasks.

The change in the mode of production will usually not only be quantitative, but also qualitative in nature: If markets are small, that is before liberalisation takes place, components are often multi-purpose. As markets become larger, that is in the course of liberalisation, intermediates

---

[56]   Since n is related to L, we could also write x as a function of overall market size measured by employment L. For details see Dluhosch (1997); for a two-factor framework with constant elasticity of substitution and endogenous choice of technology see Burda and Dluhosch (1999a,b).

[57]   The threat of potential entry is also assumed to be larger the more open and the larger the market, so that competition remains intense, even when some producers drop out of the market.

become more specific, both with regard to their function and the product for which they are designed. However, in what follows we will focus primarily on the quantitative aspect, namely the change in the number of production blocs and components respectively (and their international allocation) rather than on changes in quality, which would introduce another dimension into competition.

This subsection serves to examine the impact of integration on production processes by taking a more detailed look at the various costs of manufacturing goods and how they are affected by reorganising production. Suppose each final good is produced by use of a number of complementary components. Let x_i denote the scale of operation of an individual producer who puts the final good together (that is downstream firm). Without loss of generality it will be assumed that exactly one component of each kind from all of the different types of components enters the product. That being so, the number of identical components used for the whole output of the final good boils down to the scale of operation, that is x_i.

For ease of exposition it will further be assumed that production costs per component-unit, r^H, are equal for all types of components as long as production takes place locally.[58] If s is the (endogenous) number of different components each product is made from, total costs for the components add up to $sr^H x_i$. Finally, let $wl(s)$ stand for switching costs between the different tasks for each unit produced, so that total switching costs in the production of x_i amount to $wl(s)x_i$.

Due to switching costs between different activities, productivity at the final stage depends upon the number of complementary components. The more the product is sliced into components, the more can the factors of production concentrate on particular activities, each manufacturing a distinct component. Switching costs are thus saved, and overall productivity is higher, that is $\partial l/\partial s < 0$, the larger the number of homogeneous production blocs, even if labour productivity is the same in all activities.[59] It is reasonable, though, that this sort of productivity increases at declining rates as the slicing continues, that is $\partial^2 l/(\partial s)^2 > 0$. This is because production will first be divided among the factors of production where most of the switching costs can be saved. Nota bene: we consider the costs of manufacturing in the narrow sense of the term not to be affected by this procedure. If the factors of production differed in their productivity or if

---

[58] We do not consider the make or buy decision of a producer as long as all components of a product are manufactured either in Home or in Foreign. Pre-integration, r^H can therefore be either the price of a component or the costs of manufacturing the component in-house.

[59] This source of gains from the division of labour among equals which is only due to economies of scale has been nicely illustrated by Houthakker (1956).

they developed a routine, costs of manufacturing the various pieces would be affected. To keep the analysis as simple as possible and to concentrate on the basics, we abstract from learning though. And, as long as all of the production takes place locally, it will be assumed that all units of the factors of production are alike in their productivity. Savings in switching costs will thus be explicitly modelled rather than indicated by use of a productivity parameter attached to the costs of each component. This allows better to distinguish the different sources of productivity gains and to analyse their interaction. Otherwise, the various sources of productivity gains would feed into a single parameter. Even though the pure costs of manufacturing are not reduced by this reorganisation, production as a whole displays economies of scale.

On the one hand costs can thus obviously be curbed by rearranging the process of production into more (homogeneous) production blocs. On the other hand, increasing the number of components for rationalising production usually comes at a price as other costs are raised thereby. If products are not manufactured in one piece but made from parts, they must be put together at the final stage, usually by specialised machinery. This implies higher fixed costs, F, which add to total costs of production and which are higher the more components must be assembled, that is $\partial F/\partial s > 0$. If it is more expensive to fit the components together the smaller and the more specific they are, fixed costs climb at an increasing rate as the number of components goes up, that is $\partial^2 F/(\partial s)^2 > 0$. Even if the average cost curve can be shifted by reorganising production in this manner, higher cost reductions as regards the bloc of fixed costs are forgone. The trade-off between scale dependent and scale independent costs via the change in the number of components represents some kind of cost-reduction possibility frontier.[60]

Nonetheless, the strategy of reorganising might pay, that is, depending upon market size, producers pick a particular technology (characterised by the number of production blocs) upon entering the market.[61] The way the production mode and therefore the cost function is adapted to the increase

---

[60] Empirically, there is no way to differentiate between a sliding along the cost reduction possibility frontier and a shift of the frontier which might happen in addition if there is technological progress. However, in this study, the focus will be primarily on the direction of technological *change* rather than on technological *progress* proper. The analysis rests therefore on the assumption that the frontier stays in place and that producers slide along the curve.

[61] The assumption that producers choose a production process upon entering the market allows us to abstract from the costs of switching the production mode. Costs of adapting the mode of production currently in use to the new environment would complicate the presentation of the main driving forces without changing them in substance.

in the turf size in the course of integration can be derived from comparing the costs of production before and after rationalisation. Before rationalising, that is with the number of components $s = \tilde{s}$, producers bear total costs C according to equation (4.25):

$$C\big|_{s=\tilde{s}} = wl(s)f(\cdot) + sr^H(s)f(\cdot) + F \qquad (4.25)$$

In equation (4.25) it is already taken into account that the scale of operation is a matter of the competitive climate by substituting $f(\cdot)$ for x. As we know from Section III of this chapter, post-integration, competition can be considered as being tougher so that $f'(\cdot) > f(\cdot)$.

Post-integration, and after rationalising, overall costs shall be denoted by C'. Similarly, the number of components after integration will also be indicated by a prime, so that we can write down total costs under the new technology, that is with the number of components $s = \tilde{s}'$, as

$$C'\big|_{s=\tilde{s}'} = wl(s)f'(\cdot) + sr^H(s)f'(\cdot) + F \qquad (4.26)$$

If there are no barriers to entry, producers are forced to minimise costs by choice of the appropriate technology. In this case the appropriate technology is described by the optimal number of complementary components – or which amounts to the same – production blocs. More precisely, we have to prove that post-integration, that is with $f'(\cdot) > f(\cdot)$,

$$\tilde{s}' > \tilde{s} \quad \text{and} \quad C'\big|_{s=\tilde{s}', f'(\cdot)} < C\big|_{s=\tilde{s}, f'(\cdot)} \qquad (4.27)$$

holds true. The optimal number of components can be derived from the first order condition for a cost minimum. Differentiating equation (4.25) with respect to s, and keeping in mind that the competitive climate is described by $f(\cdot)$ and $f'(\cdot)$ respectively, yields the following first order condition:

$$\frac{\partial C}{\partial s} = s\frac{\partial l}{\partial s}f(\cdot) + \underbrace{r^H f(\cdot) + s\frac{\partial r^H}{\partial s}f(\cdot)}_{=(1+\eta_H)f(\cdot)\,r^H} + \frac{\partial F}{\partial s} \qquad (4.28)$$

With η_H indicating the elasticity of the costs of manufacturing a component r^H with respect to the extent of fragmentation s, equation (4.28) can be rewritten in a more compact manner:

$$\frac{\partial F}{\partial s} = -\left[w\frac{\partial l}{\partial s} + r^H\left(1+\eta_H\right)\right]f(\cdot) \tag{4.29}$$

According to equation (4.29), we can expect three sorts of costs to be affected by varying the number of components

- scale-independent costs incurred by rationalising production (that is LHS of equation (4.29)),
- switching costs (that is the first term in brackets on the RHS) and (probably)
- costs of manufacturing the components (that is the second term in brackets).

In any case, it is reasonable to assume that the impact of increasing the number of components on the costs of manufacturing a component, r^H, is negative. Moreover, as already indicated, at this stage of the analysis, total costs of the components are not considered to be subject to change which means that the elasticity of the costs of the components with respect to the extent of slicing is minus unity ($\eta_H = -1$).[62] With this assumption equation (4.29) reduces to:

$$\frac{\partial F}{\partial s} = -w\frac{\partial l}{\partial s}f[\cdot] \tag{4.30}$$

From (4.29) it follows that

$$f'(\cdot) = \left[-\frac{\partial F/\partial s}{\left[w\partial l/\partial s + r^H\left(1+\eta_H\right)\right]}\right]' > \left[-\frac{\partial F/\partial s}{\left[w\partial l/\partial s + r^H\left(1+\eta_H\right)\right]}\right] = f(\cdot) \tag{4.31}$$

or, in case of $\eta_H = -1$,

$$f'(\cdot) = \left(\frac{\partial F/\partial s}{-w\partial l/\partial s}\right)' > \left(\frac{\partial F/\partial s}{-w\partial l/\partial s}\right) = f(\cdot) \tag{4.32}$$

Inequality (4.32) shows that with competition being more intense, $f'(\cdot) > f(\cdot)$, and output being larger it can be reasonable for producers to employ a production mode which involves a finer fragmentation into discrete

---

[62]   Though elasticities refer to a particular point on the cost curve, the result marks the direction of change, and this is what we are interested in.

production blocs and thereby to make more intensive use of interchangeable parts. This strategy pays even if it comes at the price of higher costs for specialised machinery: the far LHS of inequality (4.32), $f'(\cdot)$, becomes increasingly positive and the slope of the cost reduction possibility frontier to the left of the inequality sign becomes steeper. At the margin, the additional gains from increasing labour productivity by slicing the product into more components are just exhausted by the additional fixed cost incurred thereby. But this exactly means that the number of production blocs increases. Thus, for any output rate, there is an optimal number of components. This number tends to be larger, the larger the scale on which the final good is produced.

$$\tilde{s}' > \tilde{s} \text{ and } C'\big|_{s=\tilde{s}',f'(\cdot)} < C\big|_{s=\tilde{s},f'(\cdot)} \text{ if } f'(\cdot) > f(\cdot) \text{ and } x' > x \qquad (4.33)$$

That is (4.30) holds true indeed. Actually, the reasoning reveals that market-led technological change is driven by the evolution of the ratio of fixed to variable costs. While the share of variable costs in total costs climbs as market size expands, inequalities (4.31) and (4.32) show that fragmenting the production process into more production blocs drives down their share again. Having derived that integration fosters the fragmentation of the production process into complementary production blocs, the next subsection will focus on outsourcing in particular.

C.   Outsourcing

As far as a foreign producer can offer the work more cheaply, integration provides an incentive to outsource parts of the production and to locally concentrate on activities which are managed comparatively well. This second source of cost savings thus differs from the one in subsection B in so far as the first primarily addresses the benefits of reorganising the production process whereas the second explicitly introduces the pay-off from cross-regional or cross-national differences in production functions. In the first case the division of labour and therefore productivity is purely driven by economies of scale whereas in the second case Ricardian differences also enter into the division of labour. As will be seen shortly, the evolution of the division of labour post-integration reflects an *interaction* between these two sources of productivity gains.

The extent of outsourcing can be captured by introducing another variable k, which denotes the fraction of components outsourced in the total number of components s. If the price of components in Foreign is denoted by r^F and a fraction k is outsourced and thus bought from foreign suppliers, total costs of the downstream producer amount to:[63]

$$C = wlx_i + sr^H x_i - sk(r^H - r^F)x_i + F + \breve{F} \qquad (4.34)$$

The price for components in Foreign (r^F) is considered to be smaller than the price at Home (r^H) which provides the very incentive for outsourcing to take place. If the difference is taken as given for a moment, then there is an optimal fraction of components k outsourced for each number of different components s which depends inter alia on the size of the integrated market. The costs of finally assembling all the components, that is $wxl(s) + F$, might nevertheless remain the same as some of the production is outsourced. What changes is that in case of outsourcing the production process needs to be coordinated at distance. Therefore, outsourcing usually requires a change in the governance structure. The new governance structure is likely to be associated with higher fixed costs which depend on the scale of outsourcing. This is because contacts with the sources of supply have to be established; a reputation for reliable collaboration has to be built up and maintained; sunk, and for the most part fixed, costs are larger because of more advertising and so on. The immaterial capital stock thus built up serves as a safeguard against opportunistic behaviour and by doing so ensures proper quality. Opportunistic behaviour might not only be cheaper to deal with in case of in-house production (because the proximity and the hierarchical relationship allows for better information). Internal safeguards and quality controls might also by and large be less of a fixed cost kind. If the foreign sources of supply are established by means of foreign direct investment, administrative costs and the gathering of information for getting a business started in an unfamiliar environment can be considered as fixed costs of outsourcing. If this holds true, there is an additional cost $\breve{F}$ in case of outsourcing which is more of a scale independent character (that is with respect to x_i) and which climbs with the extent of outsourcing k, that is $\partial \breve{F}/\partial k > 0$.[64] As the capability for handling contractual partners is usually

---

[63] In principle, outsourcing can take place both within Home and with respect to Foreign. Both of these processes could be grasped by distinguishing between k^H and k^F, that is the number of components bought from firms in Home and in Foreign respectively. However, the basic reasoning would stay the same, while the complexity would increase substantially. Thus we chose to consider that outsourcing only takes place with regard to foreign sources of supply.

[64] An increase in k shall also imply an increase in the regional entropy of the sources of supply. With the sources being more dispersed, fixed costs can be regarded as a function of k indeed. However, see also the notes on Figure 4.4.

limited, it will be assumed that these costs climb at an increasing rate the greater the fraction of production outsourced, $\partial^2 \breve{F}/(\partial k)^2 > 0.$[65]

The calculus of a producer weighing the advantages and disadvantages of outsourcing can again be described by comparing costs before and after raising the fraction of foreign sources of supply. Before trade is liberalised further, total costs of producing at a scale of x_i with $s = \hat{s}$ components and a fraction $k = \tilde{k}$ of the production outsourced amount to:

$$C\big|_{k=\tilde{k},s=\hat{s}} = wx_i l(s) + sr^H(s)x_i - skx_i\big[r^H(s) - r^F(s)\big] + F + \breve{F} \qquad (4.35)$$

Post-integration, the technology chosen shall be described by the extent of outsourcing being $k = \tilde{k}'$ and total costs C', given $s = \hat{s}$. Outsourcing is increased as integration is pushed forward if

$$\tilde{k}' > \tilde{k} \quad \text{and} \quad C'\big|_{k=\tilde{k}',s=\hat{s},f'(\cdot)} < C\big|_{k=\tilde{k},s=\hat{s},f'(\cdot)} \qquad (4.36)$$

if

$$f'(\cdot) > f(\cdot) \quad \text{and} \quad x_i' > x_i .$$

In like manner as in (4.28), one arrives for a given $\hat{s}\big(r^H - r^F\big)$ at the following rule concerning outsourcing:[66]

$$\frac{\partial C}{\partial k} = \frac{\partial \breve{F}}{\partial k} - \hat{s}\big(r^H - r^F\big)f(\cdot) = 0 \quad \text{or} \quad \frac{\partial \breve{F}}{\partial k} = \hat{s}\big(r^H - r^F\big)f(\cdot) \qquad (4.37)$$

With the local producer holding a comparative advantage in assembling and coordinating production and with the gross benefits from outsourcing $\hat{s}\big(r^H - r^F\big)$ per unit produced taken as given for the moment, outsourcing takes place until the difference in the total costs of components (RHS of (4.37)) is being matched by the additional costs (LHS of (4.37)) due to

---

[65] Becker and Murphy (1992) consider the division of labour in general to be limited by costs of coordination rather than the extent of the market. Langlois' (1988) explanation of the vertical integration of firms runs along similar lines. In the framework presented in this study integration and thus the extent of the market affects the particular point on the cost constraint chosen, though. On the factors influencing the costs of coordination see Section V of Chapter 4 of this study.

[66] Ignoring integer problems.

outsourcing. As can be immediately seen, the fraction of undertakings which are outsourced climbs with $f(\cdot)$ and the scale of operation x_i:

$$f'(\cdot) = \left[\frac{\partial \breve{F}/\partial k}{\hat{s}\left(r^H - r^F\right)}\right]' > \left[\frac{\partial \breve{F}/\partial k}{\hat{s}\left(r^H - r^F\right)}\right] = f(\cdot) \qquad (4.38)$$

Given $\hat{s}$, inequality (4.38) holds true if k is higher the more integrated the markets. For with k being larger, the expression to the left of the inequality sign is larger too, as is the value of $f'(\cdot)$.

Figure 4.3:   *Integration and outsourcing*

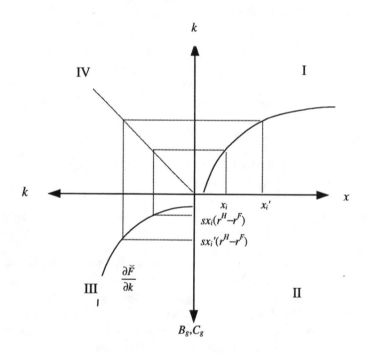

With B_g, C_g gross marginal benefits and costs from outsourcing

Figure 4.3 depicts the relationship between the extent of outsourcing, k, and the scale of operation, x_i, in the first quadrant. As shown, the fraction of components outsourced in each unit produced rises at a decreasing rate as the scale of operation increases. The forces determining the extent of outsourcing are outlined in the third quadrant. With cost differences for each component considered as given, gross benefits of outsourcing are a flat line in the third quadrant which is the farther away from the k-axis the higher the scale of operation x_i. The amount of production outsourced at each scale is thus determined by the intersection of the $sx_i(r^H - r^F)$ curve and the $\partial \breve{F}/\partial k$ curve. The optimal fraction of production outsourced k for each scale of production x_i, x_i' and so on (with $x_i' > x_i$) can be read off the k axis of quadrant III. If reflected on the 45-degree line in the fourth quadrant, we can construct in the first quadrant a graph showing how the fraction of outsourced components is related to the scale of operation x_i, or, as the scale is driven by competition, the competitive climate $f(\cdot)$.

The exact shape of the k-x_i graph surely depends upon the evolution of the costs and benefits due to outsourcing. For instance, it is reasonable that the $\partial \breve{F}/\partial k$ -curve does not go through the origin as the costs of getting a production started on an international scale can be substantial. If the additional fixed costs from outsourcing another part of production climb from the outset at increasing rates, the k-x_i curve increases at a decreasing rate (keep in mind that we have assumed that the price difference of components remains constant).

Alternatively, the $\partial \breve{F}/\partial k$ curve in the third quadrant could be shaped like a u turned upside down: at lower fractions outsourced there might be some economies of scale in coordinating production at a distance while at higher rates the law of scarce resources sets in. In this case, marginal costs of outsourcing the first production bloc are substantial. Thereafter, they first decline while later on, as outsourcing continues, they increase. Two examples why this might well hold shall suffice: first, once being established, a reputation for reliable cooperation can by and large be transferred to another component manufacturer. Second, though information costs for first going international might be substantial, the second time experience is already gained – even if the regional entropy of the sources of supply climbs. Or in different words: the reputation established and the experience gained in one line of supply also delivers services in a second line. Thus assuming some economies of scale in the process of outsourcing itself over a certain range is not that far-fetched indeed. However, in any case, the crucial part is the increasing branch of the $\partial \breve{F}/\partial k$ curve. In both cases, the parabolic and the u-shaped, the fraction of production outsourced k tends to increase with liberalisation, flattening out at higher scales of x_i as the costs of coordinating an increasingly scattered production climb exponentially.

D.   Economies of scale and differences in production functions

However, it is reasonable that the pool of ideas becomes larger with market size as more heads are involved.[67] Slicing the production process into more stages then allows an improvement on the allocation of economic activities. The regional allocation is one such dimension upon which the allocation can be improved. Suppose that ranking according to comparative advantage implied that before trade liberalisation made progress a fraction k of components was manufactured in Foreign and $(1-k)$ in Home, where the components were also assembled and where production was coordinated. Because of the fragmentation as liberalisation proceeds, Home may lose its comparative advantage in parts of the production process, thus concentrating more intensively on putting the components together and coordinating production. The key point is that the additional slicing reduces the tasks to be carried out in each production bloc by making them more specific. This allows better exploitation of regional differences in production functions. Slicing is thus fostered by the incentive to reap additional benefits from outsourcing. Since outsourcing becomes more attractive thereby as markets become more open, the fraction of production outsourced increases by even more than in (4.38).

We can capture the opportunity to refine the allocation of undertakings by assuming that the costs of components in Home and in Foreign are affected differently by fragmenting production. Differentiating (4.34) with respect to s yields

$$\frac{\partial C}{\partial s} = w\frac{\partial l}{\partial s} f(\cdot) + (1-k)r^{H}(1+\eta_{H})f(\cdot) + kr^{F}(1+\eta_{F})f(\cdot) + \frac{\partial F}{\partial s} \qquad (4.39)$$

with η_H and η_F denoting the elasticity of the costs of components with respect to the number of different components in Home and in Foreign respectively. Setting (4.39) equal to zero, we obtain the optimal extent of fragmentation as a function of k.[68] Now suppose that as the speciation of

---

[67] An additional incentive for outsourcing is due to the increase in the (local) scale of production (see Dluhosch, Freytag and Krüger (1996: 4 et seq.)). As the scale of operation is increased, local resources become scarcer. That being so, costs provide a constant pressure to move production blocs abroad, thus economising on location (an issue which is not in particular addressed in the model as the model only focuses on Ricardian, i.e. technological, differences in production functions). Interestingly, however, Ricardian models display Heckscher-Ohlin features when introducing trade in middle products. This is because home and foreign labour amount to two different factors engaged in the production of final goods as Jones (1980) has shown in a two-sector model with two stages of production.

[68] In case both elasticities are minus unity (that is $\eta_H = \eta_F = -1$), the slicing has no impact on k. This was the situation in the previous section.

undertakings is pushed on, it might be easier for a foreign producer who enjoys a specific advantage to get a foothold in the market. This is the case, for instance, if $\eta_H = 1$ and $\eta_F < -1$: whereas each unit of a component becomes cheaper in Home as the number of components climbs, the price in Foreign declines by even more. Since the term $kr^F(1+\eta_F)f(\cdot)$ is negative then, (4.39) says that marginal fixed costs due to dividing the production process into production blocs are larger than marginal benefits, that is $\partial F/\partial s > |wf(\cdot)\partial l/\partial s|$. This implies that the number of components, s, is larger for any k than in case marginal costs correspond to marginal benefits, that is $\partial F/\partial s = |wf(\cdot)\partial l/\partial s|$, as in equation (4.30), that is $\bar{s}' > \bar{s}' > \tilde{s}$. Therefore, fragmentation is also more extensive in case of the optimal k derived from (4.37), that is $\bar{s}' > \hat{s}$. Differentiating (4.34) with respect to k and setting the expression obtained equal to zero

$$\frac{\partial C}{\partial k} = s(r^H - r^F)f(\cdot) + \frac{\partial \tilde{F}}{\partial k} = 0 \qquad (4.40)$$

yields the extent of outsourcing as a function of the fragmentation of production. Inserting the extent of fragmentation as derived from (4.39) into (4.40) yields the optimal $\bar{k}'$, provided that fragmentation allows to reap gains from improving the allocation of tasks. Since fragmentation in this case is known to be more extensive than otherwise, marginal fixed costs from outsourcing, $\partial \tilde{F}/\partial k$, must be larger as well, as must be k, that is

$$\bar{s}' > \tilde{s}' > \tilde{s}, \quad \bar{k}' > \tilde{k}' > \tilde{k} \quad \text{and} \quad C'|_{k=\bar{k}', s=\bar{s}', f'(\cdot)} < C|_{k=\bar{k}', s=\bar{s}', f'(\cdot)}. \qquad (4.41)$$

In words: production becomes even more global than in the previous subsection; the opportunity to exploit Ricardian differences induces an *additional* slicing of the product into components.[69] Consequently, Ricardian differences in production functions tend to become more rather than less important as markets are opened. The result can be put more strongly: focusing more closely on what openness does to competition, it turns out that economies of scale and the exploitation of (regional) differences in production functions are positively related (rather than one being offset by the other, as for instance Baumol (1993); Baumol and Gomory (1996) claim). Or to put it the other way round: producers can exploit Ricardian differences exactly because of changing production

---

[69] The relationship between s and k is an issue arising apart from the integer problem.

methods in a way in which production is to a greater extent subject to economies of scale.

Nota bene: a growing share of production being outsourced[70] stands somewhat in contrast to the political discussion on regional economic integration which claims that the center in general attracts business at the expense of the periphery if trade is liberalised further.[71] Rather than fostering the concentration of production processes in one place, theory and data on gross product and value added, or exports and value added for that matter, back the notion that in the aftermath of integration production processes tend to be broken up into more (rather than less) geographically separated steps. A decline in outsourcing on the other hand would be indicative of the center definitely attracting industry, at least if it takes place on an international scale, referring to a country rather than a firm. However, notwithstanding that there might be forces constituting a home market effect, the observation of an increase in outsourcing suggests that there is also a substantial foreign market effect at work.

V.   Policy implications

The previous analysis has shown how integration gives rise to a foreign market effect.[72] This means that the periphery is not necessarily at a disadvantage in the process of integration, as proponents of the home market effect claim. In a larger market producers need not offer a whole range of different activities, some of which they do reasonably well, others not. Rather, they can concentrate on what they manage to do best. The narrowing of tasks makes it easier for them to gain a footing in the market.

A.   The role of supply-side policy

The interaction of economies of scale and Ricardian differences improves the chances for laggards to catch up. Since economies of scale on the supply side play an important role, they cannot be fully exploited when markets are small. Integration thus yields a dividend which can be shared among the trading parties. So far integration has had a favourable impact on absolute incomes. In contrast to models emphasising the home market effect which might suggest that catching up requires government intervention (Murphy,

---

[70] See also the 1987 World Development Report by the World Bank which devoted a whole section to the issue of outsourcing.

[71] See, for instance, the Delors Report (CEC (1989: 22)), or Baldwin (1994: part I), for a summary of the discussion.

[72] This is not to say that there is no such thing as a home market effect. Rather, our analysis expands the perspective by a foreign market effect which can also be expected to be at work as markets become more open.

Shleifer and Vishny (1989a,b); Kaldor (1970)), the previous analysis revealed how the market itself provides a development push. Notably, the development push does not depend on the usual crowding-out phenomena in advanced economies (nevertheless, these forces may also be at work).

Two caveats are in order, though: the first concerns the income distribution. As is known since Ricardo, there is no presumption that it is in general the periphery (the center) which manages to get a larger slice from the increase in real income due to the rise in overall productivity. Relative incomes may be affected in one way or the other. The balance depends on how relative productivity changes as undertakings narrow down to specific tasks. However, as a matter of fact, cross-national disparities declined in the course of European economic integration (in particular under the shock of integration, that is, shortly after removing barriers to trade and mobility). Hence, the periphery taken as a whole (and foremost the Iberian countries) did not only experience a rise in absolute per capita incomes in the process of integration. They even succeeded in improving their relative position on the European income scale. This supports the notion of market-based convergence.

Second, catching-up is not an automatic process. It is shaped by economic policy. In particular, the analysis brought the role of supply-side policies back into perspective which is of secondary importance in geography models with a home market effect because of their essentially Keynesian character. The foreign market effect crucially depends on the costs that go along with the fragmentation of production. By recognising explicitly that there are costs of assembling and coordinating the different parts of production, F and $\breve{F}$, the analysis in Section IV B-D of this chapter draws attention to these issues. In Section IV B-D both of these costs have been considered as being primarily technology-specific. However, as far as their actual amount is concerned, economic policy matters as well. This applies to both kinds of costs. As far as F, the cost of assembling different parts, is concerned, it is for instance labour market regulations which have an impact on whether integration allows for improving one's income position: if they limit production runs via imposing restrictions on the time or days worked, the capital stock is partly idle. As a result, firms suffer from excess capacity; fixed costs are higher than they otherwise would be. Regulations like these thus impede a further fragmentation of production as markets become more European, or more global for that matter. Local firms are kept from participating in the benefits a broader market offers.

Economic policy also influences the costs of coordinating production blocs internationally, that is the shape and the location of the $\partial \breve{F}/\partial k$ curve. Naturally, the curve also includes costs of distance in the narrow sense of the term as far as the latter are of a fixed cost character. Translocation costs with reference to intermediate products might well be of a fixed cost character in so far as long-term contracts in transportation are involved. Yet, for coordinating production on an international scale it requires more than transportation of intermediate products for further treatment or of final products to their markets: laws, institutions and regulations all matter to a considerable extent with regard to fixed costs. In fact, there are quite a number of regulations which raise fixed costs. Some of them are imposed by local governments, others by foreign governments, and some are due to the actual behaviour of the bureaucracy. However, they share the feature of making the international coordination of production blocs more expensive. Regulations coming under this heading are for instance those limiting competition in the airline industry, in telecommunications, and in services in general. Though many reforms have been implemented since the early 1980s in Europe – in particular privatisation was fostered[73] and communications markets were opened – a great deal remains to be done.[74] Services markets in Europe are still much more regulated than for instance those of the US, where most of the employment boom took place in the service sector (approximately 90 per cent of employment growth). This development was by no means confined to retail or personal services (gardening, health care etc.). Business-related services saw a similar expansion (Freeman (1997)). Notably, merely opening up markets is sometimes not enough for unleashing market forces, if incumbents are still free to decide about the terms on which they provide access to networks, or if they are allowed to vertically integrate into otherwise competitive markets.

Economic policy also has an impact on the administrative costs of getting a business started and keeping it going which is frequently associated with high costs. Economic policy can thus shift the $\partial \bar{F}/\partial k$ curve in Figure 4.3 up or down, making the coordination of the various activities more costly or cheaper. That being so, the model underlines the importance of economic policy in establishing a framework which allows entrepreneurs to actually make use of local or producer-specific advantages, that is $(r^H - r^F)$.

---

[73] Though less out of macroeconomic than out of fiscal reasons.

[74] Høj, Kato and Pilat (1995), for instance, provide a survey, and with reference to services in Germany see also the most recent structural report by Klodt, Maurer and Schimmelpfennig (1997). For a more theoretical investigation into the role of services in international trade see Melvin (1989) and Jones and Kierzkowski (1990).

B.   Integration and market-based convergence

Recall also that lowering coordination costs unravels a leverage effect on the division of labour and the gains therefrom: they not only imply lower costs for these services. Rather, they trigger a vertical division of labour which is associated with a pay-off that was not available before. Thus, the European Commission (1996) is wrong if it claims that the liberalisation of markets in services primarily comes to the benefit of countries ahead in per capita incomes.[75] Even the argument put forward by the European Commission that the more prosperous European countries are currently the ones which are specialised in this area and that the so-called cohesion countries all run trade deficits in services (excluding tourism) is besides the point. Apart from the fact that a sectoral perspective neglects basic macroeconomic interdependencies in the balance of payments (Dluhosch, Freytag and Krüger (1996: Ch. 3)), the argument fails to acknowledge the leverage effect of services. In light of the vertical division of labour the Commission's reasoning simply falls short of what is at hand. For the leverage effect to materialise it does not matter at all whether laggards run a trade deficit in services or not.

Hence, the model sketched out in this study emphasises local institutions in explaining differences in effective market size. If local institutions are either not appropriate for exploiting the benefits of a finer vertical division of labour or if they are not responsive to a shift in the needs of producers, they make for local differences in effective market size. In this case there is no switch in the mode of production, despite the fact that markets expand as barriers to trade are removed. Since the costs are higher than otherwise, the perceived market size is smaller than otherwise. In this case the size of the market is actually limited from the supply side rather than from the demand side.

The supply-side perspective of the previous chapter shifts away the attention from pure transportation costs as a demand-side reason for markets being segmented. The latter has been the focus of many of the models resulting in a home market effect. Taken seriously, these models suggest that catching up is difficult without a transfer scheme (either earmarked, as the one currently in place, or not) between European countries or regions.

---

[75] In the first report on economic and social cohesion in the European Union the Commission notes: 'Since the more prosperous regions seem likely to benefit most ... (all cohesion countries have trade deficits in services), the initial impact may be to widen disparities between rich and poor regions' (European Commission (1996: 74)). A few pages later, the Commission formulates slightly different: 'In general, such policies seem not to be to the *absolute* disadvantage of less favoured regions or social groups, but they tend to benefit them less *relative* to central regions of more favoured groups' (European Commission (1996: 87)).

In this framework such a scheme might even be necessary to get the periphery to agree on a further opening of markets. Otherwise, integration and the gains from integration would not come about. In fact, it is exactly this argument which is frequently called upon in defending net transfer positions in the EU. It is particularly stressed with regard to the approximately 60 per cent share of net contributions to the EU budget made by Germany. That high a contribution would be warranted since Germany is also considered to benefit the most from the single European market.[76]

Not so in the case made in this study. In the latter, the periphery does not need to be compensated to tip the cost-benefit calculus towards integration. Integration provides the opportunity to earn higher (average) per capita incomes. Whether they are realised or not depends first and foremost on whether and to what extent national economic policy allows the restructuring of the economy. In fact, the point made in this study is in line with recent empirical findings that national peculiarities carry significant weight in explaining post-integration macroperformance. Empirical studies on US-Canadian trade, for instance, came to the conclusion that national institutions matter much more than transportation costs in the division of labour. McCallum (1995), for instance, shows with the help of gravity equations that trade within Canada takes place at a 20-fold higher rate than trade across the US-Canadian border compared to what would be expected by employing the pure distance criterion. Similarly, Engel and Rogers (1996: 1120) find in explaining the volatility of prices of similar goods produced in different locations that crossing the US-Canadian border amounts to the equivalent of 1,780 miles of distance. Engel and Rogers tested three possible explanations for the different behaviour of US and Canadian markets: trade barriers, sticky prices, and the extent of the integration of labour markets. However, they recognised that most of the dispersion in prices was still left unexplained. Even the removal of trade barriers had, according to their estimates, only a minor impact on the regional dispersion of prices. Rather, they concluded that the 'width' of the border (if transformed in geographic distance) proved to be persistent even though the US-Canadian free trade agreement went into effect. Though difficult to quantify, institutions might be one explanation for the persistence of regional differences in prices.[77]

---

[76] The pay-off from integration is somewhat crudely measured by trade volume or export volume rather than changes in consumer rent, for instance. So, it is far from clear whether this holds true. Rather, standard trade theory suggests that smaller countries gain more than larger countries from integration as their free trade relative prices deviate more from their autarky prices.

[77] In terms of pure transportation costs it is in general hard to explain why some countries manage to participate on a high scale in the international division of labour whereas others,

Because of the role of economic policy and local institutions in catching up, it is also not surprising that results differ for individual countries in the EU. Recall from Chapter 2 that whereas Spain and Portugal managed to catch up after entering the EU, Greece suffered a relative decline with Greek per capita incomes dropping from 52 (1981) to 49 per cent (1996) of the EU-12 average. In addition, relative macroperformance of the laggards was subject to considerable variance through time. Spain is a case in point. Right after entering the EU, Spain was quite successful in catching up to the EU average while in the early 1990s the growth rate of the Spanish economy slowed down. In the first period of EU membership (that is 1986-89) Spain experienced by all standards an investment boom.[78] As a result, Spanish per capita income vis-à-vis the EU-12 average increased from 70 per cent in 1986 to 78 per cent in 1992. However, in 1992, the process of catch up came to a halt as the Spanish economy suffered from a more severe recession than the rest of the EU. Spanish per capita income fell to 77 per cent of the EU average. However, with labour market reforms under way, monetary stability continuing and public deficits being curbed, Spanish growth picked up again recently.

Notably, the Spanish catch-up process reveals a close link between economic reforms, and (relative) macroperformance in the EU. Spain's entry in the EU not only implied a lower effective rate of protection for the Spanish economy but was accompanied by a whole bundle of economic reforms. Overcapacities and employment in state-owned firms were reduced, legal restraints on fixed-term labour contracts and on part-time employment were lifted, and international capital flows were substantially deregulated. The failure to consolidate government finances, however, proved to be an obstacle in sustaining the impressive Spanish macroperformance of early membership. Expenditures and employment of the central government were not curbed despite political decentralisation. Moreover, Spanish labour markets continued to be characterised by rigidities. Decomposing the increase in Spanish per capita income vis-à-vis

---

being equally remote, do not. There is obviously a role for institutions. These results find additional support in studies by the IMF (1997a) which also trace differences in economic performance mainly back to differences in institutions rather than to differences in starting positions.

[78] Whereas real investment rates increased by some 5 per cent p.a. EU-wide, Spanish investment increased by approximately 10 per cent in the period 1986-89. Expectations about favourable investment opportunities led to a surge in capital imports with the Spanish current account swinging from a surplus of 4735.6 bn pts in 1985 (1.7 per cent of GDP) into a deficit of 21793.6 bn pts in 1992 (3.7 per cent of GDP). In particular, foreign direct investment climbed from an annual average of 0.7 per cent of GDP in the period 1981-85 (i.e. 9 per cent of total investment) to 1.7 per cent of GDP in the period of 1986-89 (i.e. 17 per cent of total investment). All data taken from OECD (1997b) and IMF (1996).

the EU average into the change in relative labour productivity and the change in the relative employment-population ratio shows that Spanish income growth was not driven by an increase in labour productivity (see Peñalosa (1994) for details). Instead, labour productivity was already close to the EU average in 1986. The failure to deregulate labour markets proved to be particularly detrimental in the cyclical downswing of 1993/94. Standardised unemployment rates climbed considerably and real GDP shrank. However, as labour market reforms in the mid-1990s allow for more flexibility in contracts and new laws regarding protection against dismissal reduce compensation payments, Spanish macroperformance improves again. Seeing the correlation of Spanish macroperformance and economic policy reforms shows that EU membership does not provide a windfall gain. What integration provides is the *opportunity* of earning higher incomes. Reaping the benefits from participating in the EU division of labour as competition becomes more intense *requires* economic policy reforms. In fact, locational competition in the EU is a dynamic process requiring continuous efforts by all participants.[79] In addition, finding out which services prove to be the most productive for the local economy requires a search process which flourishes best in a competitive rather than a centralised climate.

C. The EU-approach to convergence

Note the difference as compared to the European approach to catching up: the pro-competitive impact of integration suggests that it is primarily the responsibility of national economic policy to implement supply-side measures supporting individual producers in competing themselves into the market. Whether they succeed is thus not a matter of transfers. Art. 130a of the Treaty on European Union, however, considers it a European task to even out differences in economic development between regions and in particular vis-à-vis the most disadvantaged. EU-wide transfers are regarded

---

[79] The role of coordination costs in the division of labour does not imply that an EU-wide ex-ante harmonisation of national policies proves to be beneficial or even necessary for capturing the benefits of a finer vertical division of labour. From a welfare economic point of view policy makers themselves should have an incentive to ensure the compatibility and adaptability of local institutions without an explicit (institutionalised) international coordination. On the one hand, producers (and consumers) want to reap the benefits from a finer division of labour, so there is demand for appropriate institutions. On the other hand, their supply should become cheaper as well. Because of the increase in market size and new markets for middle products and mediating services emerging, institutions become sustainable which have not paid beforehand (actually, this is a Demsetzian (1967/1988) approach to the emergence of institutions). Vested interests may try to influence policy to their advantage, though. But since all governments face this problem, harmonisation of policies provides no solution to the problem either. Quite the contrary is the case as harmonisation may lend even more power to their interests (on this issue see Vaubel (1995)).

as an appropriate measure in achieving this goal. Though regional problems are deemed a national matter, the European Commission (1996: 54) claims that they cannot be left to national policies. This is because, so the argument runs, national policies would put those regions at an advantage which are located in more prosperous EU member countries.[80] Therefore, regional problems are considered a European issue.

For equilibrating regional development, the EU implemented its own EU-wide transfer scheme providing earmarked aid for special programs which are considered to foster local economic development.[81] Funds were expanded substantially in the 1980s and 1990s which is astonishing as the European periphery succeeded in catching up. Currently, there are four funds in place which are explicitly geared towards structural problems (apart from the cohesion fund and EIB loans), the Regional Development Fund, the Social Fund, the EAGGF-Guidance and the Financial Instrument for Fisheries Guidance with their total volumes having climbed considerably, namely from 10.8 bn ECU in 1988 to a projected 27.4 bn ECU in 1999 (1992 prices).[82] Concerning eligibility for funds, the EU differentiates between so-called objective-1, 2, 3, 4, 5a, 5b and 6 regions. Most of the structural funds, that is approximately 70 per cent, are devoted to objective-1 regions which are classified as lagging in economic development. Following the Agenda 2000 adopted by the European Commission in 1997 (see European Commission (1997)), the European Council reached in March 1999 an agreement on the 'reform' of the Union's policies, in particular the common agricultural policy and structural policies. The reform aims at concentrating funds on regions which are lagging the most either in terms of per capita incomes or because of suffering from structural change. At the same time, the number of objectives is reduced from 6 to 3. From the year 2000 onwards EU policy distinguishes between

---

[80] As the European Commission points out (disapprovingly), two regions with exactly the same income may be net beneficiary or net contributor – depending on the country in which they are situated (European Commission (1996: 55)). However, if the Commission takes its own argument seriously, it applies equally well to citizens of different countries.

[81] In addition, the EU has fixed thresholds for maximum member state aid varying between 75 per cent and 10 per cent of eligible expenditures depending on their relative standing within the EU income scale.

[82] European Commission (1996: Table 23 (p. 143)). In deflating the 1988 numbers we used the GDP deflator for the European Union as published by the OECD (1997b: Annex Table 14). Begg, Gudgin and Morris (1995), Cuny (1997), Diekmann and Breier (1993), Dignan (1995), Waniek (1994) and the European Commission (1996: Ch. 5) provide surveys on EU structural policies, each from a different perspective.

- Objective 1 shall promote the development and structural adjustment of regions whose development is lagging behind. Objective 1 status for the period 2000-2006 will be conferred on:

  - current NUTS level II regions whose *per capita* GDP is less than 75% of the Community average;
  - the most remote regions..., which are all below the 75% threshold;
  - areas eligible under Objective 6 for the period 1995-1999 pursuant to Protocol No. 6 to the Act of Accession of Finland and Sweden.

- Objective 2 shall support the economic and social conversion of areas facing structural difficulties....

- Objective 3 will lend support to the adaptation and modernisation of policies and systems of education, training and employment... (European Council (1999: notes 32-9)

Though consolidating the six objectives because of formerly overlapping eligibility criteria, the basic concept is not supposed to change. In total, the European Council at its meeting in Berlin considered 195 bn Euros as 'the appropriate level of commitment' for the period 2000-2006 with annual expenditures ranging from 29.4 bn Euros to 26.7 bn Euros in 1999 prices. As before, the majority of funds (that is 69.7 per cent) is allocated to objective-1 regions (European Council (1999: notes 29 and 30)). Consequently, the conclusions of the presidency point out, that 'this overall level of expenditure will enable the Union to maintain the present average aid intensity levels' (European Council (1999: note 28)).

The cohesion fund, though officially being implemented to ease adjustment problems following the fiscal consolidation in preparation for European Monetary Union and conditioned thereupon add another 2-3 bn ECU annually to these funds (1.5 bn ECU in 1993, 2.6 bn ECU in 1999, both in 1992 prices; European Commission (1996: 143)). As the beneficiaries already pointed out (*Handelsblatt* June 2, 1997 and June 10, 1997), they consider these transfers by no means as transitory. This view has been emphasised at the Berlin summit by the decision of the European Council to continue funding under the roof of the cohesion fund. For the period 2000-2006 a total of 18 bn Euros is earmarked for the cohesion fund with expenditures of approximately 2.6 bn Euros annually in 1999 prices (European Council (1999: note 52)).

A fair amount of scepticism is in order as regards the motives of EU regional policies. First, European policies are lacking consistency with respect to their regional incidence. Some of the policies and programs in effect undo what others have accomplished,[83] however, at quite high a

---

[83] The theory of bureaucracy might provide an explanation to this.

price.[84] The guarantee section of the CAP (EAGGF), for instance, which absorbs almost 50 per cent of the EU budget comes to the benefit of northern countries such as Denmark and France, whereas Portugal is according to the European Commission's own estimates a net contributor to the CAP. In fact, in terms of the standard farm unit, it is Denmark which receives the highest support, though being ranked second in terms of per capita incomes in the EU-12 (1996 numbers in 1985 international prices).

Second, looking for an argument for market failure, EU policy basically seems to share in the horizontal perspective of the new economic geography which stresses the home market effect of integration. Interpreted from this perspective, EU policy wants to achieve a level playing field for producers no matter where they are located, either by enlarging local markets or by actively promoting individual competitiveness. However, acknowledging that the division of labour also has a *vertical* dimension, evolving endogenously, suggests (a) that the notion of a level playing field is a dubious goal for economic policy and (b) that catching up is not a matter of transfers.

Hence, the notion that without proper political steering by the EU, that is an EU-wide transfer scheme, laggards are not able to participate in the gains from integration turned out to be false. That being so, EU transfers cannot be interpreted as a side-payment which is necessary for ensuring the cohesion of the Community by tipping the periphery's cost-benefit calculus towards a further opening of markets. Notably, income distribution – as opposed to absolute gains – is another matter. This raises the question whether an EU-wide transfer scheme can be considered to foster the cohesion of the Community out of distributional reasons.

---

[84] Their effectiveness or non-effectiveness is still another matter. For a detailed assessment of the common regional policies which is not at the heart of this study see, for instance, Klodt, Stehn et al. (1992) and Franzmeyer, Seidel and Weise (1993).

5.   EU Cohesion: a Matter of Income Distribution?[*]

In a recent article appearing in *Slate*, a Microsoft-sponsored online magazine, Krugman (1996b) argued that it is not absolute income levels people are concerned about, but their performance in terms of income received vis-à-vis others. He cites the example of the United States. Judged by all ordinary measures of standards of living (absolute income levels, TVs, telephones, cars, showers, etc.), the twenty-fifth percentile in the United States today would be much better off than the fiftieth percentile were in 1950. People would not necessarily consider themselves to be better off today, though. If they were able to choose, they might, according to Krugman, 'almost surely' prefer the situation of 1950 to the one prevailing today; they simply would feel more comfortable being middle class rather than belonging to the lowest quartile, despite the difference in material terms.

But is it really an economic issue whether individuals are actually personally concerned about how they do relative to others? They might, or they might not. From an economic perspective, there is hardly anything to say about this. Whether for instance people are primarily concerned about keeping up with the Joneses rather than simply improving their absolute income level is purely a matter of personal judgment and individual decision. Individually, somebody can decide to deviate from the notion that it is absolute income that matters. This in itself does not pose any particular economic problem.

The choice of distributional norms for the society at large is quite a different matter, however. The reason is that in this case, it is not merely an individual decision as regards to keeping up with the Joneses or not which can be tailored to individual tastes. Rather, as the norm is supposed to apply to all members of the society, individuals of a community have to 'choose' the same norm. They have to agree on a norm, either implicitly or explicitly. The institutional choices based thereupon are supposed to reflect individual attitudes towards distributional matters. Thus, we are confronted with a public choice problem. It is here, where the economic perspective enters the picture.

Take EU regional policy. Though not geared towards the personal income distribution, EU policy is driven by considerations of achieving

[*]   This chapter was initially published in *Constitutional Political Economy*, Vol. 8 (1997), pp. 337-52. Permission to reprint the paper is gratefully acknowledged.

more equality in per capita incomes across its member states. In fact, EU policy is committed to a particular distributional norm. Recall that under the Single European Act, adopted in July 1987, regions of the European Union earning a per capita income of less than 75 per cent vis-à-vis the EU average (so-called objective-1 regions) are eligible for EU transfers. The 75 per cent rule is applied to regions on the so-called NUTS II level. Yet, despite having a regional focus, EU policy is in effect channeling transfers between poorer and richer EU countries. Funds are raised in proportion to national GDPs, and net beneficiaries are those on the bottom of the national income scale within the EU.[1]

Despite the fact that they are not considered an outright incomes policy, these transfers are geared towards actively curbing the income dispersion across EU member states. They are earmarked either for increasing public expenditures or for promoting private investment locally, both of which are considered to have a leverage effect on incomes on the spot. By reducing the EU-wide income dispersion, they are considered to further the cohesion of the Union. Thus, even if there are absolute gains from integration, the income distribution is, in any case, deemed to be a policy issue. More precisely, even if the lowest percentile on the regional income scale is made better off by market-led integration, the goal is not considered to be achieved if not accompanied by a reduction in the dispersion – or even worse – if the higher income is associated by an increase in dispersion. Hence, it is not only the change in absolute income levels which is at the heart of the policy concerns but the evolution of the distribution, i.e. the change of particular income positions vis-à-vis others.[2] Moreover, it is not just plain convergence in real incomes towards which EU policy is geared.

---

[1]   Recently, the EU has once more increased its financial support for countries lagging behind the EU average in per capita incomes by putting into effect a special cohesion fund. These transfers come to the benefit of the so-called 'cohesion-4', that is countries earning an average per capita income of less than 90 per cent of the EU average (Greece, Portugal, Spain, Ireland). Even though officially designed to cushion the hardship of fiscal consolidation in lagging economies on their way to EMU, they nonetheless are tied to the EU income distribution. In addition, it remains an open question whether these funds run out (as scheduled) with the implementation of EMU. Despite their conditionality, experience suggests not. Expanding interjurisdictional transfers is deemed necessary by many in preparation for Monetary Union. With all member-countries sharing a single currency, asymmetric shocks, so the argument runs, are not cushioned anymore by a change in the nominal exchange rate. Rather, with sticky prices they are said to increase unemployment. This being so, income gaps are said to widen as compared to a flexible exchange rate regime. Transfers are considered to counterbalance the impact on incomes.

[2]   To be more precise, EU policy is characterised by a 'constant (relative) inequality aversion' (Atkinson (1970: 251)) as it is not sensitive with regard to movements of the mean. The income distribution stays an issue regardless of whether average per capita income climbs or not.

The EU has formulated two specific goals: first, an improvement of the position of those who are the least well off; and second, the least well off should reach 75 per cent of the average per capita income in the EU.

While economic theory can say little about the goals themselves, it can say a lot about the feasibility. Does the focus on distributional matters generally foster the cohesion of the Community? Or does it provide the seeds of conflict? The answer to these questions depends crucially on whether the distributional norm employed by the EU can be considered as being in line with individual preferences. However, as will be shown shortly, whether or not the EU focus on distributional matters fosters the cohesion of the Community cannot be answered in the affirmative since it faces a substantial measurement problem.

A theoretic argument in favour of an EU-wide transfer scheme being guided by the notion of real convergence seems to be that some norms, in particular distributional norms, are not considered to be subjectable to competition. Rather, so the argument runs, distributional issues call for centralisation. The decentralisation of these policies would trigger a process of 'ruinous' competition driving down transfers, thereby making it de facto impossible to sustain distributional norms (Sinn (1996)).[3] However, even though distributional norms clearly fall into the realm of public choice, does this already provide a good argument for their centralisation, i.e. a good reason for assigning the EU a competence in distributional matters?

By focusing on the measurement problems involved, this section argues that there is actually no good argument for centralisation. The reason is that exactly because distributional norms fall into the realm of public choice, competition in distributional norms is indispensable. As we will point out, competition in distributional norms is necessary for reconciling public choice with individual choice; or, to put it differently, competition in distributional norms is necessary for coping with the measurement problem. EU-wide transfers, however, eliminate this kind of competition.

Though interest in and contributions to matters of income distribution have mushroomed recently (see Atkinson (1997) and Gottshalk and Smeeding (1997) for surveys), the measurement problem and the institutional questions raised as a result have been largely neglected. There has been quite a surge in contributions focusing on explanations of the dynamics of income distributions, either in a growth-theoretic (Barro and Sala-í-Martin (1992); Baumol, Nelson and Wolff (1994)) or in a trade-theoretic setting (Burtless (1995); Wood (1994); Krugman (1995b);

---

[3]   However, this argument is not undisputed. For a dissenting view see Donges et al. (1996), and referring to the example of US states with widely differing, though quite stable, institutions, Majone (1993: 160).

Krugman and Venables (1995)). In particular, studies concentrated on the impact of technology and/or openness on the performance of different regions, or on the earnings of various skill groups of the local labour force. Equally intense has been the debate on the relationship between income inequality and the rate of growth and the direction of influence between both factors (e.g. Alesina and Rodrik (1991); Frank and Cook (1995); Deininger and Squire (1997); Robson and Wooders (1997)). Besides these empirical and theoretical investigations into the sources shaping the income distribution across countries and regions, there has been some controversy about the measurement of convergence (Friedman (1992); Quah (1993; 1996)). However, the authors have mainly pointed out that the convergence towards a mean on the one hand and the convergence of individual positions on the other hand makes for a difference in results.[4] This section aims at putting a different measurement problem into focus; namely that there is no objective measurement in distributional matters.

In discussing the EU focus on a particular kind of real convergence, we will not analyse the consequences of transfer schemes for incentives and the tendency of aid to promote perpetual dependence (as in fact the Mezzogiorno problem has shown). Neither will we investigate the ruinous competition argument. Rather, we will deal with the issue of comparing distributions and choosing a distributional norm in particular.

This chapter is organised into four sections. In Section I, we argue that the choice of distributional norms, though normative in nature, is accessible to economic reasoning. In Section II, we show that any notion of real convergence implies normative considerations. Though on the face of it requiring two scales, one for comparing distributions and one for evaluating, the aggregation necessary for comparing distributions already faces severe measurement problems. In Section III, we employ some indices developed by Shannon (1948); Theil (1967); Atkinson (1970); and Sen (1973) on EU data to show more explicitly that there is no unique ranking of income distributions. Rather, different forms of aggregation involve conflicting views about whether the goal is achieved or not. This has to be kept in mind when evaluating the particular kind of measuring stick employed by the EU. Although generally speaking, the EU concept of convergence and other equally general norms may yield conflicting results. In face of the measurement problem, the goal to promote cohesion rather than conflict can only be reached if there is good reason to assume that individuals of all EU member states share ex ante the same view on

---

[4] When applying this insight to the issue of cross-national or cross-regional evolutions, the authors analyse the question whether an economy tends towards its own steady state or whether it succeeds in catching up vis-à-vis other economies.

distributional matters. Fourth, and finally, we will derive some conclusions which emanate from the fact of ambiguity in the ranking of distributions for the constitutional design of the EU. In particular, we will point out that the ambiguity is in support of competition in distributional rules rather than their centralisation by means of an EU-wide transfer scheme.

I.   Distributional norms: the economic perspective

EU cohesion policy appears to be motivated by notions of what constitutes an 'appropriate' distribution. Whether a distribution is considered as 'appropriate' or not is mainly a matter of (individual) preferences. Tastes, however, are usually considered by economists as a given. One case in point is Sen's (1973; 1992/1995: 136 et seq.) critique of Paretian welfare economics. His main objection is that it is blind with regard to the distribution of incomes. This is because Paretian welfare economics is concerned with singling out all those allocations where nobody can be made better off without making somebody else worse off. But, as Sen rightly stresses, Paretian welfare economics provides no criterion for choosing a particular point on the contract curve representing the set of Pareto-optimal allocations in the well-known Edgeworth box diagram. The only way to discriminate among these points is to draw on distributional considerations. Paretian reasoning is of no help here as it only focuses on the question of how to achieve *given ends* with as low a cost as possible. By doing so, it is concentrating on the *means*, not the *ends*. However, when it comes to the choice of distributional norms, *ends* matter as well. Yet, ends are evaluated on the basis of individual preferences. From this perspective, distributional norms seem to be outside of the realm of economic reasoning. But, the very fact that Paretian welfare economics is blind with regard to distributional issues does not yet imply that economic reasoning in general cannot provide any guidance in the choice of distributional norms.

That distributional and economic reasoning can be reconciled is straightforward in all those cases in which the distributional norm can be interpreted as being based on an individual calculus weighing the costs and benefits of the respective norm while the pay-off in particular situations is uncertain (Sugden (1986); Frank (1988); Vanberg (1994)). Some distributional norms might thus be derived from a cost-benefit calculus in so far as they can be put in terms of an insurance against individually suffered income fluctuations, provided that they are not correlated with those experienced by the society at large.

At first glance, the link to European economic integration might not be that far fetched. In providing a more competitive environment, integration might increase the risk of suffering from income fluctuations. The latter might induce a demand for an insurance which operates EU-wide. The removal of barriers to trade fosters the specialisation of trading partners. Being less diversified, regions (or countries for that matter) may be more prone to structural change. This would not affect the regional income distribution in case resources are mobile. However, there is no such thing as perfect mobility. Rather, specialisation usually involves incurring sunk costs so that part of the regional capital stock is destroyed in case of structural change. With costs being sunk, the income distribution is affected in case of asymmetric shocks.[5] As the division of labour is promoted by EU integration, regions as well as the member states themselves become more specialised. Thus, they might ex ante agree on a norm which cushions income fluctuations and which works on an insurance basis. If this holds true, such a norm may be considered ex ante to further the cohesion of the Community. Conflict might arise on an ex post basis, though, once the event giving rise to a claim has occurred. In this case, the cohesion versus conflict issue amounts to an ex ante/ex post incentive problem: Ex ante, not knowing the exact future position on the income scale, all might be in favour of a rule which is geared towards avoiding the worst; ex post, once the position is known, there might be an incentive not to comply with the rules, though. However, even the latter need not arise, as the discussion about the chain-store paradox (Selten (1978)) and the folk theorem (Axelrod (1984) is one application) has shown. Whether there is an incentive to comply with the rules or to defect crucially depends upon the time horizon (i.e. the rate of discount) and the expected frequency of fluctuations within the income distribution.[6]

However, EU policy can only be traced back to an insurance-reasoning along these lines if two conditions are satisfied. First, EU policy must operate on an insurance basis indeed. Second, integration must have triggered a trend of rising income fluctuations across member states.

---

[5] A fact that was already pointed out by Ohlin (1924: 84; transl. by Flam and Flanders (1991)), who noted that 'With perfect mobility the spatial distribution of productive factors would be completely arbitrary. Interlocal trade would exist because of indivisibilities of factors, that is, the advantages of large-scale production, but it would be uninteresting. Exchange of this nature, permitting large scale production and reducing the disadvantages of the indivisibilities, is highly important in and of itself ... But its spatial aspect would, under the circumstances described above, have no influence on the structure of prices ... [I]t is the imperfect mobility of factors of production that necessitates an extension of price theory to the spatial aspect of exchange.' The lack of mobility can have several reasons. Specialisation is only one of them. Another one is lack of flexibility of labour-market institutions or non-pecuniary differences.

[6] The whole reputation and signaling issue is closely connected with the chain-store paradox and the folk theorem.

Leaving the question open as to whether the latter is the case or not, a closer look at EU policy reveals that EU transfer schemes are not geared towards cushioning fluctuations. This is not the case for two reasons. First, if so, the variance of particular income positions would be the appropriate perspective rather than relative incomes in general. The focus would be on the mobility of particular incomes with respect to their own mean. In contrast, EU policy is focusing on overall real convergence, i.e. on the average of all per capita incomes taken together. Second, in the case of an insurance, the members think of themselves as being probably unfortunate and thus future beneficiaries of the insurance scheme.[7] Nevertheless, though some countries have managed to catch up while others have suffered from a setback, nobody would seriously expect the cross-national income scale in the EU being turned upside down within a few years or so. The veil of ignorance that an insurance scheme is driven by ex ante is pretty transparent in this case. In addition, there might be in general doubts as to what extent regional economic performance is an insurable risk or whether incentives are spoiled by the insurance scheme to such a magnitude that it cannot work properly.

Summarising, the focus on real convergence by EU policy cannot be considered an insurance. Rather, it must be regarded as being primarily motivated by normative considerations about the 'appropriate' distribution of incomes. Thus, we are in the realm of preferences indeed. But even in this case, economic and thus cost considerations are to be considered. For institutional arrangements differ with respect to the link between public choice and individual preferences. The looser the link, the higher the costs that go along with a particular institutional arrangement and the more it is prone to conflict. Note that in this case, the issue of conflict not only arises ex post as is (probably) the case with an insurance scheme. Notwithstanding the fact that the institutional arrangement might give rise to conflict ex post, members of a group have to decide ex ante on a norm. Hence, the issue of conflict versus cohesion already arises ex ante. The more the norm employed already deviates from individual preferences ex ante, the more it gives rise to conflict and thereby threatens rather than safeguards the cohesion of the EU.

Now individual preferences can differ as regards the 'appropriate' income distribution, both across individuals and through time. So can the notion of what constitutes an appropriate income distribution across sets of individuals, e.g. EU member countries. In any case, to agree on a particular

---

[7]   See Atkinson (1997: 317). Though dynamic, the Weizsäckerian (1984) notion of a general compensation is based on similar reasoning.

distributional norm ex ante, notions have to converge to a consistent preference order about income distributions. Ordering distributions requires two steps. The first step deals with the comparison of distributions. The second step comprises the evaluation of the difference between (at least) two distributions. Both, however, involve a serious measurement problem to which we will now turn before drawing policy conclusions with respect to the EU approach to cohesion.

II. Aggregation and normative measurement

Distributional norms can be considered to be derived from a mapping of income and its dispersion into the domain of welfare. On the face of it, the mapping requires two scales, one for describing and summarising the pattern of the income distribution and one for evaluating it. It is the latter which is supposed to carry normative content and it is the latter where subjective evaluations are supposed to enter. The first scale, in contrast, is supposed to measure and compare distributions with regard to their characteristics. The measurement, however, requires some sort of aggregation of individual situations. Problems of reaching an agreement on a distributional norm ex ante already start with this aggregation of incomes. In fact, the usual measuring sticks employed for ordering distributions differ with regard to the aggregation. That being so, the choice of the indicator which is supposed to measure the dispersion in per capita incomes is not free from normative considerations. Deciding upon the indicator is much more than a mere matter of technique and convenience. It is also a matter of content.

The measurement problem arises even if the point of departure of all measures of the change in income dispersion is considered the same. Usually, the indicators are based upon a comparison of two frequency distributions at different points in time, recognising the principle of Dalton. Dalton (1920) claimed that the redistribution of a unit of income in favour of a lower income percentile ought to reduce the degree of inequality the income distribution displays without, however, changing its order. While probably not controversial, this is clearly a normative condition. The Dalton condition is met by a whole family of measures which have two mathematical characteristics in common. They are continuously increasing and Schurr-concave.[8] The group of indicators comprises for instance the

---

[8] Their mathematical properties are examined in Lambert (1989) and Cowell (1995). For the recent theoretical discussion of measuring dispersion see, for instance, Howes (1996) and Tam and Zhang (1996).

standard deviation of logarithms and the indices developed by Shannon, Theil, and Gini, to name but a few.[9]

However, as can be seen from Table 5.1, the picture they draw of the income dynamics within the EU is by no means the same (see also Estebán (1994) for a more regional focus). All of the calculations refer to the Europe of 12.

Table 5.1: Measuring the income distribution across EU member states:
conflicting views of ordinary scales

| | Year | | | | | | | | | | |
	1983	1984	1985	1986	1987	1988	1989	1990	1991	1992	1993
SDL	0.441	0.435	**0.439**	**0.455**	**0.454**	0.423	0.388	0.380	0.350	0.348	**0.383**
GC	0.226	0.216	0.212	0.236	**0.236**	0.206	0.185	**0.189**	0.146	**0.164**	**0.203**
TI											
– IS	0.046	0.043	0.042	0.047	**0.046**	0.039	0.032	0.031	0.016	0.015	**0.020**
– PS	0.055	0.052	0.050	0.055	**0.054**	0.046	0.038	0.036	0.034	**0.036**	**0.047**

Key: SDL: Standard Deviation of Logarithms; GC: Gini coefficient; TI: Theil index; –IS: Theil index weighted by income shares; –PS: Theil index weighted by population shares. Calculations are based on average per capita incomes in ECU at current prices and exchange rates. A rise of the respective indicator signals an increase in dispersion.
Source: EUROSTAT REGIO Data Tape, Edition April 1997, own calculations.

Notably, the indicators differ with regard to their sensitivity. The standard deviation of logarithms, for instance, moves only slightly compared to the entropy as measured by the Theil index. However, the scales do not only differ with regard to linear transformations, as for instance, when measuring temperature either in degrees celsius or fahrenheit where one scale can actually be converted into the other. They differ also with regard to the ranking which is much less demanding, but more fundamental. Differences in the ranking of distributions are shown in Table 5.1 as bold entries in the rows going from one column to the next on the right. Time and again, the direction of change differs. This is, for instance, the case in 1984-85. The Gini coefficient and the entropy-based Theil index of cross-national disparities in the EU took a downturn, even though, according to the standard deviation of logarithms, dispersion was still on the rise. Similarly, the measuring sticks disagree on the convergence of income distributions in the EU in 1989-90 and 1991-92.

---

[9] The Rawlsian (1971) leximin principle does not satisfy the condition of concavity since it focuses at the lowest income percentile only (Lambert (1989)). However, being the extreme of the Atkinson coefficient, it in principle belongs to this class of measures of dispersion.

Implicitly, the summarising measures attach different weights to changes in incomes, depending upon the position on the income scale which is actually affected (see Atkinson (1970: 256); Lambert (1989), for technical details). Hence, the scales for measuring and comparing distributions differ as regards to whose well-being is at stake.[10] In summary, there is a substantial ambiguity with respect to the ranking of distributions. This applies both within and across time. First, measuring sticks differ with regard to the amount of dispersion they ascribe to a particular distribution. Second, there is frequently dissent about whether the dispersion increased or declined from one year to another. As there is no unique order of distributions, the costs associated with a particular distributional norm cannot be inferred from any objective measurement. It is already the aggregation of individual income positions for purposes of evaluating the income distribution which faces normative measurement. Hence, the scale for describing a distribution and the scale for evaluating a distribution can actually not be completely separated from each other.

III. The fundamental problem in ranking distributions

This leaves us with two related issues; namely (1) *whose* welfare is at stake in evaluating a particular distribution; and (2) *which* basket of goods should be used as reference. Both of these issues are related insofar as both are a matter of preferences and are thus subjective in nature.

Let us consider the first issue, i.e. whose welfare is at stake. EU policy, for instance, attaches more weight to those who are the least well off in terms of income levels. A development in which incomes further in the middle of the scale pull forward calls for more rather than less correction of the income distribution as those on the bottom of the distribution suffer from a relative set back, despite the fact that both cases are somehow characterised by convergence.

The fact that the ranking of distributions depends upon whose situation counts to what extent can be handled more explicitly by drawing upon an index developed by Atkinson (1970) and Sen (1973). The index can actually be traced back to the same concept of entropy employed in Table 5.1.[11]

---

[10] This difference occurs despite the fact that all of them suppose that well-being is a function of income levels and that the function is the same for everybody, independent of particular circumstances (an issue Sen (1992;1995) dwells on).

[11] This index for measuring relative economic performance of the periphery vis-à-vis the rest of the EU was already employed in Chapter 2. The index was first introduced for capturing the informational content of a message by Shannon (1948) and later refined by Theil (1967). In fact, the index was modified by Atkinson (1970: 257 et seq.); (see also Cowell (1995)) for the

Recall from Chapter 2 that the Atkinson index attaches different weights to countries in the measurement of dispersion with the weights depending upon the countries' place on the income scale. This is achieved by introducing a parameter $\in$ which is supposed to capture the attitude (of the person evaluating the income distribution) vis-à-vis the dispersion of the subject matter. If $\in$ is zero, the person is indifferent as regards to the distribution of incomes. The higher $\in$ is, the more the person is averse to inequality. Finally, if $\in$ reaches infinity only the evolution experienced by the lowest percentile counts. In fact, this is the approach Rawls (1971) takes in his notion of distributional justice.[12] In this respect, the Rawlsian notion has some resemblance to the EU approach to distributional matters which focuses on those who do not beat the 75 per cent line.[13]

The idea behind Atkinson's measure is to estimate the per capita income which, if equally distributed, provides the same (social) utility as the one actually observed. The shape of the (social) utility function in turn depends upon the aversion against inequality. The more even the actual income distribution, the lower is the Atkinson index for a given aversion. The lower the index, the higher the overall income needed for achieving the same level of social well-being as that actually experienced. As can be seen from Figure 5.1, the graph is s-shaped.

In case of a low degree of aversion, it is only the absolute numbers which matter. As the degree of aversion is increased, the curve flattens out. Hence, the index covers a whole family of positive as well as normative indicators and thereby provides, in effect, a set of distributional norms.

However, for different parameter values, the ranking changes quite frequently. The evaluation is repeatedly turned upside down as the parameter adopts different values. That being so, the time series covering the period from 1978 to 1993 displays no unique order. Swings in evaluation while going from one column to another are marked by bold entries in Table 5.2.

---

purpose of associating a particular distribution with the notion of social welfare. Atkinson (1970: 257) consequently refers to it as the 'social welfare function approach'. The 'accounting' approach to the choice of norms by the notion of 'social welfare' shall serve our purposes, i.e. illustrating the tension between individual preferences on distributions on the one hand and institutional choice in the EU on the other hand. However, we draw on it to show that particular distributions cannot be associated with some sort of 'social welfare' as the society as a whole provides no maximand. If there was a maximand, measurement and agreement in distributional matters would pose no problem.

[12] For a critical appraisal of the notion of 'distributive justice' in a market-led economy, see Hayek (1976/1982).

[13] In setting $\in = 100$ in Chapter 2, we focused the index quite closely on the country with the lowest per capita income in the EU-12.

Figure 5.1: Cross-national dispersion of per capita incomes in the EU-12 1978-93: a welfare-theoretic evaluation based on Atkinson indices

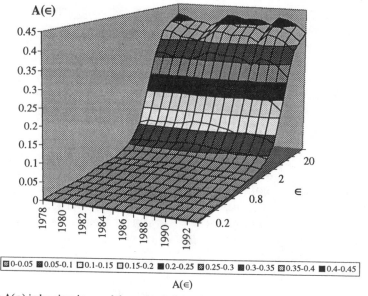

0-0.05 ▨0.05-0.1 □0.1-0.15 ▨0.15-0.2 ■0.2-0.25 ▨0.25-0.3 ■0.3-0.35 ▨0.35-0.4 ■0.4-0.45

A(∈)

The A(∈) index rises in ∈ and the regional dispersion observed. The parameter ∈ is ranked on an ordinal scale.
Source: See Table 5.2.

The ambiguity with respect to the ranking of distributions in the EU is due to the fact that any procedure of aggregation contains value judgements. These value judgements are embodied in the weights given to different income positions. Implicitly, a social welfare function is specified in aggregating individual circumstances. Parameter values listed in Table 5.2 are confined to an ∈ of 10 or less as the pattern becomes quite stable thereafter. However, as long as ∈ is below 10, the time series covering the period from 1978 to 1993 displays no unique order. For instance, in 1978/79, the index decreases when the aversion parameter is lower than 5, while it increases as the parameter reaches higher numbers. The ranking of distributions can already be reversed by a minor change in inequality aversion. The change that took place between 1989 and 1990 is evaluated differently even though the inequality aversion parameter is only increased slightly, namely from ∈ = 0.2 to ∈ = 0.4.

Table 5.2: Ranking of EU income distributions according to inequality aversion (ϵ)

ϵ	Year							
	1978	1979	1980	1981	1982	1983	1984	1985
0.2	0.0137	0.0117	0.0099	0.0088	0.0083	**0.0096**	0.0089	0.0088
0.4	0.0277	0.0237	0.0233	0.0179	0.0169	**0.0197**	0.0183	0.0180
0.8	0.0565	0.0488	0.0425	0.0377	0.0356	**0.0418**	0.0390	0.0383
2	0.1460	0.1325	0.1206	0.1086	0.1032	**0.1236**	0.1171	0.1148
5	0.3541	**0.3731**	0.3484	0.3173	0.3130	**0.3627**	**0.3662**	0.3540
10	0.5364	**0.5725**	0.5403	0.5031	**0.5058**	0.5457	**0.5598**	0.5442

ϵ	Year							
	1986	1987	1988	1989	1990	1991	1992	1993
0.2	**0.0096**	0.0095	0.0080	0.0066	**0.0068**	**0.0115**	**0.0136**	**0.0178**
0.4	**0.0198**	0.0196	0.0164	0.0135	0.0135	**0.0165**	**0.0187**	**0.0245**
0.8	**0.0417**	0.0413	0.0347	0.0287	0.0280	0.0275	**0.0297**	**0.0385**
2	**0.1211**	0.1199	0.1032	0.0859	0.0815	0.0692	0.0691	**0.0854**
5	0.3481	0.3471	0.3209	0.2840	0.2655	0.2266	0.2040	**0.2206**
10	0.5255	0.5228	0.5039	0.4720	0.4493	0.4086	0.3718	0.3717

The numbers are calculated as follows: $A(\epsilon) = 1 - \left[\sum_{i=1}^{12} x_i (y_i / x_i)^{1-\epsilon} \right]^{1/(1-\epsilon)}$. x_i and y_i refer to the population share and the income share of country i. Income shares are based on GDPs at current prices and exchange rates.
Source: EUROSTAT REGIO Data Tape Edition April 1997, own calculations.

Differences in evaluation indicate that the Lorenz curves of two subsequent years intersect rather than shift either totally inward or outward.[14] This means that different income segments managed to pull forward in the distribution. During the years 1978-79, for instance, percentiles in the middle of the income distribution got a bigger slice from the normalised cake. In the years 1985-86, it was the other way round. The lowest percentiles managed to get more. If the Lorenz curves of two distributions cross, we can always think of two distributional preferences ranking them differently (Atkinson (1970: 247); Lambert (1989: 54 et seq.); Davies and

---

[14] The so-called principle of Lorenz-curve dominance (that is the Lorenz curve shifting either inward or outward) is a partial order in effect minimising the specification of the social welfare function (Shorrocks (1983); Shorrocks and Foster (1987); Lambert (1989: 62 et seq.); Cowell (1995: 41 et seq.), Davies and Hoy (1995)). However, there are not that many policy measures or changes of the state of the world which pass the test of Lorenz-curve dominance. This reduces its usefulness for practical policy.

Hoy (1995)). Individuals attaching different weights to income positions will thus order the states of the world differently. One might prefer a distribution like the one prevailing in 1978-79; whereas the other might be in favour of a distribution such as in 1985-86. Consequently, distributions cannot be ranked unambiguously, not even on an ordinal scale. Rather, the ranking depends on individual preferences. As preferences are subjective, we face a measurement problem indeed.[15]

There is another point worth noting as regards to whose welfare is at stake. EU regional policy is directed towards balancing the spatial distribution of per capita incomes in the EU. However, transfers based on rankings of countries or regions according to average per capita incomes neglect the personal distribution of incomes in the EU and within countries and regions (see Majone (1993: 163) on this issue). This is in line with models of the new economic geography. As discussed in Chapter 3, the new economic geography claims that everybody located at the periphery is worse off compared to the center since everybody would suffer from higher costs of transportation. However, in so far as costs of transportation are not the primary factor in shaping the distribution of incomes or when individuals are differently affected, in sum: if the distribution within countries or regions is not uniform, the personal rather than the regional income distribution might matter for the social cohesion of the Community.[16] This is the case for two reasons: first, the beneficiaries of EU money are not necessarily those least well off. Second, it is not automatically the majority of people living in a lagging area which is favoured by EU transfers. Interpreting EU cohesion as an implicit or explicit agreement of individuals to EU integration based on a cost-benefit calculus, that is adopting a procedural approach to EU cohesion, EU regional policy thus might well fail to achieve the goal of cohesion.[17]

Pretty much the same measurement problem arises with respect to the second issue, namely with regard to the basket of goods chosen as reference-basket. Statistics can only take into account money income. In contrast, what matters from a welfare point of view is income in real rather

---

[15] Note that the notion of risk aversion as regards to those bringing up the rear falls a bit short of what is at hand. The point is that the whole shape of the distribution can be subject to evaluation, not merely its tails. In designing his 'measure of equally distributed equivalent income', Atkinson (1970: 244 et seq.; 249) was inspired by a parallel reasoning in decisionmaking under uncertainty though.

[16] Even the personal income distribution, however, may be irrelevant if people care more about the absolute gains from integration than about relative movements.

[17] This holds true even when leaving aside issues of reduced incentives to work and invest on the side of the contributors and induced perpetual dependence on the side of the recipients or of rent-seeking on both sides.

than nominal terms. It is purchasing power that matters. However, the evolution of purchasing power also depends upon individual preferences. Individuals are concerned about the basket of goods they can buy for the income they receive. This requires eliminating pure movements in the price level. This is not that much of a problem as long as there is one basket of goods which is not subject to change. If everybody bought the same (scaled up or down) basket of goods, regardless of the evolution of relative prices, and everybody had the same ability to enjoy the goods bought, (in short: if everybody was like everybody else), the difference between nominal and real numbers for the evolution of incomes would not be that much of an issue. In this case, the nominal value would simply be deflated with the respective price index. However, in addition to the price level, relative prices usually change over time as well. And moreover, everybody is not like everybody else. Rather, habits differ and people behave differently in reaction to changes of relative prices. This feeds into a problem of comparing income positions in real terms. For in this case, the evolution of incomes in real terms depends upon the basket of goods the individual prefers to buy which clearly differs across individuals and usually even more so across inhabitants of different countries.[18]

The issue at hand can already be illustrated by comparing the evolution of incomes in the EU at actual exchange rates (AER) and at purchasing power parities (PPP). The latter are said to reflect more closely the price movements of locally supplied goods. Following Balassa (1964), locally supplied goods, i.e. non-tradables, are cheaper in countries in which productivity and thus incomes are lower. A comparison in terms of actual nominal exchange rates which reflect the prices of tradables would thus underrate their position on the income scale. However, whether this holds true or not depends again upon individual preferences. PPP would be the appropriate measuring stick if individuals across EU member states were indeed concerned about the same basket of goods. Whether they do or do not makes for a substantial difference. Take for instance an evaluation of the evolution in dispersion based on the particular aversion parameter ϵ = 0.2. Table 5.3 summarises the respective calculations.

---

[18] Apart from this and the fact that national statistics differ conceptionally, comparisons are also spoiled by differences in the size of the informal sector or differences in the importance of capital gains across countries. Institutional differences matter as well, such as for instance participation rates, the organisation of the labour market and so on. Moreover, lifetime incomes should be the basis of comparison rather than income flows received in a particular span of time. The latter would at least eliminate, for instance, differences in the age structure across EU member countries.

Table 5.3: Ranking of EU income distributions with reference to different baskets of goods

Basket	1978	1979	1980	Year 1981	1982	1983	1984	1985
PPP	0.00309	**0.00336**	**0.00337**	**0.00349**	0.00340	**0.00343**	**0.00358**	0.00355
AER	0.01372	0.01171	0.00994	0.00875	0.00825	**0.00956**	0.00889	0.00875

Basket	1986	1987	1988	Year 1989	1990	1991	1992	1993
PPP	0.00343	0.00316	0.00301	0.00277	**0.00289**	0.00284	0.00283	0.00242
AER	**0.00964**	0.00953	0.00796	0.00658	**0.00678**	**0.01146**	**0.01359**	**0.01778**

Key: PPP: Purchasing Power Parities; AER: Actual Exchange Rates.
Source: EUROSTAT REGIO Data Tape Edition April 1997, own calculations.

Bold entries within a row (while moving from left to right) indicate that the dispersion of incomes has climbed from one year to the other. This was for instance the case between 1978 and 1979, if measured in PPP. The same holds true for the change between 1979 and 1980. The dispersion declined, however, between 1981 and 1982 and so on. Though being based on the same parameter, the evaluation of the evolution of the distribution of incomes differs fundamentally depending upon which basket of goods is being chosen.

The evolution depends crucially on whether the basket of goods is measured in PPP or actual exchange rates of national currencies vis-à-vis the ECU. Income disparities throughout the period 1978-93 are substantially smaller if measured in PPP. But, results differ not only with regard to the absolute amount of dispersion. As can be seen from Table 5.3, the measurement even disagrees in 8 out of 15 cases with respect to the ranking. Compared at actual exchange rates inequality declined from 1979 to 1980. It increased though if compared at PPP. The same holds true for the measurement in 1980/81, 1983/84. Similarly, but with the sign reversed, the same is found for the years 1985/86, 1990/91, 1991/92, and again in 1992/93.

Now consider the EU approach to cohesion. EU policy employs a particular form of aggregation of individual circumstances and associates a particular distribution with the 'appropriate income distribution'. Interjurisdictional transfers, being intended to achieve this particular distribution, are considered to foster the cohesion of the Community. However, as there is actually no unique ranking of income distributions, applying a particular norm which is supposed to hold for all in the EU embodies considerable value judgements. Clearly, in evaluating a particular distribution everybody somehow attaches weights to individual income positions.[19] Yet, the presumption that one particular set of weights is the prevailing one and that everybody shares this notion in the EU is quite a strong assumption.[20] If it cannot be taken for granted that all individuals share in the same evaluations of distributional matters, public choice does not boil down to the choice of a representative individual. Instead, because of the subjectivity of weights, a considerable measurement problem is involved in the choice of distributional norms.[21]

IV.   Conclusions and institutional consequences

The choice of distributional norms thus faces a dilemma. On the one hand, the question whether EU policy promotes cohesion or conflict (from an ex ante perspective) by employing a particular notion of an 'appropriate' income distribution depends crucially upon whether and to what extent it is in line with individual preferences. On the other hand, there is no unique measuring stick for comparing distributions. This is not a measurement problem which arises once. Rather, preferences can shift through time. In principle, the measurement problem cannot be solved. However, institutions differ as regards to how they cope with the measurement problem.

Assigning the EU a competence in distributional matters means facing the measurement problem with full force. Presenting constitutionally distributional issues as a national matter would instead allow for a diversity of designs and submit the choice of distributional norms to additional competition. The variety would permit individual preferences to be revealed not only by means of the voting booth but also by mobility.[22]

---

[19]   Hammond (1976) goes even one step further by proposing that they are based on interpersonal comparisons of utilities. In principle, Harsanyi (1955) raises a similar point.

[20]   Lachmann (1986: 24) has put the basic problem even stronger in noting: '(A) ... sinister development has to be seen ... in the tendency ... to assume "given" tastes of individuals, that is, an ordered comprehensive preference field for each individual, and to proceed to the solution of economic problems of all kinds, which have thus been surreptitiously turned into merely technical ones, on this slippery basis.'

[21]   This issue has been pointed out by Buchanan (1969/1978: 70 et seq.) when drawing on the example of Pigovian norms and the internalisation of externalities. If there is no market place for trading and no perfect competition, individual preferences can neither be objectively measured nor can they be amalgamated. Their aggregation to some kind of 'social distributional norm' would require interpersonal hedonic comparisons for which there is actually no theoretical basis (Arrow (1951/1963)).

[22]   The measurement problem with regard to the distribution of incomes and its evaluation surely arises in every instance. However, EU institutions are still in the process of being designed. Compared to institutions which are already established, it is thus much easier to introduce

Though most of the inhabitants of EU member states consider themselves 'Europeans', first and foremost, most of them consider themselves to be French, Italian, German and so on. Obviously, the EU member states themselves display a greater homogeneity than the EU as a whole when considering which policy is 'appropriate' indeed. In this case, group-specific institutional arrangements can reflect more closely preferences of individuals. In doing so, they lower dissent and therefore conflict. Thus, in effect, they safeguard the cohesion of the EU. In addition, group-specific institutions can exploit competition for coping with the problem of measurement.

---

elements of competition between EU member states by designing EU institutions accordingly. Though in cases involving those already established there might also be more room for competition than currently allowed for, their reform faces considerable opposition from those who are afraid of losing rents.

On the benefits of competition among EU regions and member-states as opposed to current EU regional policy see also Eekhoff (1995).

6.   Reprise: History is not Destiny

Though the overall trend seems to indicate that integration has a favourable impact on average per capita incomes, some countries and regions have never managed to make it. Differences in post-integration performance already crop up within the European Union (EU): by and large, Spain and Portugal managed to catch up, whereas Greece suffered a set-back.

Within economic theory there is no consensus about the prospects of different regions and countries participating in economic integration either. Reasoning along traditional trade theory (in particular Heckscher-Ohlin-Samuelson) suggests that specialisation tends not only to promote income growth in absolute terms but also works towards a more even development. This optimistic outlook at least applies with regard to countries with the same cone of diversification, i.e. with sufficiently similar factor endowments.

The new economic geography, however, paints a rather different picture. Many models of this strand suggest that nations, and regions in particular, might benefit in different ways from integration. Whole countries or regions might even be worse off because of integration. Instead of promoting a more even development EU-wide, any centre-periphery pattern observable pre-integration might even become more pronounced as integration proceeds. This result rests on two premises, namely (1) that the spatial distribution of industries is driven by economies of scale on the demand side and (2) that there has been a change in transportation costs. Since transportation costs play an important role in this framework, real GDP per capita depends on the distribution of industries. A decline in the costs of transportation, so the argument runs, reinforces any centre-periphery bias in the distribution of industries present beforehand, as in the distribution of incomes. Taken seriously, this would imply that laggards cannot expect a development push from market-led integration. If this were true, economic prospects of countries and regions would be pretty much a matter of the starting position. History would be destiny.

The basic argument is not new: the suspicion that relative backwardness is in itself a stumbling bloc for development was already raised by early development economics. However, in development economics policy recommendations based on this reasoning by and large failed to provide the development push they ought to have provided. Though at the very start these failures were considered to be a matter of wrong implementation of a basically right policy, development policy started to realise that an outward-oriented strategy provides more of a development push. The experience in developing countries already casts doubts on whether the new theory is in fact addressing the crucial issues in economic development.

As a matter of fact, a detailed analysis reveals that neither the distribution of industries is solely driven by economies of scale on the demand side, nor that there has been a substantial change in the costs of transportation recently. Transportation costs have hardly declined in the last twenty years. Rather, there has been a substantial decline in the costs of communication. In contrast to costs of transportation, costs of communication are more of a fixed cost kind with respect to the scale of output. Because of the fixed costs involved, a larger market at any rate sustains a mode of production which is more coordination and communication intensive. Diminishing costs of communication actually reinforce the trend towards a production which is more spread out internationally.

The notion that integration is primarily shaped by economies of scale on the demand side is not convincing either. Claiming that the pattern of industries is primarily a matter of economies of scale on the demand side is tantamount to saying that – contrary to all experience – integration is not accompanied by structural change. Adjustment in this framework occurs with regard to the location of industries. But apart from that, the theory suggests that production takes place on the same scale and in the same manner before and after integration. In fact, any role of cost competition is lacking in this approach. Though local consumers are not, producers are in effect sheltered from this sort of competition. Yet, this can only be part of the story. Experience tells us something different, namely that openness is crucial both for static and dynamic efficiency. Actually, this is what deregulation (which is a form of integration) is all about. Whether markets are open or whether there are barriers to entry does matter for market performance. This, however, means that integration does trigger structural change on the supply side. Consequently, no serious analysis of the impact of integration on the intra-European division of labour can neglect the supply side.

Bringing the supply side and coordination costs into perspective shows how producers in fact reorganise the mode of production as markets become more integrated. Cost competition and the larger market provide an incentive to employ a production mode which is characterised (a) by a greater fragmentation for the whole production process into different activities and (b) by a more regionally scattered distribution of the various activities. Since a larger market allows the exploitation of economies of scale (on the supply side) to a greater extent, it permits producers to split production into a larger number of production blocs, each manufacturing a different component. Finally, goods tend to be made from a larger number of components the more open the economy. However, the greater the number of components, the more specific are the tasks required in manufacturing a particular component. This makes it easier for producers who are located at the periphery but who enjoy a specific advantage to participate in the division of labour. Instead of being built from a small number of components which are produced locally, commodities are assembled from a greater number of components whose production is regionally scattered. In fact, by allowing the exploitation of economies of scale to a greater extent, a larger market allows the exploitation of Ricardian differences in production functions better as well. A foreign market effect thus crops up. Hence, it does not take Heckscher-Ohlin-Samuelson to be optimistic about the economic prospects of laggards. A supply-side perspective shows how a centrifugal force is arising endogenously in the course of integration. The supply-side perspective is actually supported by trade statistics showing that a considerable amount of trade takes place in intermediates. In fact, trade nowadays reached a scale that can hardly be explained without openness inducing some sort of fragmentation of production.

The concern that integration per se promotes a centre-periphery pattern in industries and incomes because of centripetal forces dominating also finds no support in EU-income data. In the long run, the cross-national dispersion of real per capita incomes (in constant international prices) shows no increase for the EU of 12. Rather, the income share weighted Theil index and the Gini coefficient both declined almost continuously from the early 1950s to the mid-1970s. In the 1990s they even reached their lowest level for these countries since the European Community was founded. The Atkinson index shows that by and large the periphery succeeded in catching up vis-à-vis the EU. In particular in the second half of the 1980s, the polarisation of incomes in the EU-12 was on the decline. The broad picture within Europe thus is more in line with the supply-side perspective than the divergence hypothesis which focuses on the demand side.

However, there is no automatism in catching up. Rather, integration provides the opportunity to reap the benefits of a finer (vertical) division of labour which can be shared among trading partners. Whether or not producers are able to make use of their specific advantages is a matter of economic policy. This can best be illustrated by the example of Spain, showing that Spain was not only able to realise gains from integration, but also to catch up vis-à-vis the more advanced European economies when integration was accompanied by policy reforms. Generally speaking, the fact that different countries in the EU fared differently well when joining the EU lends additional support to the notion that the supply side matters. Otherwise it is hard to explain why Spain and Portugal managed to catch up whereas Greece did not. If the notion that relative backwardness in itself is a stumbling block for development were true, one would expect that all peripheral countries have a hard time in improving their income position. Obviously, there is a role for economic policy, and for supply-side policy in particular. History is not destiny.

In the new economic geography the supply side plays virtually no role. Rather, due to its Keynesian character it seems to call for a policy of achieving a level playing field for all producers in the EU. This is supposed to provide for a development push in lagging economies. Notably, this is also the EU approach to convergence as EU policy is concerned about the distributional impact of integration. For equilibrating regional development, the EU has implemented a transfer scheme between richer and poorer regions of the Community. Since poorer regions happen to be regionally concentrated, EU policy is in fact channelling transfers between richer and poorer member countries. If not traced back to a purely distributional motive, this policy is obviously driven by the notion of achieving a level playing field for firms EU-wide.

Taking the fragmentation of production into account, this perspective fails to hold. Producers need not compete on all terms. Rather, integration allows them to concentrate on their specific advantages. Since the notion that laggards are not able to participate in the gains from integration turns out to be wrong, EU regional policy cannot be interpreted as a side payment which is necessary for the periphery sharing in the gains from integration.

Arguing in favour of an EU transfer scheme out of purely distributional considerations is not convincing either. The argument that distributional matters call for a common policy because of national policies otherwise triggering a process of ruinous competition fails to hold as well. Rather, competition is in particular indispensable in the realm of public choice. An EU-wide transfer scheme would reduce rather than promote competition in economic policy. This suggests that EU regional policy is the outcome of successful rent-seeking and logrolling within Europe rather than of an economically sound policy.

Bibliography

Abramovitz, Moses and Paul A. David (1995): 'Convergence and Deferred Catch-up: Productivity Leadership and the Waning of American Exceptionalism', mimeo: Stanford; forthcoming in: *Growth and Development: The Economics of the 21st Century*, ed. by Ralph Landau, Timothy Taylor and Gavin Wright, Stanford, CA: Stanford University Press.

Alesina, Alberto and Dani Rodrik (1991): 'Distributive Politics and Economic Growth', NBER Working Paper #3668.

Allen, P.M. (1982): 'Self-Organization in the Urban System', in: *Self-Organization and Dissipative Structures*, ed. by W.C. Schieve and P.M. Allen, Austin, 132-57.

Allen, P.M. and M. Sanglier (1979): 'A Dynamic Model of a Central Place System', *Geographical Analysis* 13: 149-64.

Amiti, Mary (1997): 'Specialization Patterns in Europe', CEP Discussion Paper #363.

Amiti, Mary (1998): 'New Trade Theories and Industrial Location in the EU: A Survey of Evidence', *Oxford Review of Economic Policy* 14 (2): 45-53.

Amsden, Alice H. (1985): 'The Division of Labor is Limited by the Rate of Growth of the Market: The Taiwan Machine Tool Industry in the 1970s', *Cambridge Journal of Economics* 9: 271-84.

Anderson, F.J. (1991): 'Trade, Firm Size, and Product Variety Under Monopolistic Competition', *Canadian Journal of Economics* 24: 12-20.

Armington, Paul S. (1969): 'A Theory of Demand for Products Distinguished by Place of Production', *IMF Staff Papers* 16: 159-76.

Armstrong, Harvey W. (1995): 'Convergence among Regions of the European Union 1950-90', *Papers in Regional Science* 74: 143-52.

Arndt, Sven W. (1996): 'Globalization and the Gains from Trade', in: *Trade, Growth, and Economic Policy in Open Economies*, Festschrift in Honor of Hans-Jürgen Vosgerau, ed. by K. Jaeger and K.-J. Koch, New York: Springer.

Arrow, Kenneth J. (1951/1963): *Social Choice and Individual Values*, 2nd ed., Yale: Cowles Foundation.

Arthur, Brian (1994): *Increasing Returns and Path Dependence in the Economy*, Ann Arbor: University of Michigan Press.

Atkinson, Anthony B. (1970): 'On the Measurement of Inequality', *Journal of Economic Theory* 2: 244-63.

Atkinson, Anthony B. (1996): 'Income Distribution in Europe and the United States', *Oxford Review of Economic Policy* 12: 15-28.

Atkinson, Anthony B. (1997): 'Bringing Income Distribution in From the Cold', *Economic Journal* 107: 297-321.

Axelrod, Robert (1984): *The Evolution of Cooperation*, New York: Basic Books.

Babbage, Charles (1832): *On the Economy of Machinery and Manufactures*, reprint 1963, New York: M. Kelly.

Balassa, Bela (1964): 'The Purchasing-Power Parity Doctrine: A Reappraisal', *Journal of Political Economy* LXXII: 584-96.

Baldwin, Richard E. (1994): *Towards an Integrated Europe*, London: CEPR.

Baldwin, Richard E. and Phillipe Martín (1999): 'Globalization: A New Phenomenon?', in: *Globalization and Labor*, ed. by Horst Siebert, Tübingen: Mohr, 3-58.

Baldwin, Richard E.; Francois, Joseph F. and Richard Portes (1997): 'The Costs and Benefits of Eastern Enlargement: The Impact on the EU and Central Europe', *Economic Policy* 24, April: 127-76.

Barber, Lionel (1995): 'Brussels Keeps Shut the Gates to the East', *Financial Times*, Nov. 16: 17.

Barber, Lionel and Anthony Robinson (1997): 'Uncertain Map of the Future', *Financial Times* March 12: 13.

Barro, Robert J. and Xavier Sala-í-Martin (1991): 'Convergence Across States and Regions', *Brookings Papers on Economic Activity* 1/1991: 107-82.

Barro, Robert and Xavier Sala-í-Martin, (1992): 'Convergence', *Journal of Political Economy* 100: 223-51.

Barro, Robert and Xavier Sala-í-Martin (1995): *Economic Growth*, New York: McGraw Hill.

Baumol, William J. (1977): 'Say's (at Least) Eight Laws, or What Say and James Mill May Really Have Meant', *Economica* 44: 145-62.

Baumol, William J. (1993): 'On Location of Industries Among Trading Countries: Scale Economies as Possible Offset to Comparative Advantage', in: *Does Economic Space Matter?*, ed. by. Hiroshi Ohta and Jacques-François Thisse, Houndmills and London: St. Martin's Press, 187-206.

Baumol, William J. and Ralph E. Gomory (1996): 'Inefficient and Locally Stable Equilibria Under Scale Economies: Comparative Advantage Revisited', *Kyklos* 49: 509-40.

Baumol, William J.; Blackman, Sue Anne Batey and Edward N. Wolff (1991): *Productivity and American Leadership: The Long View*, Cambridge: MIT Press.

Baumol, William J.; Nelson, Richard R. and Edward N. Wolff (1994): *Convergence of Productivity: Cross-National Studies and Historical Evidence*, Oxford: Oxford University Press.

Baumol, William J.; Panzar, John C. and Robert D. Willig (1982): *Contestable Markets and the Theory of Industry Structure*, New York: Harcourt Brace Jovanovich.

Becker, Gary S. and Kevin M. Murphy (1992): 'The Division of Labor, Coordination Costs, and Knowledge', *Quarterly Journal of Economics* CVII: 1137-60.

Begg, Iain and David Mayes (1993): 'Cohesion in the European Community: A Key Imperative for the 1990s?', *Regional Science and Urban Economics* 23: 427-48.

Begg, Iain; Gudgin, Graham and Derek Morris (1995): 'The Assessment: Regional Policy in the European Union', *Oxford Review of Economic Policy* 11, No. 2: 1-17.

Ben-David, Dan (1993): 'Equalizing Exchange: Trade Liberalization and Income Convergence', *Quarterly Journal of Economics* 108: 653-79.

Ben-David, Dan (1996): 'Trade and Convergence Among Countries', *Journal of International Economics* 40: 279-98.

Berman, Eli; Bound, John and Stephen Machin (1998): 'Implications of Skill-Biased Technological Change: International Evidence', *Quarterly Journal of Economics* 113, 1245-79.

Blanchard, Olivier Jean and Lawrence F. Katz (1992): 'Regional Evolutions', *Brookings Papers on Economic Activity* 1/92: 1-75.

Bletschacher, Georg and Henning Klodt (1992): *Strategische Handels- und Industriepolitik: Theoretische Grundlagen, Branchenanalysen und wettbewerbspolitische Implikationen*, Tübingen: Mohr.

Blien, Uwe (1994): 'Konvergenz oder dauerhafter Entwicklungsrückstand? Einige theoretische Überlegungen zur empirischen Regionalentwicklung in den neuen Bundesländern', in: *Informationen zur Raumentwicklung*, H. 4: 273-85.

Blundell, Richard; Preston, Ian and Ian Walker (1994): *The Measurement of Household Welfare*, New York: Cambridge University Press.

Brakman, Steven and Harry Garretsen (1993): 'The Relevance of Initial Conditions for German Unification', *Kyklos* 46: 163-81.

Brander, James A. and Barbara J. Spencer (1981): 'Tariffs and the Extraction of Foreign Monopoly Rents under Potential Entry', *Canadian Journal of Economics* 14: 371-89.

Brander, James A. and Barbara J. Spencer (1984): 'Tariff Protection and Imperfect Competition', in: *Monopolistic Competition and International Trade*, ed. by Henryk Kierzkowski, Oxford: Oxford University Press, 194-206.

Brander, James A. and Barbara J. Spencer (1985): 'Export Subsidies and International Market Share Rivalry', *Journal of International Economics* 18: 83-100.

Broadberry, Steven N. (1993): 'Manufacturing and the Convergence Hypothesis: What the Long-Run Data Show', *The Journal of Economic History* 53: 772-95.

Broadberry, Steven N. (1994): 'Technological Leadership and Productivity Leadership in Manufacturing Since the Industrial Revolution: Implications for the Convergence Debate', *Economic Journal* 104: 291-302.

Brülhart, Marius and Johan Torstensson (1996): 'Regional Integration, Scale Economies and Industry Location in the European Union', CEPR Discussion Paper #1435.

Bruton, Henry J. (1989): 'Import Substitution as a Development Strategy', in: *Handbook of Development Economics*, ed. by Hollis Chenery and T.N. Srinivasan, Vol. I, Ch. 30, Amsterdam: North Holland, 1601-44.

Bruton, Henry J. (1998): 'A Reconsideration of Import Substitution', *Journal of Economic Literature* 36: 903-36.

Buchanan, James M. (1969/1978): *Cost and Choice – An Inquiry in Economic Theory*, Midway Reprint 1978, Chicago: University of Chicago Press.

Buchanan, James M. and Gordon Tullock (1962): *The Calculus of Consent*, Ann Arbor: University of Michigan Press.

Buchanan, James M. and Yong J. Yoon (1994): *The Returns to Increasing Returns*, Ann Arbor: The University of Michigan Press.

Buchanan, James M. and Yong J. Yoon (1995): 'Constitutional Implications of Alternative Models of Increasing Returns', *Constitutional Political Economy* 6: 191-6.

Burda, Michael C. (1997): 'Persistently High Irish Unemployment: Some Lessons from the UK', forthcoming in: *International Perspectives on Irish Economic Issues*, ed. by Allan Gray, Dublin: INDECON, 85-111.

Burda, Michael C. and Barbara Dluhosch (1999a): 'Globalization and European Labor Markets', in: *Globalization and Labor*, ed. by Horst Siebert, Tübingen: Mohr, 181-207.

Burda, Michael C. and Barbara Dluhosch (1999b): 'Globalization and Labor Markets', mimeo: Berlin and Munich.

Burenstam Linder, Staffan (1961): *An Essay on Trade and Transformation*, Stockholm: Almqvist & Wiksell and New York: John Wiley & Sons.

Burkhauser, Richard V. and John G. Poupore (1997): 'A Cross-National Comparison of Permanent Inequality in the United States and Germany', *Review of Economics and Statistics* LXXIX: 10-17.

Burtless, Gary (1995): 'International Trade and the Rise in Earnings Inequality', *Journal of Economic Literature* 33: 800-816.

Busch, Berthold; Lichtblau, Karl and Claus Schnabel (1997): 'Kohäsion in der Europäischen Union: Eine empirische Analyse', *iw-trends* 24, 1/97: 1-16.

Busch, Berthold; Lichtblau, Karl and Claus Schnabel (1998): 'Kohäsionspolitik, Konvergenz und Arbeitslosigkeit in der Europäischen Union', *Jahrbuch für Wirtschaftswissenschaften* 49: 1-25.

Campa, José and Linda S. Goldberg (1997): 'The Evolving External Orientation of Manufacturing: A Profile of Four Countries', *Federal Reserve Bank of New York Economic Policy Review* 3, No. 2 (July): 53-81.

Carlino, G.A. (1992): 'Are Regional Per Capita Earnings Diverging?', in: *Business Review*, Federal Reserve Bank of Philadelphia, 3-12.

CEC (Commission of the European Communities) (1989): *Report on Economic and Monetary Union in the European Community*, Luxembourg: Office of Official Publications of the European Communities.

CEC (Commission of the European Communities) (1991): *The Regions in the 90s*, Luxembourg: Commission of the European Communities.

CEC (Commission of the European Communities) (1993): *European Economy: The Economics of Community Public Finance*, Luxembourg: Commission of the European Communities.

CEC (Commission of the European Communities) (1994): *White Paper: Growth, Competitiveness, and Employment*, Luxembourg: Commission of the European Communities.

Chamberlin, Edward H. (1933): *The Theory of Monopolistic Competition*, Cambridge, Mass.: Harvard University Press.

Chandler, Alfred D. (1977): *The Visible Hand: The Managerial Revolution in American Business*, Cambridge and London: Harvard University Press.

Chandler, Alfred D. (1990): *Scale and Scope: The Dynamics of Industrial Capitalism*, Cambridge and London: Harvard University Press.

Chenery, Hollis B. (1955): 'The Role of Industrialization in Development Programmes', reprinted in *The Economics of Underdevelopment*, ed. by.

A.N. Agarwala and S.P. Singh (1958), Oxford: Oxford University Press, 450-71.

Chenery, Hollis B. and Paul Clark (1959): *Interindustry Economics*, New York: John Wiley.

Christaller, Walter (1933): *Die zentralen Orte in Süddeutschland*, Jena: G. Fischer.

Coase, Ronald H. (1937): 'The Nature of The Firm', *Economica* N.S. 4: 386-405.

Corsetti, Giancarlo; Pesenti, Paolo and Nouriel Roubini (1998): 'What Caused the Asian Currency and Financial Crisis?', mimeo: New York.

Corsi, Marcella (1991): *Division of Labor, Technical Change and Economic Growth*, Aldershot: Avebury.

Cortes, Olivier and Sébastian Jean (1997): 'International Trade Spurs Productivity', paper presented at the 1997 EEA Annual Meeting in Toulouse.

Courant, Paul N. and Alan V. Deardorff (1992): 'International Trade with Lumpy Countries', *Journal of Political Economy* 100: 198-210.

Cowell, Frank A. (1995): *Measuring Inequality*, LSE Handbooks in Economics, 2nd ed., London etc.: Prentice Hall.

Cox, David and Richard Harris (1985): 'Trade Liberalization and Industrial Organization: Some Estimates for Canada', *Journal of Political Economy* 93: 115-45.

Crafts, Nicholas F.R. (1985): 'Industrial Revolution in England and France: Some Thoughts on the Question "Why England was First"', in: *The Economics of the Industrial Revolution*, ed. by Joel Mokyr, Totowa: Rowman and Allanheld, 119-31.

Crandall, Robert W. (1993): *Manufacturing on the Move*, Washington, DC: Brookings Institution.

Cuadrado, Juan Ramón; Dehesa, Guillermo de la and Andrés Precedo (1993): 'Regional Imbalances and Government Compensatory Financial Flows: The Case of Spain', in: *Finance and Development: Issues and Experience*, ed. by Alberto Giovannini, Cambridge: Cambridge University Press, 261-93.

Cuny, Reinhard H. (1997): 'Reform der Europäischen Strukturfonds', *Wirtschaftsdienst*, 77: 227-33.

Dalton, Hugh (1920): *Some Aspects of the Inequality of Incomes in Modern Communities*, London: Routledge.

Danziger, Sheldon and Peter Gottshalk (eds) (1994): *Uneven Tides: Rising Inequality in America*, New York: Russell Sage Foundation.

David, Paul A. (1975): *Technical Choice, Innovation, and Economic Growth: Essays on American and British Experience in the Nineteenth Century*, Cambridge: Cambridge University Press.

David, Paul A. (1985): 'Clio and the Economics of QWERTY', *American Economic Review* (Papers and Proceedings) 75: 332-7.

David, Paul A. and Joshua L. Rosenbloom (1990): 'Marshallian Factor Market Externalities and the Dynamics of Industrial Localization', *Journal of Urban Economics* 28: 349-70.

Davies, James and Michael Hoy (1995): 'Making Inequality Comparisons When Lorenz Curves Intersect', *American Economic Review* 85: 980-86.

Deardorff, Alan V. (1994): 'Exploring the Limits of Comparative Advantage', *Weltwirtschaftliches Archiv* 130: 1-19.

Deardorff, Alan V. (1998): 'Fragmentation in Simple Trade Models', paper presented at the 1998 Meeting of the North American Economics and Finance Association.

De Groot, Henri L.F. (1997): 'Macroeconomic Consequences of Outsourcing: An Analysis of Growth, Welfare, and Product Variety', mimeo: Tilburg University.

Dehesa, Guillermo de la and Paul R. Krugman (1993): *EMU and the Regions*, Group of Thirty Occasional Paper No. 39: Washington D.C.: Group of Thirty.

Deininger, Klaus and Lyn Squire (1997): 'Wirtschaftswachstum und ungleiche Einkommensverteilung: Neue Zusammenhänge?', *Finanzierung und Entwicklung*: 36-9.

Demsetz, Harold (1967/1988): 'Toward a Theory of Property Rights', *American Economic Review* 57, reprinted in: *Ownership, Control and the Firm: The Organization of Economic Activity Vol. I*, Oxford and Cambridge, Mass.: Basil Blackwell, 104-16.

Dicken, Peter (1986): *Global Shift, Industrial Change in a Turbulent World*, London: Harper&Row.

Diekmann, Berend (1998): 'Neuordnung der EU-Finanzen: Die Nettozahlerposition als Hebel?', *Wirtschaftsdienst* 78: 89-96.

Diekmann, Berend and Siegfried Breier (1993): 'Der Kohäsionsfonds – ein notwendiges Gemeinschaftsinstrument?', *Wirtschaftsdienst* 73: 258-65.

Dignan, Tony (1995): 'Regional Disparities and Regional Policy in the European Union', *Oxford Review of Economic Policy* 11, No. 2: 64-95.

DIW (1997a): 'Europäische Union: Osterweiterung beschleunigt Konvergenz', *DIW Wochenbericht* 64, 14/97: 223-31.

DIW (1997b): 'Globalisierung: Falle oder Wohlstandsquelle?', *DIW Wochenbericht* 64, 23/97: 413-19.

DIW (1997c): 'Dienstleistungsdynamik in der Europäischen Union uneinheitlich', *DIW Wochenbericht* 64, 16/97: 273-80.

Dixit, Avinash and Joseph E. Stiglitz (1977): 'Monopolistic Competition and Optimum Product Diversity', *American Economic Review* 67: 297-308.

Dluhosch, Barbara (1995): 'Eine neue europäische Spaltung? Zur Dynamik wirtschaftlicher Integration aus Sicht der Außenhandelstheorie', *Zeitschrift für Wirtschaftspolitik* 44: 233-54.

Dluhosch, Barbara (1996): 'On the Fate of Newcomers in the European Union: Lessons from the Spanish Experience', Bank of Spain Working Paper #9602.

Dluhosch, Barbara (1997): 'Trade Liberalization, Technological Change, and the Economics of Outsourcing', paper presented at the 1997-98 conferences of the EEA and AEA.

Dluhosch, Barbara; Freytag, Andreas and Malte Krüger (1996): *International Competitiveness and the Balance of Payments: Do Current Account Deficits and Surpluses Matter?*, Cheltenham and Brookfield: Edward Elgar.

Dolado, Juan J. and José Viñals (1990): 'Macroeconomic Policy, External Targets and Constraints: The Case of Spain', in: *External Constraints on Macroeconomic Policy: The European Experience*, ed. by George Alogoskoufis, Lucas Papademos and Richard Portes, Cambridge, Mass.: Cambridge University Press, 304-38.

Dolado, Juan J.; González-Páramo, José M. and José M[a] Roldán (1994): 'Convergencia Económica Entre las Provincias Españolas: Evidencia Empírica (1955-1989)', in: *Moneda y Credito*, Segundo Epoca 198: 81-119.

Dollar, David and Edward N. Wolff (1993): *Competitiveness, Convergence and International Specialization*, Cambridge: MIT Press.

Donges, Juergen B. (1994): 'Kritisches zu den Forderungen nach einer strategischen Industriepolitik', in: *Ordnung in Freiheit*, Festgabe für Hans Willgerodt zum 70. Geburtstag, ed. by Rolf H. Hasse, Josef Molsberger and Christian Watrin, Stuttgart, Jena and New York: Gustav Fischer, 182-99.

Donges, Juergen B. and Ulrich Hiemenz (1985): 'Export Liberalization and the Outward-Oriented Trade Regime', Kiel Working Paper No. 241, Kiel: Institut für Weltwirtschaft.

Donges, Juergen B. et al. (1982): *The Second Enlargement of the European Community: Adjustment Requirements and Challenges for Policy Reform*, Kieler Studie No. 171, Tübingen: Mohr.

Donges, Juergen B. et al. (Kronberger Kreis) (1996): *Sozialunion für Europa?*, Bad Homburg: Frankfurter Institut.

Dornbusch, Rudi; Fischer, Stanley and Paul A. Samuelson (1977): 'Comparative Advantage, Trade, and Payments in a Ricardian Model with a Continuum of Goods', *American Economic Review* 67: 823-39.

Economic Report of the President (1994), Washington, DC: US Government Printing Office.

Edwards, Sebastian (1993): 'Openness, Trade Liberalization and Growth in Developing Countries', *Journal of Economic Literature* 31: 1358-93.

Eekhoff, Johann (1995): 'Regionale Strukturpolitik in der Europäischen Union versus Wettbewerb der Regionen', in: *Europa zwischen Ordnungswettbewerb und Harmonisierung*, ed. by Lüder Gerken, Berlin and Heidelberg: Springer, 315-28.

Eichengreen, Barry (1990): 'One Money for Europe? Lessons from the US Currency Union', *Economic Policy* 10: 118-66.

Elberfeld, Walter (1997): 'Market Size and the Degree of Vertical Integration', mimeo: University of Cologne.

Engel, Charles and John H. Rogers (1996): 'How Wide is the Border?', *American Economic Review* 86: 1112-25.

Engerman, Stanley L. and Kenneth L. Sokoloff (1994): 'Factor Endowments, Institutions, and Differential Paths of Growth Among New World Economies: A View From Economic Historians of the United States', NBER Working Papers on Historical Factors in Long Run Growth No. 66; forthcoming in: *How Latin America Fell Behind: Essays on the Economic Histories of Brazil and Mexico*, ed. by Steve Haber, Stanford: Stanford University Press.

Estebán, Joan Mª (1994): 'La Desigualdad Interregional en Europa y en España: Descriptión y Análisis, in: *Crecimiento y Convergencia Regional en España y en Europa Vol. II*, Barcelona: Instituto de Análisis Economico (CSIC), 13-84.

Estebán, Joan Mª and Debraj Ray (1994): 'On the Measurement of Polarization', *Econometrica* 62: 819-51.

Ethier, Wilfried J. (1979): 'Internationally Decreasing Costs and World Trade', *Journal of International Economics* 9: 1-24.

Ethier, Wilfried J. (1982): 'National and International Returns to Scale in the Modern Theory of International Trade', *American Economic Review* 72: 950-59.

European Commission (1996): *First Report on Economic and Social Cohesion 1996*, preliminary edition, Luxembourg: Office for Official Publications of the European Communities.

European Commission (1997): *Agenda 2000: For a Stronger and Wider Union*, Strasbourg, July 15, 1997 (DOC/97/6).

European Commission (1998): *Financing the European Union: Commission Report on the Operation of the Own Resources System*, Brussels, Oct. 1998.

European Council (1999): *Presidency Conclusions of the Berlin European Council 24 and 25 March 1999* (SN 100/99).

EUROSTAT (1997): *EUROSTAT REGIO Data Tape*, ed. April 1997.

Fagerberg, Jan and Bart Verspagen (1996): 'Heading for Divergence? Regional Growth in Europe Reconsidered', *Journal of Common Market Studies* 34: 431-48.

Feenstra, Robert C. and Gordon H. Hanson (1996a): 'Globalization, Outsourcing, and Wage Inequality', *American Economic Review* (Papers and Proceedings) 86: 240-45.

Feenstra, Robert C. and Gordon H. Hanson (1996b): 'Foreign Investment, Outsourcing, and Relative Wages', in: *The Political Economy of Trade Policy*, Papers in Honor of Jagdish Bhagwati, ed. by Robert C. Feenstra, Gene M. Grossman and Douglas A. Irwin, Cambridge, Mass. and London: Cambridge University Press, 89-127.

Feenstra, Robert C. and James R. Markusen (1994): 'Accounting for Growth with New Inputs', *International Economic Review* 35: 429-47.

Feenstra, Robert C.; Markusen, James R. and William Zeile (1992): 'Accounting for Growth with New Inputs: Theory and Evidence', *American Economic Review* (Papers and Proceedings) 82: 415-21.

Feix, Thorsten (1996): *Räumliche Wirtschaftsstruktur und Industriepolitik*, Wiesbaden: Dt. Univ. Verlag.

Fels, Gerhard and Klaus-Dieter Schmidt (1980): *Die deutsche Wirtschaft im Strukturwandel*, Kieler Studie #166, Tübingen: Mohr.

Fisch, Gerhard (1993): 'Außenhandels- und entwicklungstheoretische Aspekte der Kohäsionspolitik in der EU', *Konjunkturpolitik* 39: 349-75.

Fisch, Gerhard (1994): *Integration und Kohäsion heterogener Staaten in der EU: außenhandels- und entwicklungsrelevante Probleme*, Wiesbaden: Dt. Univ. Verlag.

Fisher, Franklin; McGowan, John and Joen Greenwood (1985): *Der Anti-Trust-Fall US gegen IBM*, Mohr: Tübingen.

Fishlow, Albert (1973): 'Comparative Consumption Patterns, the Extent of the Market, and Alternative Development Strategies', in: *Micro-Aspects of Development*, ed. by Eliezer Ayal, New York: Praeger.

Flam, Harry and M. June Flanders (eds.) (1991): *Eli Heckscher and Bertil Ohlin: Heckscher-Ohlin Trade Theory*, translated, edited and introduced by Harry Flam and M. June Flanders, Cambridge and London: MIT Press.

Francois, Joseph (1990a): 'Producer Services, Scale, and the Division of Labor', *Oxford Economic Papers* 42, 715-29.

Francois, Joseph (1990b): 'Trade in Producer Services and Returns Due to Specialization under Monopolistic Competition', *Canadian Journal of Economics* 23, 109-24.

Frank, Robert H. (1988): *Passions Within Reason*, New York and London: Norton.

Frank, Robert H. and Philip J. Cook (1995): *The Winner-Take-All Society*, New York: Free Press.

Frankel, Jeffrey A.; Stein, Ernesto and Shang-Jin Wei (1996): 'Regional Trading Arrangements: Natural or Supernatural?', *American Economic Review* (Papers and Proceedings) 86: 52-6.

Franzmeyer, Fritz; Seidel, Bernhard and Christian Weise (1993): *Die Reform der EG-Strukturfonds von 1988*, DIW-Beiträge zur Strukturforschung, H. 141, Berlin: Duncker & Humblot.

Freeman, Richard B. (1997): 'Low Wage Employment: Is more or less better?', mimeo: Harvard, NBER, CEP.

Friedman, Milton (1992): 'Do Old Fallacies Ever Die?', *Journal of Economic Literature* 30: 2129-32.

Fujita, Masahisa (1989): *Urban Economic Theory*, Cambridge: Cambridge University Press.

Fujita, Masahisa and Jacques-François Thisse (1996): 'Economics of Agglomeration', CEPR Discussion Paper #1344.

Galy, Michel (1993): 'Opening Up of the Spanish Economy in the Context of EC Integration', in: *Spain: Converging with the European Community*, IMF Occasional Paper #101, Washington, DC, 2-12.

Georgescu-Roegen, Nicholas (1972): 'Process Analysis and the Neoclassical Theory of Production', *American Journal of Agricultural Economics* LIV: 279-94; reprinted in: Nicholas Georgescu-Roegen (1976): *Energy and Economic Myths: Institutional and Analytical Economic Essays*, New York etc.: Pergamon Press, 37-52.

German Statistical Office (1996): *Data Tape*, Wiesbaden.

Giersch, Herbert (1949): 'Economic Union Between Nations and the Location of Industries', *The Review of Economic Studies* XVII: 87-97.

Gottshalk, Peter and Timothy M. Smeeding (1997): 'Cross-National Comparisons of Earnings and Income Inequality', *Journal of Economic Literature* 35: 633-87.

Greene, H.A. John (1964): *Aggregation in Economic Analysis: An Introductory Survey*, Princeton, NJ: Princeton University Press.

Grossman, Gene M. (1990): 'Promoting New Industrial Activities: A Survey of Recent Arguments and Evidence', in: *OECD Economic Studies*, No. 14, Spring: 87-125.

Grossman, Gene M. and Elhanan Helpman (1991/1995): *Innovation and Growth in the Global Economy*, Cambridge: MIT Press.

Habbakkuk, H.J. (1962): *American and British Technology in the Nineteenth Century: The Search for Labor Saving Inventions*, Cambridge: Cambridge University Press.

Haberler, Gottfried (1933): *Der internationale Handel*, reprint 1970, Berlin: Springer.

Hagen, Jürgen von (1991): 'Fiscal Arrangements in a Monetary Union: Evidence from the US', Diskussionsbeiträge des Giessener Arbeitskreises für wirtschaftspolitische Studien #9.

Hagen, Jürgen von and George Hammond (1994): 'Industrial Localization: An Empirical Test for Marshallian Localization Economies', CEPR Discussion Paper # 917.

Hammond, Peter (1976): 'Why Ethical Measures of Inequality Need Interpersonal Comparisons', *Theory and Decision* 7: 263-74.

Handelsblatt: 'Keine EU-Erweiterung auf Kosten der Südstaaten', Interview of José María Aznar by Joachim Hoenig and Christian Potthoff, *Handelsblatt* June 2, 1997: 9.

Handelsblatt: 'Aznar besteht auf weiterhin hohen EU-Finanzhilfen für Spanien', *Handelsblatt* June 10, 1997: 14.

Handelsblatt: 'Waigel will ab 2000 gerechte Beiträge', *Handelsblatt* July 28, 1997: 3.

Hanson, Gordon H. (1996): 'Localization Economies, Vertical Organization, and Trade', *American Economic Review* 86: 1266-78.

Hanson, Gordon H. (1998): 'North American Economic Integration and Industry Location', *Oxford Review of Economic Policy* 14(2): 30-44.

Harris, Richard G. (1993): 'Globalization, Trade and Income', *Canadian Journal of Economics* 26: 755-76.

Harris, Richard G. (1995): 'Trade and Communication Costs', *Canadian Journal of Economics* 28: S46-S75.

Harsanyi, John C. (1955): 'Cardinal Welfare, Individualistic Ethics, and Interpersonal Comparisons of Utility', *Journal of Political Economy* 63: 309-21.

Havrylyshyn, Oli (1990): 'Trade Policy and Productivity Gains in Developing Countries: A Survey of the Literature', *World Bank Research Observer* 5, No. 1.

Hayek, Friedrich A. von (1976/1982): *Law, Legislation and Liberty*, one-volume ed., London, Melbourne and Henley: Routledge & Kegan Paul.

Heckscher, Eli and Bertil Ohlin (1991 (1919/24)): *Heckscher-Ohlin Trade Theory*, ed. and transl. by Harry Flam and M. June Flanders, Cambridge: MIT Press.

Helpman, Elhanan (1981): 'International Trade in the Presence of Product Differentiation, Economies of Scale and Imperfect Competition: A Chamberlin-Heckscher-Ohlin Approach, *Journal of International Economics* 11: 305-40.

Helpman, Elhanan (1984): 'Increasing Returns, Imperfect Markets and Trade Theory', *Handbook of International Economics* Vol. I, ed. by Ronald W. Jones and Peter B. Kenen, Amsterdam: North Holland, 325-65.

Helpman, Elhanan (ed.) (1992): *Imperfect Competition and International Trade*, Cambridge: MIT Press.

Helpman, Elhanan and Paul R. Krugman (1985): *Market Structure and Foreign Trade*, Cambridge: MIT Press.

Henderson, J. Vernon (1988): *Urban Development: Theory, Fact and Illusion*, Oxford: Oxford University Press.

Herring, Richard J. and Robert E. Litan (1995): *Financial Regulation in the Global Economy*, Washington, DC: Brookings Institution.

Heston, Alan and Robert Summers (1997): *Penn World Tables 5.6 Data Tape*, ed. 1996, http://datacentre.epas.utoronto.ca:5680/pwt/pwt.html.

Hicks, John R. (1932): *The Theory of Wages*, London: Macmillan.

Hicks, John R. (1973): 'The Austrian Theory of Capital and its Rebirth in Modern Economics', in: *Carl Menger and the Austrian School of Economics*, ed. by John R. Hicks and W. Weber, Oxford: Clarendon Press, 190-206.

Hirschman, Albert O. (1958): *The Strategy of Economic Development*, New Haven: Yale University Press.

Høj, Jens; Kato, Toshiyasu and Dirk Pilat (1995): 'Deregulation and Privatisation in the Service Sector', *OECD Economic Studies* 25 (1995/II): 37-74.

Hoover, E.M. (1948): *The Location of Economic Activity*, New York: McGraw Hill.

Hort, Peter (1997): 'Die Milliarden für Europa', *Frankfurter Allgemeine Zeitung*, August 1: 13.

Houthakker, Hendrik S. (1956): 'Specialization and Speciation', *Kyklos* 9: 181-89.

Howes, Stephen (1996): 'The Influence of Aggregation on the Ordering of Distributions', *Economica* 63: 253-72.

Hummels, David; Rapoport, Dana and Kei-Mu Yi (1997): 'Globalization and the Changing Nature of World Trade', in: *FRBNY Economic Policy Review* 4 (2) 1998, 79-99.

IMF (1996): *International Financial Statistics, Yearbook*, Washington, DC: IMF.

IMF (1997a): *World Economic Outlook: Globalization – Opportunities and Challenges*, May 1997, Washington, DC: IMF.

IMF (1997b): *International Financial Statistics, edition June 1997*, Washington, D.C.: IMF.

Innis, H.A. (1936/1956): 'Unused Capacity as a Factor in Canadian Economic History, *Canadian Journal of Economics and Political Science* 2: 1-15; reprinted in H.A. Innis (1956), *Essays in Canadian Economic History*, Toronto: University of Toronto Press.

Ippolito, Richard A. (1977): 'The Division of Labor in the Firm', *Economic Inquiry* 15: 469-92.

Irwin, Douglas A. (1996): 'The United States in a New Global Economy? A Century's Perspective', *American Economic Review* (Papers and Proceedings) 86: 41-6.

Isçan, Talan (1998): 'Trade Liberalisation and Productivity: A Panel Study of the Mexican Manufacturing Industry', *Journal of Development Studies* 34: 123-48.

Ishii, Jun and Kei-Mu Yi (1997): 'The Growth of World Trade', Federal Reserve Bank of New York Research Paper #9718, May 1997.

Jackman, Richard (1995): 'Regional Policy in an Enlarged Europe', *Oxford Review of Economic Policy* 11, No. 2: 113-25.

Jenkins, Stephen P. (1996): 'Recent Trends in the UK Income Distribution: What Happened and Why?', *Oxford Review of Economic Policy*, Vol. 12, No. 1, Spring: 29-46.

Johnson, Harry G. (1967): *International Trade and Economic Growth: Studies in Pure Theory*, Cambridge, Mass.: Harvard University Press.

Johnson, Paul (1996): 'The Assessment: Inequality', *Oxford Review of Economic Policy* 12, No. 1, Spring: 1-14.

Jones, Ronald (1980): 'Comparative and Absolute Advantage', *Schweizerische Zeitschrift für Volkswirtschaft und Statistik* 116: 235-60.

Jones, Ronald (1996): 'Vertical Markets in International Trade', Diskussionsbeiträge SFB 178, Univ. Konstanz, Serie II, #318.

Jones, Ronald and Henryk Kierzkowski (1990): 'The Role of Services in Production and International Trade: A Theoretical Framework', in: *The Political Economy of International Trade: Essays in Honor of Robert E. Baldwin*, ed. by Ronald W. Jones and Anne O. Krueger, Cambridge and Oxford: Basil Blackwell, 31-48.

Jones, Ronald and Henryk Kierzkowski (1997): 'Globalization and the Consequences of International Fragmentation', paper prepared for the Festschrift in Honor of Robert A. Mundell, Washington, DC: The World Bank MC12-121.

Jorgenson, Dale W. (ed.) (1995): *Productivity Vol. 2: International Comparisons of Economic Growth*, Cambridge: MIT Press.

Junius, Karsten (1996): 'Economic Development and Industrial Concentration: An Inverted U-Curve', *Kieler Arbeitspapier #770*, Kiel: Institut für Weltwirtschaft.

Kaldor, Nicholas (1970): 'The Case for Regional Policies', *Scottish Journal of Political Economy* 17: 337-48.

Kaldor, Nicholas (1972): 'The Irrelevance of Equilibrium Economics', *Economic Journal* 82: 1237-55.

Kauffman, Stuart (1993): *The Origins of Order*, New York: Oxford University Press.

Kelly, Morgan (1997): 'The Dynamics of Smithian Growth', *Quarterly Journal of Economics* CXII: 939-64.

Kennedy, C. (1964): 'Induced Bias in Innovation and the Theory of Distribution', *Economic Journal* 74: 541-7.

Kierzkowski, Henryk (1998): 'Trade Restructuring and Globalization: New Challenges for the Transition Economies', report prepared for the WTO: Geneva.

Klein, Benjamin and Keith B. Leffler (1981): 'The Role of Market Forces in Assuring Contractual Performance', *Journal of Political Economy* 89: 615-41.

Klodt, Henning; Stehn, Jürgen et al. (1992): *Die Strukturpolitik der EG*, Kieler Studie No. 249, Tübingen: Mohr.

Klodt, Henning; Maurer, Rainer and Axel Schimmelpfennig (1997): *Tertiarisierung der deutschen Wirtschaft*, Kieler Studie No. 283, Tübingen: Mohr.

Kol, Jacob and Paul Rayment (1989): 'Allyn Young Specialisation and Intermediate Goods in Intra-Industry Trade', in: *Intra Industry Trade: Theory, Evidence and Extensions,* ed. by P.K.M. Tharakan and Jacob Kol, London: Macmillan, 51-68.

Krishna, Kala and Anne O. Krueger (1995): 'Rules of Origin and Hidden Protection', in: *New Directions in Trade Theory*, ed. by Jim Levinsohn, Ann Arbor: University of Michigan Press.

Krueger, Anne O. (1980/1990): 'Trade Policy as an Input to Development', *American Economic Review* (Papers and Proceedings) 70: 288-92; reprinted in: Anne O. Krueger, *Perspectives on Trade and Development*, New York etc.: Harvester Wheatsheaf, 95-102.

Krueger, Anne O. (1984/1990): 'Comparative Advantage and Development Policy Twenty Years Later', reprinted in: Anne O. Krueger, *Perspectives on Trade and Development*, New York etc.: Harvester Wheatsheaf, 49-70.

Krueger, Anne O. (1995a): 'Policy Lessons from Development Experience since the Second World War', in: *Handbook of Development Economics* III, ed. by Jere R. Behrman and T.N. Srinivasan, Amsterdam: Elsevier.

Krueger, Anne O. (1995b): 'Free Trade Agreements Versus Customs Unions', mimeo: Stanford University.

Krueger, Anne O. (1997): 'Trade Policy and Economic Development: How We Learn', *American Economic Review* 87, 1-22.

Krugman, Paul R. (1980): 'Scale Economies, Product Differentiation, and the Pattern of Trade', *American Economic Review* 70: 950-59; reprinted in: Krugman, Paul R. (1990): *Rethinking International Trade*, Cambridge: MIT Press, 22-37.

Krugman, Paul R. (1984): 'Import Protection as Export Promotion: International Competition in the Presence of Oligopoly and Economies of Scale', in: *Monopolistic Competition in International Trade*, ed. by Henryk Kierzkowski, Oxford: Oxford University Press, 180-93.

Krugman, Paul R. (1990): 'Industrial Organization and International Trade', in: *Rethinking International Trade*, Cambridge and London: MIT Press, 226-68.

Krugman, Paul R. (1991a): *Geography and Trade*, Cambridge: MIT Press.

Krugman, Paul R. (1991b): 'The Move Toward Free Trade Zones', *Federal Reserve Bank of Kansas City Economic Review*, November/December: 5-25.

Krugman, Paul R. (1993): 'The Hub Effect: Or, Threeness in Interregional Trade', in: *Theory, Policy and Dynamics in International Trade: Essays in Honor of Ronald W. Jones*, ed. by Wilfried J. Ethier, Elhanan Helpman and J. Peter Neary, Cambridge: Cambridge University Press, 29-37.

Krugman, Paul R. (1994): 'Urban Concentration: The Role of Increasing Returns and Transport Costs', Paper prepared for the World Bank's Annual Conference on Development Economics, April 1994.

Krugman, Paul R. (1995a): 'How the Economy Organizes Itself in Space: A Survey of the New Economic Geography', mimeo: Stanford.

Krugman, Paul R. (1995b) 'Technology, Trade, and Factor Prices', NBER Working Paper #5355.

Krugman, Paul R. (1995c): 'Growing World Trade: Causes and Consequences', *Brookings Papers on Economic Activity*, Vol. 1, Washington, DC: Brookings: 327-62.

Krugman, Paul R. (1995d): 'Increasing Returns, Imperfect Competition and the Positive Theory of International Trade', in: *Handbook of International Trade, Vol. III*, ed. by G. Grossman and K. Rogoff, Amsterdam: North-Holland, 1243-77.

Krugman, Paul R. (1996a): *The Self-Organizing Economy*, Cambridge: Basil Blackwell.

Krugman, Paul R. (1996b): 'The CPI and the Rat Race: New Evidence on the Old Question of Whether Money Buys Happiness', *Slate* 12/21/96, http://www.slate.com/Dismal/96-12-21/Dismal.asp.

Krugman, Paul R. (1996c): *Development, Geography, and Economic Theory*, Cambridge: MIT Press.

Krugman, Paul R. (1997): 'Space: The Final Frontier?', mimeo: MIT.

Krugman, Paul R. (1998a): 'What's New about the New Economic Geography?', *Oxford Review of Economic Policy* 14 (2), 7-17.

Krugman, Paul R. (1998b): 'What Happened to Asia?', mimeo: Cambridge, Mass.

Krugman, Paul R. and Maurice Obstfeld (1994): *International Economics: Theory and Policy*, 3rd ed., New York: Harper Collins.

Krugman, Paul R. and Anthony Venables (1990): 'Integration and the Competitiveness of Peripheral Industry', in: *Unity with Diversity: the Community's Southern Frontier*, ed. by Christopher Bliss and Jorge Braga de Macedo, Cambridge: Cambridge University Press, 56-75.

Krugman, Paul R. and Anthony J. Venables (1995): 'Globalization and the Inequality of Nations', *Quarterly Journal of Economics* 110: 857-80.

Kubo, Y. (1985): 'A Cross-Country Comparison of Inter-Industry Linkages and the Role of Imported Intermediates', *World Development* 13: 1287-98.

Lachmann, Ludwig M. (1986): *The Market as a Process*, Oxford and New York: Basil Blackwell.

Lagendijk, Arnoud (1993): *The Internationalisation of the Spanish Automobile Industry and its Regional Impact: The Emergence of a Growth-Periphery*, Tinbergen Institute Research Series #59, Amsterdam: Thesis Publishers.

Lambert, Peter (1989): *The Distribution and Redistribution of Income: A Mathematical Analysis*, Cambridge, Mass.: Basil Blackwell.

Lancaster, Kelvin (1979): *Variety, Equity, and Efficiency*, Oxford: Basil Blackwell.

Lancaster, Kelvin (1996): *Trade, Markets and Welfare*, Cheltenham and Brookfield: Edward Elgar.

Langlois, Richard N. (1988): 'Economic Change and the Boundaries of the Firm', *Journal of Institutional and Theoretical Economics* 144: 635-57.

Larre, Bénédicte and Raymond Torres (1991): 'Is Convergence a Spontaneous Process? The Experience of Spain, Portugal and Greece', *OECD Economic Studies*, No. 16, Spring: 169-98.

Lawrence, Colin and Pablo T. Spiller (1983): 'Product Diversity, Economies of Scale, and International Trade', *Quarterly Journal of Economics* 93: 63-83.

Leijonhufvud, Axel (1986): 'Capitalism and the Factory System', in: *Economics as a Process: Essays in the New Institutional Economics*, ed. by Richard N. Langlois, Cambridge: Cambridge University Press, 203-23.

Leonardi, Robert (1995): *Convergence, Cohesion and Integration in the European Union*, Houndmills and London: Macmillan.

Letzner, Volker (1997): *Integrationstheorie und monopolistische Konkurrenz*, Wiesbaden: Dt. Univ. Verlag.

Lösch, August (1938): 'Wo gilt das Theorem der komparativen Kosten?', *Weltwirtschaftliches Archiv* XLVIII: 45-65.

Lösch, August (1943): *Die räumliche Ordnung der Wirtschaft*, Jena: G. Fischer.

Maddison, Angus (1991): *Dynamic Forces in Capitalist Development: A Long-Run Comparative View*, Oxford and New York: Oxford University Press.

Maddison, Angus (1994): 'Explaining the Economic Performance of Nations, 1820-1989', in: *Convergence of Productivity: Cross-National Studies and Historical Evidence*, ed. by William J. Baumol; Richard R. Nelson and Edward N. Wolff, Oxford and New York: Oxford University Press, 20-61.

Magill, Michael and Martine Quinzii (1996): *Theory of Incomplete Markets, Vol. 1*, Cambridge, Mass. and London: MIT Press.

Majone, Giandomenico (1993): 'The European Community Between Social Policy and Social Regulation', *Journal of Common Market Studies* 31: 153-70.

Markusen, James R. (1990): 'Micro-foundations of External Economies', *Canadian Journal of Economics* 23: 493-508.

Marshall, Alfred (1919): *Industry and Trade: A Study of Industrial Techniques and Business Organization; and of their Influences on the Conditions of Various Classes and Nations*, London: Macmillan.

Martin, Philippe and Gianmarco I.P. Ottaviano (1995): 'The Geography of Multi-Speed Europe', CEPR Discussion Paper Series #1292.

Martin, Ron (1997): 'The New "Geographical Turn" in Economics: Some Critical Reflections', forthcoming in *Cambridge Journal of Economics*.

Matusz, Steven J. (1996): 'International Trade, the Division of Labor, and Unemployment', *International Economic Review* 37: 71-84.

McCallum, John (1995): 'National Borders Matter: Canada-U.S. Regional Trade Patterns', *American Economic Review* 85: 615-23.

Melvin, James R. (1985a): 'Domestic Taste Differences, Transportation Costs, and International Trade', *Journal of International Economics* 18: 65-82.

Melvin, James R. (1985b): 'The Regional Economic Consequences of Tariffs and Domestic Transportation Costs', *Canadian Journal of Economics* 18: 237-57.

Melvin, James R. (1989): *Trade in Services: A Theoretical Analysis*, Halifax: The Institute for Research on Public Policy.

Melvin, James R. (1991): Presidential Address: 'Time and Space in Economic Analysis', *Canadian Journal of Economics* 23: 725-47.

Mokyr, Joel (1977): 'Demand Versus Supply in the Industrial Revolution', *Explorations in Economic History* 37: 981-1008.

Mokyr, Joel (1990): *The Lever of Riches: Technological Creativity and Economic Progress*, New York and Oxford: Oxford University Press.

Molle, Willem (1997): 'The Regional Economic Structure of the European Union', in: *Zentrum und Peripherie – Zur Entwicklung der Arbeitsteilung in Europa*, ed. by Hans-Jürgen Vosgerau, Schriften des Vereins für Socialpolitik No. 250, Berlin: Duncker & Humblot, 13-27.

Monopolkommission (1992): *Wettbewerbspolitik oder Industriepolitik*, Hauptgutachten 1990/1991, Baden-Baden: Nomos.

Morawetz, David (1981): *Why the Emperor's New Clothes are not Made in Columbia. A Case Study in Latin American and East Asian Manufactured Exports*, Oxford: Oxford University Press.

Mowery, David Charles and Nathan Rosenberg (1989): *Technology and the Pursuit of Economic Growth*, Cambridge, Mass.: Cambridge University Press.

Murphy, Kevin M.; Schleifer, Andrei and Robert W. Vishny (1989a): 'Industrialization and the Big Push', *Journal of Political Economy* 97: 1003-26.

Murphy, Kevin M.; Shleifer, Andrei and Robert W. Vishny (1989b): 'Income Distribution, Market Size and Industrialization', *Quarterly Journal of Economics* 104: 537-64.

Myrdal, Gunnar (1957): *Economic Theory and Underdeveloped Regions*, London: Duckworth.

Neven, Damien and Claudine Gouyette (1995): 'Regional Convergence in the European Community', *Journal of Common Market Studies* 33: 47-65.

Nunnenkamp, Peter (1997): 'Aufhol- und Abkopplungsprozesse im europäischen Binnenmarkt', *Die Weltwirtschaft*, H. 2: 190-203.

Nunnenkamp, Peter; Gundlach, Erich and Jamuna Agarwal (1994): *Globalisation of Production and Markets*, Kieler Studie #262, Tübingen: Mohr.

Nurkse, Ragnar (1953): *Problems of Capital Formation in Underdeveloped Countries*, New York: Oxford University Press.

OECD (1997a): *National Accounts, Main Aggregates 1960-1995*, Vol. I, Paris: OECD.

OECD (1997b): *Economic Outlook*, edition June 1997, Vol. 61, Paris: OECD.

OECD (1997c): *Main Economic Indicators*, edition July 1997, Paris: OECD.

Ottaviano, Gianmarco and Diego Puga (1997): 'Agglomeration in the Global Economy: A Survey of the "New Economic Geography"', CEPR Discussion Paper #1699.

Ottaviano, Gianmarco and Jacques-François Thisse (1998): 'Agglomeration and Trade Revisited', CEPR Discussion Paper #1903.

Peñalosa, Juan María (1994): *The Spanish Catching-Up Process: General Determinants and Contributions of the Manufacturing Industry*, Madrid: Banco de España.

Pratten, Clifford F. (1980): 'The Manufacture of Pins', *Journal of Economic Literature* 18: 93-6.

Prigogine, Ilya and Isabelle Stengers (1984): *Order Out of Chaos*, New York: Bantam Books.

Puga, Diego and Anthony J. Venables (1996): 'The Spread of Industry: Spatial Agglomeration in Economic Development', CEPR Working Paper #1354.

Quah, Danny (1993): 'Galton's Fallacy and Tests of the Convergence Hypothesis', *Scandinavian Journal of Economics* 95: 427-43.

Quah, Danny (1996): 'Twin Peaks: Growth and Convergence in Models of Distribution Dynamics', *Economic Journal* 106: 1045-55.

Rauch, James E. (1991): 'Comparative Advantage, Geographic Advantage and the Volume of Trade', *Economic Journal* 101: 1230-44.

Rawls, John (1971): *A Theory of Justice*, Cambridge: Harvard University Press.

Reichenbach, Horst and Hans-Ulrich Beck (1997): 'Die Regionalpolitik der Europäischen Union: Auf dem Wege zu verbesserter Kohäsion', in: *Zentrum und Peripherie – Zur Entwicklung der Arbeitsteilung in Europa*, Schriften des Vereins für Socialpolitik #250, ed. by Hans-Jürgen Vosgerau, Berlin: Duncker & Humblot, 129-45.

Ricci, Luca A. (1996): 'A Ricardian Model of New Trade and Location Theory', SFB 178 'Internationalisierung der Wirtschaft' Diskussionsbeitrag #309 (Serie II), Univ. Konstanz.

Richardson, G.S. (1972): 'The Organization of Industry', *Economic Journal* 82: 883-96.

Rivera-Batiz, L.A. and Paul M. Romer (1991): 'Economic Integration and Endogenous Growth', *Quarterly Journal of Economics* 106: 531-56.

Robson, Arthur J. and Myrna Wooders (1997): 'On the Growth Maximizing Distribution of Income', *International Economic Review* 38: 511-26.

Rodrik, Dani (1997): *Has Globalization Gone Too Far?*, Washington, DC: Institute for International Economics.

Romer, Paul (1986): 'Increasing Returns and Long Run Growth', *Journal of Political Economy* 94: 1002-37.

Romer, Paul (1987): 'Growth Based on Increasing Returns to Specialization', *American Economic Review* (Papers and Proceedings) 77: 56-62.

Romer, Paul M. (1996): 'Why, Indeed, in America? Theory, History, and the Origins of Modern Economic Growth', *American Economic Review* (Papers and Proceedings) 86: 202-6.

Rosenberg, Nathan (1965): 'Adam Smith on the Division of Labor: Two Views or One?', *Economica* 32: 127-39.

Rosenberg, Nathan (ed.) (1969): *The American System of Manufactures. The Report of the Committee on the Machinery of the United States 1855 and the Special Reports of George Wallis and Joseph Whitworth 1854*, ed. with an introduction by Nathan Rosenberg, Edinburgh: Edinburgh University Press.

Rosenberg, Nathan (1977): 'American Technology: Imported or Indigenous?', *American Economic Review* (Papers and Proceedings) 67: 21-6.

Rosenberg, Nathan (1981/1994): 'Why in America?', in: *Yankee Enterprise, the Rise of the American System of Manufactures*, ed. by Otto Mayr and Robert C. Post, Washington, DC: Smithsonian Institution Press; reprinted in Nathan Rosenberg (1994), *Exploring the Black Box: Technology, Economics, and History*, Cambridge: Cambridge University Press, 109-20.

Rosenberg, Nathan (1982): *Inside the Black Box*, Cambridge: Cambridge University Press.

Rosenberg, Nathan (1994a): 'Charles Babbage: Pioneer Economist', in: *Exploring the Black Box: Technology, Economics, and History*, ed. by Nathan Rosenberg, Cambridge: Cambridge University Press, 24-46.

Rosenberg, Nathan (1994b): *Exploring the Black Box: Technology, Economics, and History*, Cambridge: Cambridge University Press.

Rosenstein-Rodan, Paul N. (1943): 'Problems of Industrialization of Eastern and South-Eastern Europe', *Economic Journal* 53: 202-11.

Rothenberg, Winifred B. (1979): 'A Price Index for Rural Massachusetts', 1750-1855, *Journal of Economic History* 39: 975-1001.

Rothenberg, Winifred B. (1992): 'The Productivity Consequences of Market Integration: Agriculture in Massachusetts, 1771-1801', in: *American Economic Growth and Standards of Living Before the Civil War*, ed. by Robert E. Gallman and John Joseph Wallis, NBER Conference Report, Chicago and London: University of Chicago Press, 311-38.

RWI (1996): *Der Wirtschaftsstandort Deutschland vor dem Hintergrund regionaler Entwicklungstendenzen in Europa*, report for the German Ministry of Economic Affairs, Essen: RWI.

Sachs, Jeffrey D. and Steven Radelet (1998): 'The Onset of the East Asian Financial Crisis', mimeo: Cambridge, Mass.

Sachs, Jeffrey D. and Sala-í-Martin, Xavier (1991): 'Fiscal Federalism and Optimum Currency Areas: Evidence from Europe and the United States', NBER Working Paper #3855.

Sachs, Jeffrey D. and Andrew Warner (1995): 'Economic Reform and the Process of Global Integration', *Brookings Papers on Economic Activity* 1/95: 1-118.

Sala-í-Martin, Xavier (1990): 'Lecture Notes on Economic Growth: Five Prototype Models of Endogenous Growth', Economic Growth Center Discussion Paper #622, New Haven: Yale University.

Sala-í-Martin, Xavier (1994): 'La Riqueza de las Regiones: Evidencia y Teorías Sobre Crecimiento Regional y Convergencia', *Moneda y Crédito* 198: 13-54.

Sala-í-Martin, Xavier (1996a): 'Regional Cohesion: Evidence and Theories of Regional Growth and Convergence', *European Economic Review* 40: 1325-52.

Sala-í-Martin, Xavier (1996b): 'The Classical Approach to Convergence Analysis', *Economic Journal* 106: 1019-36.

Samuelson, Paul (1948): 'International Trade and the Equalization of Factor Prices', *Economic Journal* 58: 163-84.

Samuelson, Paul (1949): 'International Factor Price Equalization Once Again', *Economic Journal* 59: 181-197; reprinted 1987 in: *International Trade: Selected Readings*, ed. by Jagdish N. Bhagwati, 2nd ed., Cambridge: MIT Press, 5-20.

Samuelson, Paul (1954): 'The Transfer Problem and Transport Costs, II: Analysis of Effects of Trade Impediments', *Economic Journal* 64: 264-89.

Samuelson, Paul A. (1965): 'A Theory of Induced Innovation Along Kennedy-Weizsäcker Lines', *Review of Economic and Statistics* XLVII: 343-56.

Sanyal, Kalyan K. (1983): 'Vertical Specialization in a Ricardian Model with a Continuum of Stages of Production', *Economica* 50: 71-8.

Sanyal, Kalyan K. and Ronald W. Jones (1982): 'The Theory of Trade in Middle Products', *American Economic Review* 72: 16-31.

Saul, S.B. (ed.) (1970): *Technological Change: The United States and Britain in the Nineteenth Century*, London: Methuen and Co.

Schelling, Thomas C. (1978): *Micromotives and Macrobehavior*, New York: Norton.

Scherer, F.M. (1992): *International High-Technology Competition*, Cambridge, Mass.: Harvard University Press.

Scitovsky, Tibor (1954): 'Two Concepts of External Economies', *Journal of Political Economy* LXII: 143-51.

Scotchmer, Suzanne and Jacques-François Thisse (1992): 'The Implications of Space for Competition', CEPR Discussion Paper #724.

Seitz, Konrad (1991): *Die japanisch-amerikanische Herausforderung: Deutschlands Hochtechnologie-Industrien kämpfen ums Überleben*, Stuttgart: Verlag Bonn Aktuell.

Selten, Reinhard (1978): 'The Chain-Store Paradox', *Theory and Decision* 9: 127-59.

Sen, Amartya (1973): *On Economic Inequality*, Oxford: Oxford University Press.

Sen, Amartya (1992/1995): *Inequality Reexamined*, 3rd ed. New York and Cambridge, Mass.: Russell Sage Foundation and Harvard University Press.

Shannon, Claude E. (1948): 'The Mathematical Theory of Communication', *Bell System Technical Journal* 27: 379-423, 623-56.

Shorrocks, Anthony F. (1983): 'Ranking Income Distributions', *Economica* 50: 3-17.

Shorrocks, Anthony F. and James E. Foster (1987): 'Transfer Sensitive Inequality Measures', *Review of Economic Studies* LIV: 485-97.

Shubik, Martin (1971): 'Pecuniary Externalities: A Game Theoretic Analysis', *American Economic Review* 61: 713-18.

Shultz, George P. and William E. Simon (1998): 'Who Needs the IMF?', *Wall Street Journal* (Europe), February 4th: 10.

Siebert, Horst (1988): 'Strategische Handelspolitik – Theoretische Ansätze und wirtschaftspolitische Empfehlungen', *Aussenwirtschaft* 43: 549-84.

Sinn, Hans-Werner (1996): 'The Subsidiarity Principle and Market Failure in Systems Competition', NBER Working Paper #5411.

Slaughter, Matthew J. (1995): 'Multinational Corporations, Outsourcing, and American Wage Divergence', NBER Working Paper #5253.

Slaughter, Matthew J. (1997): 'Per Capita Income Convergence and the Role of International Trade', *American Economic Review* (Papers and Proceedings) 87: 194-9.

Smith, Adam (1776): *An Inquiry into the Nature and the Causes of the Wealth of Nations*, ed. by R.H. Campbell and A.S. Skinner (1976), Oxford: Clarendon Press.

Smith, John M. (1982): *Evolution and the Theory of Games*, Cambridge: Cambridge University Press.

Sokoloff, Kenneth L. (1986): 'Productivity Growth in Manufacturing During Early Industrialization: Evidence from the American Northeast, 1820-1860', in: *Long-Term Factors in American Economic Growth*, ed. by Stanley L. Engerman and Robert E. Gallman, NBER Studies in Income and Wealth #51, Chicago: University or Chicago Press, 679-736.

Sokoloff, Kenneth L. (1988): 'Inventive Activity in Early Industrial America: Evidence From Patent Records, 1790-1846', *Journal of Economic History* XLVIII: 813-50.

Sokoloff, Kenneth L. (1992): 'Invention, Innovation, and Manufacturing Productivity Growth in the Antebellum Northeast', in: *American Economic Growth and Standards of Living Before the Civil War*, ed. by Robert E. Gallman and John Joseph Wallis, NBER Conference Report, Chicago and London: University of Chicago Press, 345-78.

Solow, Robert (1956): 'A Contribution to the Theory of Economic Growth', *Quarterly Journal of Economics* 70: 65-94.

Stackelberg, Heinrich von (1934): *Marktform und Gleichgewicht*, Wien: Springer.

Stadler, Manfred (1995): 'Geographical Transaction Costs and Regional Quality Ladders', *Journal of Institutional and Theoretical Economics* 151: 490-504.

Stahl, Konrad (1997): 'Divergenz und Konvergenz der regionalen Wirtschaftsentwicklung aus Sicht der Raumwirtschaftstheorie', in: *Zentrum und Peripherie – Zur Entwicklung der Arbeitsteilung in Europa*, ed. by Hans-Jürgen Vosgerau, Schriften des Vereins für Socialpolitik #250, Berlin: Duncker & Humblot, 53-72.

Stegemann, Klaus (1988): 'Wirtschaftspolitische Rivalität zwischen Industriestaaten: Neue Erkenntnisse durch Modelle strategischer

Handelspolitik?', in: *Wirtschaftspolitik zwischen ökonomischer und politischer Rationalität: Festschrift für Herbert Giersch*, Wiesbaden: Gabler, 3-25.

Stiglitz, Joseph (1998): 'Restoring the Asian Miracle', *Wall Street Journal* (Europe), February 3rd: 6.

Stigler, George J. (1951): 'The Division of Labor is Limited by the Extent of the Market', *Journal of Political Economy* LIX: 185-202.

Stolpe, Michael (1995): *Technology and the Dynamics of Specialization in Open Economies*, Kieler Studie #271, Tübingen: Mohr.

Störmann, Wiebke (1993): *Agglomeration aus Sicht der evolutorischen Ökonomik*, Berlin: Köster.

Strack, D; Helmschrott, H. and S. Schönherr (1997): 'Internationale Einkommensvergleiche auf der Basis von Kaufkraftparitäten: Das Gefälle zwischen Industrie- und Entwicklungsländern verringert sich', *Ifo Schnelldienst* 50, 10/97: 7-14.

Sugden, Robert (1986): *The Economics of Rights, Co-operation and Welfare*, Oxford: Basil Blackwell.

Sugden, Robert (1995): 'The Co-existence of Conventions', *Journal of Economic Behavior and Organization* 28: 241-56.

Tam, Mo-Yin S. and Renze Zhang (1996): 'Ranking Income Distributions: The Tradeoff between Efficiency and Equality', *Economica* 63: 239-52.

Teece, David J. (1980): 'Economies of Scope and the Scope of the Enterprise', *Journal of Economic Behavior and Organization* 1: 223-47.

Temin, Peter (1971): 'Labor Scarcity in America', *Journal of Interdisciplinary History* 1 (2): 251-64.

Theil, Henry (1967): *Economics and Information Theory*, Amsterdam and Chicago: North Holland and Rand McNally.

Thomas, Ingo P. (1995): 'Konvergenz und Divergenz in der Europäischen Union: Theoretischer Überblick, empirische Evidenz und wirtschaftspolitische Implikationen', *Kieler Arbeitspapier* #682, Kiel: Institut für Weltwirtschaft.

Thomas, Ingo P. (1997): *Ein Finanzausgleich für die Europäische Union?*, Kieler Studie # 285, Tübingen: Mohr.

Thünen, Johann Heinrich von (1990 (1818-42)): *Der isolierte Staat in Beziehung auf Landwirtschaft und Nationalökonomie*, kommentierte Gesamtausgabe von 1990, Berlin: Akademie-Verlag.

Torstensson, Johan (1997): 'Country Size and Comparative Advantage: An Empirical Study', CEPR Discussion Paper #1554.

Townsend, Robert M. (1993): *The Medieval Village Economy: A Study of the Pareto Mapping in General Equilibrium*, Princeton: Princeton University Press.

Tryon, Rolla Milton (1917): *Household Manufactures in the United States, 1640-1860*, New York: Augustus M. Kelley.

Tyson, Laura D'A. (1992): *Who's Bashing Whom: Trade Conflict in High-Technology Industries*, Washington, DC: International Institute.

United Nations (1993): *Trends in International Distribution of Gross World Product, National Accounts Statistics Special Issue*, New York: United Nations.

US Bureau of the Census (1994): *Statistical Abstract of the United States*, Washington, DC: Government Printing Office.

US Department of Commerce (1975): *Historical Statistics of the United States*, Two Volumes, Washington, DC: Government Printing Office.

Vanberg, Viktor J. (1994): 'Morality and Economics: De Moribus est Disputandum', in: *Rules and Choice in Economics*, ed. by Viktor J. Vanberg, London and New York: Routledge, 41-59.

Van Bergeijk, Peter A.G. and Nico W. Mensink (1997): 'Measuring Globalization', *Journal of World Trade* 31: 159-68.

Van Suntum, Ulrich (1986): 'Internationale Wettbewerbsfähigkeit einer Volkswirtschaft: Ein sinnvolles wirtschaftspolitisches Ziel?', *Zeitschrift für Wirtschafts- und Sozialwissenschaften* 106: 495-507.

Vaubel, Roland (1995): *The Centralisation of Western Europe: The Common Market, Political Integration, and Democracy*, Hobart Paper #127, London: IEA.

Venables, Anthony J. (1987): 'Trade and Trade Policy with Differentiated Products: A Chamberlain-Ricardian Model', *Economic Journal* 97: 700-717.

Venables, Anthony J. (1996): 'Equilibrium Locations of Vertically Linked Industries', *International Economic Review* 37: 341-59.

Venables, Anthony J. (1997): 'Economic Integration and Centre-Periphery Inequalities: The View from Trade Theory', in: *Zentrum und Peripherie – Zur Entwicklung der Arbeitsteilung in Europa*, Schriften des Vereins für Socialpolitik #250, Berlin: Duncker & Humblot, 33-51.

Venables, Anthony J. (1998a): 'The Assessment: Trade and Location', *Oxford Review of Economic Policy* 14 (2): 1-6.

Venables, Anthony J. (1998b): 'The International Division of Industries: Clustering and Comparative Advantage in a Multi-Industry Model', CEPR Discussion Paper #1961.

Viñals, José (1992): 'La Economía Española Ante el Mercado Unico: Las Claves del Proceso de Integratión en la Comunidad Europea', in: *La Economía Española Ante el Mercado Unico Europeo*, ed. by José Viñals, Madrid: Alianza Editorial, 15-116.

Viñals, José et al. (1990): 'Spain and the "EC cum 1992" Shock', in: *Unity with Diversity in the European Economy: The Community's Southern Frontier*, ed. by Christopher Bliss and Jorge Braga de Macedo, Cambridge, 145-235.

Waniek, Roland (1994): 'EG-Regionalpolitik für die Jahre 1994 bis 1999', *Wirtschaftsdienst* 74: 43-9.

Weber, Alfred (1909): *Über den Standort der Industrien. Erster Teil: Reine Theorie des Standorts*, Tübingen: Mohr; engl. transl. by C.J. Friedrich (1929) *Theory of the Location of Industries*, Chicago: University of Chicago Press.

Weimer, Wolfram (1997): 'Europas teurer Süden', *Frankfurter Allgemeine Zeitung*, June 11: 13.

Weizsäcker, Carl Christian von (1984): 'Was leistet die Property Rights Theorie für aktuelle wirtschaftspolitische Fragen?', in: *Ansprüche, Eigentums- und Verfügungsrechte (Schriften des Vereins für Socialpolitik, N.F. Band 140)*, ed. by Manfred Neumann Berlin: Duncker & Humblot, 123-52.

Weizsäcker, Carl Christian von (1991): 'Antitrust and the Division of Labor', *Journal of Institutional and Theoretical Economics* 147: 99-113.

Weizsäcker, Carl Christian von and Franz Waldenberger (1992): 'Wettbewerb und strategische Handelspolitik', *Wirtschaftsdienst* 72: 403-9.

Welter, Patrick (1997a): 'Gerechtigkeit läßt sich nicht berechnen', *Handelsblatt* July 28, 1997: 2.

Welter, Patrick (1997b): 'Gerechtigkeit auf Kosten des Südens', *Handelsblatt* July 29, 1997: 8.

Willgerodt, Hans (1992): 'Armut als Integrationshindernis? Zum Konflikt zwischen Vertiefung und Erweiterung der Europäischen Gemeinschaft', *Zeitschrift für Wirtschaftspolitik* 41: 95-123.

Williamson, Harold F. (1960): 'Mass Production, Mass Consumption, and American Industrial Development', in: *First International Conference of Economic History: Contributions and Communications*, Paris: Mouton, 137-47.

Williamson, Jeffrey G. (1996): 'Globalization, Convergence, and History', *Journal of Economic History* 56: 277-306.

Williamson, Oliver E. (1980): 'The Organization of Work: A Comparative Institutional Assessment', *Journal of Economic Behavior and Organization* 1: 5-38.

Williamson, Oliver E. (1996): *The Mechanisms of Governance*, New York: Oxford University Press.

Wood, Adrian (1994) *North-South Trade, Employment and Inequality*. Oxford: Oxford University Press.

World Bank (1987): *World Development Report 1987*, Washington, DC: World Bank.

World Bank (1995): *World Development Report 1995*, Washington, DC: World Bank.

Yang, Xiaokai and Yew-Kwang Ng (1993): *Specialization and Economic Organization: A New Classical Microeconomic Framework*, Amsterdam etc.: North Holland.

Yang, Xiaokai and He-Ling Shi (1992): 'Specialization and Product Diversity', *American Economic Review* (Papers and Proceedings) 82: 392-98.

Young, Allyn (1928): 'Increasing Returns and Economic Progress', *Economic Journal* 38: 527-42.

Young, Alwyn (1992): 'A Tale of Two Cities: Factor Accumulation and Technical Change in Hong Kong and Singapore', in: *NBER Macroeconomics Annual 1992*, ed. by Olivier Jean Blanchard and Stanley Fischer, Cambridge and London: MIT Press, 13-54.

Subject Index